D1521482

EVELYN UNDERHILL

Spirituality for Daily Living

Annice Callahan, R.S.C.J.

In gratitude,
annice Callahan rscj.

University Press of America,® Inc.
Lanham • New York • Oxford

Copyright © 1997 by
University Press of America,® Inc.
4720 Bóston Way
Lanham, Maryland 20706

12 Hid's Copse Rd.
Cummor Hill, Oxford OX2 9JJ

Library of Congress Cataloging-in-Publication Data

Callahan, Annice
Evelyn Underhill : spritualilty for daily living / Annice Callahan.
p. cm.
Includes bibliographical references and index.
1. Underhill, Evelyn, 1875-1941. 2. Theologians--England--
Biography. 3. Spirituality--Church of England--History--20th
century. 4. Church of England--Doctrines--History--20th century.
5. Anglican Communion--Doctrines--History-20th century. I. Title.
BX5199.U53C35 1997 248.2'2'092--dc21 97-17958 CIP
(B)

ISBN 0-7618-0849-3 (cloth: alk. ppr.)

⊖™ The paper used in this publication meets the minimum
requirements of American National Standard for information
Sciences—Permanence of Paper for Printed Library Materials,
ANSI Z39.48—1984

Evelyn Underhill (1875-1941)

To the Canadian Anglican Sisters of Saint John the Divine

in gratitude for their living and sharing of faith, hope, and

love in the Spirit

Contents

Abbreviations

Abba
Evelyn Underhill. *Abba: Meditations on the Lord's Prayer.* Harrisburg, Pa: Morehouse, 1996.

Adornment

C.A.
Evelyn Underhill. Introduction. John of Ruysbroeck. *Adornment of the Spiritual Marriage.* Trans. Dom Wynschenk. London: John M. Watkins, 1951.

Armstrong
Christopher J.R. Armstrong. *Evelyn Underhill (1875-1941): An Introduction to her Life and Writing.* London: Mowbrays, 1975.

Artist
Dana Greene. *Evelyn Underhill: Artist of the Infinite Life.* New York: Crossroad, 1990.

Cloud
Evelyn Underhill. Introduction. *A Book of Contemplation the Which is Called the Cloud of Unknowing, in the Which a Soul is Oned with God.* Ed. Evelyn Underhill. 7th ed. London: Stuart & Watkins, 1970.

Cropper
Margaret Cropper. *Life of Evelyn Underhill.* New York: Harper & Bros., 1958.

DGC
Dana Greene Collection based on Dana Greene's research in the Underhill archives at King's College, London, and now part of the Evelyn Underhill Collection of the Archives of Bishop Payne Library at Virginia Theological Seminary.

Essentials
Evelyn Underhill. *The Essentials of Mysticism and Other Essays.* New York: E.P. Dutton & Co., 1960.

Fragments
Evelyn Underhill. *Fragments from an Inner Life.* Ed. Dana Greene. Harrisburg, Pa.: Morehouse, 1993.

Fruits
Evelyn Underhill. *The Fruits of the Spirit.* Harrisburg, Pa.: Morehouse, 1996.

Golden	Evelyn Underhill. *The Golden Sequence: A Fourfold Study of the Spiritual Life.* London: Methuen & Co., 1932.
Guide	*Evelyn Underhill: Modern Guide to the Ancient Quest for the Holy.* Ed. Dana Greene. Albany, N.Y.: State University of New York Press, 1988.
House Press,	Evelyn Underhill. *The House of the Soul and Concerning the Inner Life.* Minneapolis: Seabury 1984.
Jacopone	Evelyn Underhill. *Jacopone da Todi Poet and Mystic 1228-1306: A Spiritual Biography.* Freeport, N.Y.: Books for Libraries Press, 1972.
Kabir	*One Hundred Poems of Kabir.* Trans. Rabindranath Tagore assisted by Evelyn Underhill. London: Macmillan Co., 1915.
Light	Evelyn Underhill. *Light of Christ.* Harrisburg, Pa.: Morehouse, 1989.
Lt	Evelyn Underhill. *The Letters of Evelyn Underhill.* Ed. Charles Williams. Westminster, Md.: Christian Classics, 1989.
Man	Evelyn Underhill. *Man and the Supernatural* London: Methuen & Co., Ltd., 1927.
Milos	Joy Milos. "The Role of the Spiritual Guide in the Life and Writings of Evelyn Underhill." Ph.D. diss., Catholic University of America, 1988.
Mixed	Evelyn Underhill. *Mixed Pasture: Twelve Essays and Addresses.* London: Methuen & Co. Ltd., 1933.
Mysticism	Evelyn Underhill. *Mysticism: The Preeminent Study in the Nature and Development of Spiritual*

	Consciousness. 13th ed. New York: Doubleday Image, 1990.
Mystics	Evelyn Underhill. *The Mystics of the Church.* Harrisburg, Pa.: Morehouse, 1997.
Papers	Evelyn Underhill. *Collected Papers of Evelyn Underhill.* Ed. Lucy Menzies. New York: Longmans, Green and Co., Inc., 1946.
Practical	Evelyn Underhill. *Practical Mysticism: A Little Book for Normal People.* New York: E.P. Dutton & Co., 1914.
Ruysbroeck	Evelyn Underhill. *Ruysbroeck.* London: G. Bell and Sons Ltd., 1914.
School	Evelyn Underhill. *The School of Charity: Meditations on the Christian Creed.* Harrisburg, Pa.: Morehouse, 1991.
Spirit	Evelyn Underhill. *The Life of the Spirit and the Life of Today.* Harrisburg, Pa.: Morehouse, 1995.
Spiritual Life	Evelyn Underhill. *The Spiritual Life.* Harrisburg, Pa.: Morehouse, 1996.
Tagore	Evelyn Underhill. Introduction. The Autobiography *of Maharishi Devendranth Tagore.* Trans. Satyendranath Tagore and Indira Devi. London: Macmillan, 1916, ix-xlii.
TI 3	Karl Rahner. *Theological Investigations.* Vol. 3. Trans. Karl H. and Boniface Kruger. Baltimore: Helicon Press, 1967.
TI 4	Karl Rahner. *Theological Investigations.* Vol. 4. Trans. Kevin Smyth. Baltimore: Helicon Press, 1966.

TI 6   Karl Rahner. *Theological Investigations.* Vol. 6.
              Trans. Karl -H. and Boniface Kruger. Baltimore:
              Helicon Press, 1969.

TI 7   Karl Rahner, *Theological Investigations.* Vol.
              7.Trans. David Bourke. NewYork:Herder and Herder,
              1971.

TI 9   Karl Rahner. *Theological Investigations.* Vol. 9.
              Trans. David Bourke. New York: Herder and Herder,
              1972.

TI 16   Karl Rahner. *Theological Investigations.* Vol.
              16.Trans. David Morland. New York: Seabury Press,
              1979.

TI 19   Karl Rahner. *Theological Investigations.* Vol. 19.
              Trans. Edward Quinn. New York: Crossroad, 1983.

TI 20   Karl Rahner. *Theological Investigations.* Vol. 20.
              Trans. Edward Quinn. New York: Crossroad, 1981.

TI 23   Karl Rahner. *Theological Investigations.* Vol. 23.
              Trans. Joseph Donceel and Hugh M. Riley. New
              York: Crossroad, 1992.

Visions   Karl Rahner. *Visions and Prophecies.* Tr. Charles
              Henkey and Richard Strachan. New York: Herder
              and Herder, 1963.

Way   Evelyn Underhill. *The Mystic Way: A Psychological
              Study in Christian Origins.* Folcroft, Pa.: Folcroft
Library   Editions, 1975.

Ways   Evelyn Underhill. *The Ways of the Spirit.* Ed. Grace
              Adolphsen Brame. New York: Crossroad, 1990.

Worship   Evelyn Underhill. *Worship.* New York: Crossroad,
              1985. 2nd ed.: Guildford, Surrey: Eagle, 1991; and
              Wheaton, Il.: Harold Shaw, 1992.

Acknowledgements

The topic of my book is Evelyn Underhill's spirituality for daily living. Evelyn Underhill, (1875-1941), an Anglican poet, novelist, scholar of mysticism, spiritual writer, retreat preacher, and spiritual director in England, is most famous for her two classics, one called *Mysticism* and the other called *Worship*.

This book has been in preparation for more than a decade. For the last eleven years, I have taught units on Evelyn Underhill in my courses on mysticism and spirituality. In the spring of 1989 on a research leave in Boston, I wrote a chapter on "Evelyn Underhill (1875-1941): Pathfinder for Our Way to God" in a book I called *Spiritual Guides for Today* which Crossroad published in 1992. In recent years I have given lectures and workshops on her to Anglicans and Roman Catholics in Spokane, Montreal, Toronto, and Washington, D.C.

In the spring of 1993, I took a half-sabbatical in the Resident Scholar Program of the Institute for Ecumenical and Cultural Research, Collegeville, Minnesota to do further research on Evelyn Underhill in an ecumenical setting. I am grateful for those who furthered my project: Patrick Henry, executive director, Dolores Schuh, C.H.M., executive associate, and the other scholars in the program. I particularly appreciated their questions and comments at the seminar I presented on Evelyn Underhill's contribution to mysticism, April 13, 1993, and at the public lecture I delivered on Evelyn Underhill's practical advice for living the Christian life in the world according to her letters, May 13, 1993. On April 19, 1993, Shawn Madigan, C.S.J., and I spoke on "Mystics: Off the Pedestal, On to the Ground," at the University of Saint Thomas, Minneapolis, at which I presented Underhill's everyday mysticism.

Research for this project was made possible through two generous grants. One grant to help promote research on Underhill was awarded by the Evelyn Underhill Association. The other was offered by the Elizabeth Ann Bogert Memorial Fund of the Friends World Committee for Consultation, Section of the Americas, which helps support research on mysticism.

In preparation for my work, I made a trip in the summer of 1992 to the Evelyn Underhill "archives" in the United States which then resided at the home of Dana Greene, a professor of history at St. Mary's College of Maryland who wrote a definitive biography of Evelyn Underhill published by Crossroad in 1990, and edited a collection of her essays and a collection of her journals. There I was able to xerox many of Dr. Greene's holdings on Underhill which she collected during her time of research at King's College, London, St. Andrews University, Scotland, and the House of Retreat, Pleshey, where Underhill gave many retreat talks in her latter years. Since I had read Underhill's books and letters, this was the missing piece in my research. I am deeply indebted to Dr. Greene for her sharing of these materials which I have coded in this book as DGC, her substantive biography, her editing of Underhill's journal, her encouraging support of my research, and her critical reading of the manuscript. She donated these materials to form the beginnings of the Evelyn Underhill Collection of the archives of Bishop Payne Library at Virginia Theological Seminary. Julia E. Randle, archivist, kindly sent me recent additions to this collection.

I was also assisted by Grace Adolphsen Brame, whose theological dissertation on Underhill was followed by her collection of four previously unknown Underhill retreats which she discovered and edited under the title *The Ways of the Spirit*. She shared with me her version of the Underhill-von Hügel collection of letters, and was very helpful in answering questions about Underhill's life and works.

Margaret Guider, O.S.F., associate professor of religion and society at Weston School of Theology, Cambridge, Massachusetts, read the manuscript critically. Anne Carr, B.V.M., professor of theology at the University of Chicago Divinity School, and Joan Nuth, associate

professor of religious studies at John Carroll University, graciously
offered feedback on Chapters Two and Seven.

Claire Kondolf, R.S.C.J., editor of the *RSCJ Newsletter*, exercised her
journalistic skills liberally with the entire text. Phyllis Braceland,
R.S.C.J., who worked at the Jesuit Mission Office in Toronto at the time,
read and proofread the document, picking up fine points of grammar,
punctuation, and spelling, and did the final proofreading. Anne Leonard,
R.S.C.J., who works in the General Archives of the Society of the Sacred
Heart in Rome, read the text and helped significantly with the final
editing.

I am grateful to the Regis College community for giving me time and
support during my sabbatical to write this. In particular, I want to thank
Jack Costello, S.J., president, Ron Mercier, dean in 1997, and Terry
Prendergast, S.J., dean in 1993, for making it possible; Cathleen Flynn,
C.S.J., for helping me prepare the draft for mailing, Naomi Gold for
reconfiguring the Index, Mary Jo Leddy, for inspiring me through her
new book, John Olney, S.J., for formatting and laser-printing the final
version, George Schner, S.J., for suggesting ways to trim the Index, and
Jean Zadorian, S.N.J.M., for proofreading the laser-printed version.

The Canadian Anglican Sisters of Saint John the Divine have provided
interest and support during the writing of this manuscript. I value our
ongoing Anglican-Roman Catholic dialogue during my weekends of
prayer at their motherhouse in Toronto, and for our mutual love of
Evelyn Underhill.

Morehouse's reprinted editions of works by Evelyn Underhill have
been useful resources for this book. In particular, I am indebted to the
following publishers for copyright material from their publications:
Morehouse for the use of the photograph of Evelyn Underhill;
Morehouse and Cassell/Mowbray for: *The School of Charity*;
Christian Classics for: *The Letters of Evelyn Underhill*.

I treasure the privilege of collaborating with Nancy Ulrich and Helen
Hudson, my editors at University Press of America. Their encouragement
and advice have been invaluable.

Introduction

Evelyn Underhill (1875-1941), was one of the leading authorities on mysticism and the spiritual life of her time. Born in England of a well-to-do barrister family, she was an Anglican poet, novelist, spiritual writer, and spiritual director. She was a trailblazer in opening up certain positions and ministries to women. She became the first woman outside lecturer in religion at Oxford University, the first to become a Fellow of King's College, London, one of the few awarded a Doctor of Divinity by the University of Aberdeen, the first Anglican woman asked to preach a clergy conference and a retreat to Anglican priests, and certainly one of the first Anglican women to give retreats and spiritual direction.

One can speak of two developments in her adult life: her study of mysticism which began to evolve in her major work *Mysticism* first published in 1911, and an articulation of the spiritual life which emerged in the latter part of her life when she was asked to give retreats and spiritual direction to her fellow Anglicans. Her spirituality was theocentric. She emphasized the interpenetration of the life of the Spirit in day-to-day living. Her openness to inter-religious dialogue demonstrated this consciousness. My book focuses on Underhill's spirituality for daily living which integrated her interpretation of the mystics and her awareness of the need to make the spiritual life accessible to Christians living in the world.

Before her marriage, Underhill joined for a brief time the occultist Hermetic Society of the Golden Dawn which was dedicated to a communal search for the world of spirits through ritual. She was attracted to its mystery. She left, however, because it was about magic and control, and sought mysticism because that was about love. Years later she continued a communal search for the world of the Spirit by rejoining the Anglican communion.[1]

The experience of and search for beauty and truth led her to write her first novel at age twenty-seven, *The Grey World*, with the theme of beauty and truth pointing to a world beyond; it was published in 1904, the same year in which five of her short stories on similar themes were published in *Horlick's Magazine*. Her fascination with medieval legends and with Roman Catholicism led her to write her first scholarly work, *The Miracles of Our Lady, St. Mary*, in which she translated twenty-five medieval legends about Mary, the Mother of God.[2]

When she was thirty-two, although she had decided to become a Roman Catholic, this decision was postponed, and she married Hubert Stuart Moore, a childhood companion and prosperous barrister, and published her second novel, *The Lost Word*. Unlike the central character of her first novel who pursued the "perfect" alone, the central character of her second novel chooses the ordinary and the communal way to God, based on love and sacrifice within marriage.

This emphasis on the power of sacrificial love is also the theme of her third and last novel, *The Column of Dust*, published in 1909. In this work the central character dies a sacrificial death for her unlovable daughter.

Her aesthetic sensitivities to art and architecture were exercised in her iconographical study of *The Fountain of Life*, a painting in a church at Ghent portraying the Trinity with various prophets, saints, and martyrs, contributing their blood to the fountain of mercy and holding their hearts to receive blood from it. She insisted that these allegories represent the doctrine of grace which includes our cooperative response to God's gift.[3]

Underhill wrote some devotional literature under the pseudonym John Cordelier, publishing two works: *The Path of Eternal Wisdom: A Mystical Commentary on the Way of the Cross*, 1911, and *The Spiral Way*, 1912, which treated the fifteen mysteries in our ascent to God. These are of limited worth and appeal. Since Vatican II, biblical and liturgical spirituality have undergirded and, in many cases, replaced devotional spirituality.[4]

Poetry was another mode of expression for Underhill's spirituality. Her first book of poems called *A Bar-Lamb's Ballad Book*, 1902, was about law, the subject dearest to her father's heart and to that of Hubert, her future husband. *Immanence: A Book of Verses* was a collection of her poems published in 1912, followed by *Theophanies* in 1916. Her writings reflected her fascination with magic, beauty, truth, and the invisible world. But soon she began to focus on mysticism as such. Underhill made a significant contribution to the study of mysticism. She translated some works of the major British medieval mystics into modern English adding scholarly introductions and notes. Conversant with European Christian mysticism, she worked in 1913 with the non-Christian mystic, Rabindranath Tagore, to help compile and translate the poems of Kabir, another non-Christian mystic, into English. After having worked with the mystics many years, she returned to traditional, institutional, sacramental religion by pledging herself to the Anglican communion. In 1924, the year of the Conference on Politics, Economics, and Christianity (COPEC), she was a member of the commission which wrote the report on the nature and purpose of God. Although she was self-taught for the most part, she became a fellow of King's College, Cambridge, in 1928, and was given an honorary doctorate in divinity from the University of Aberdeen in 1938.

Underhill also made a significant contribution to what we call today spiritual guidance. After exploring the mystic way, she turned to the practical implications of relating to God in the world. In 1922, she was invited to make a retreat at Pleshey, an Anglican retreat house in the country, where she experienced the strength and joy of a community of shared faith; two years later she was invited to conduct her first retreat at Pleshey. In 1926, she was asked to address the clergy conference from the Liverpool diocese, a pioneer work for a laywoman of her time, the talks of which were later published in *Concerning the Inner Life*. The following year she served on a commission chaired by the bishop of Liverpool for the deepening of the spiritual life of laity and clergy; she encouraged laypeople to commit themselves to God. Her 1929 retreat addresses were published in a volume called *The House of the Soul,* and subsequent retreat talks to the Wives' Fellowship and address to the Anglican Fellowship were published as *The Golden Sequence.* Her retreat addresses published as *The School of Charity* became the Bishop of London's Lent Book for 1934. Three broadcasts of her talks for the BBC were published as *The Spiritual Life.* Her revised retreat addresses were published in 1940 as *Abba.*[5]

Those who sought her out for spiritual counsel either in formal retreat talks, one-to-one conversations, or the reading of her books urged her to develop the pastoral implications of her scholarly grasp of mysticism. It is on these pastoral implications that I plan to dwell in order to show her contemporary relevance.

One formative influence on her view of the Christian life was Baron Friedrich von Hügel. Recognizing that she was thoroughly theocentric and to some extent Unitarian in her spirituality, he helped her to experience Christ personally. He realized also that she emphasized the mystical aspect of Christianity in a Neoplatonic way, and facilitated her shifting this approach to an acknowledgement of the historical basis of Christianity.

Keenly aware of the personal imbalance which a very serious pursuit of mysticism and mystical experience can create, von Hügel urged Underhill to develop some hobbies and to follow a regular but minimal devotional program. She began scriptwriting and continued gardening. Baron von Hügel encouraged her to do some work with the poor, as she herself had encouraged a spiritual directee years before. She visited poor families in North Kensington two days a week, and helped a young widow with children who was interested in the spiritual life. Von Hügel led Underhill to new depths of an incarnational spirituality.

Her interest in and commitment to ecumenical and interreligious dialogue began, I suggest, with her study of mysticism. It may seem that the topic of mysticism is not related to ecumenism but let us recall that people of faith are in the process of recovering, understanding, and deepening the rich variety of their liturgical and spiritual traditions. Many are nervous about mysticism believing it to be a flight from reality to be alone with the alone. Underhill, however, was convinced that mysticism is the art of union with reality. For her the central fact of mysticism is the mystic's consciousness of a living God and of a personal self capable of communion with God through mutual self-giving. How mystics feel about God and their relationship with God is more important to them than how they view God in images, creeds, or doctrines. How their mystical experiences enhance their lives and the lives of those they served is more important than their content, duration, or frequency.

Her study of mystics included Roman Catholic saints, Moslem Sufi poets, Protestants like Jacob Boehme, John Wesley, and George Fox, and Indian Hindus. She helped Rabindranath Tagore translate poems by a Hindu mystic whom they thought to be Kabir. She belonged to the Spiritual Entente, a group committed to praying for Christian unity. Her participation in the liturgies of the Russian Orthodox Church intensified her ecumenical spirit. She joined the Fellowship of St. Alban and St. Sergius. Her second major classic, *Worship*, 1936, reflected on the practice of Christian liturgy in several rites. She chose and arranged a collection of eucharistic prayers from ancient liturgies, drawing not only on the Roman and Gallican rites of the Western church, but also the rites of the Byzantine liturgies, the Egyptian church, and the west Syrian church. She invited people to respect their own religious experience as well as the diverse doctrines of different churches.[6]

After experiencing the devastation caused by the bombing of London during World War II, Underhill became a pacifist. She joined the Anglican Pacifist Fellowship and wrote for them a pamphlet entitled *The Church and War*. At the same time, she wrote a *Meditation of Peace* for the Fellowship of Reconciliation. She and her husband moved from London to her friend Marjorie Vernon's home, Lawn House, Hampstead, which was her last home until her death on June 15, 1941.[7]

I have applied an approach that I use in many of my courses on the mystics whereby I invite students to reflect on their own experiences and images of self, God, Christ, the church, and the world, and then to reflect on each mystic's experiences and images. This focus has led me to present Underhill's material according to the different genres in which she wrote.[8] Although her emphasis was on the life and power of the Spirit, I have traced her experiences and images of Christ as a way of highlighting the Christian dimension of her spirituality.

Part One looks at her own religious experience. Since she wrote so much on the lives and writings of the mystics, it next explores her reflection on the mystics' descriptions of their religious experiences. Since she spent the latter part of her life exploring new vistas of the spiritual life in a more pragmatic and less scholarly way, Part Two summarizes the practical advice she gave in her letters, in her retreat addresses, and then in her other works concerning the spiritual life. Part Three evaluates Evelyn Underhill's contribution to the study of mysticism, describes her contribution to the ministry of spiritual guidance, and assesses the pastoral and ecumenical relevance of her spirituality. It is clear that Underhill used experience, her own and that of others, as the point of departure for her reflection.

In each chapter material is presented chronologically under each sub-section, rather than thematically. In so doing, I hope to show the development of her thought. At the end of each chapter are an exercise and a set of questions for prayerful reflection and faith-sharing which can be used as a guide for solitary reading and for group discussion. Many of the suggested readings of reprinted editions of Underhill's books reveal the resurgence of interest in her life and writings.

This work is not meant to be exhaustive. Underhill was too prolific a writer for one to synthesize effectively her thirty-nine books and more than three hundred and fifty articles and reviews. Rather, this work is meant to be illustrative of her life, her study of the mystics, her spirituality for daily living, and her legacy to us. Her practical mysticism discovered and revealed the transcendent in what she loved to call the homely, or we might say homey, details of daily life. She noticed how the mystics found God in their lives and invited us to do likewise.

Evelyn Underhill was a woman of God, a woman of the church, and a woman of her times. Let us explore together what she can say to Christians in the third millennium.

In order to present her spirituality in the context of her culture in Edwardian England at the turn of the century, I retain the gender exclusive language of her works and of other works written in her day. My preference is for inclusive language.

Notes

1. It is important to distinguish between spirituality and spiritualism. Spirituality has to do with our personal and communal experience of God, reflection on the experience, and the articulation of that reflection, all of which are historically and culturally conditioned. It concerns our search for the living mystery of God. Spiritualism, on the other hand, is based on a belief in the possibility of the living contacting and communicating with the spirits of the dead.

On my use of the term spirituality, see Annice Callahan, "The Relationship between Spirituality and Theology," *Horizons* 16/2 (1989): 266-74. On spiritualism, see Alex Owen, *The Darkened Room: Women, Power and Spiritualism in Late Victorian England* (London: Virago Press, 1989), esp. "Chapter 1. Power and Gender: The Spiritualist Context," 1-17; and "Chapter 8. Spiritualism and the Subversion of Femininity," 202-35. For this reference, I am indebted to Margaret Guider in a conversation in Cambridge, Massachusetts, on August 18, 1993. For a clarification of Underhill's motivations for entering and leaving the Golden Dawn, I am indebted to Dana Greene in a letter of September 8, 1993. See *Artist,* 17-18.

On the Golden Dawn, see, for example, R.A. Gilbert, *The Golden Dawn: Twilight of the Magicians* (Wellingborough, Northamptonshire: Aquarian Press, 1983); Ellic Howe, *The Magicians of the Golden Dawn: A Documentary History of a Magical Order 1887-1923* (London: Routledge & K. Paul, 1972); and Israel Regardie, *The Golden Dawn: An Account of the Teachings, Rites and Ceremonies of the Order of the Golden Dawn,* rev. ed. (St. Paul, Mn.: Llewellyn Pub., 1978), 4 vols.

2. See, for example, "A Green Mass," "The Death of a Saint," "The Ivory Tower," and "Our Lady of the Gate," *Horlick's Magazine* (1904): 173-77, 207-211, 243-247, and 445-448, DGC; and idem, "Two Miracles of Our Lady Saint Mary," *The Fortnightly Review* (September 1905): 496-506, DGC.

3. See E. Underhill, *"The Fountain of Life:* An Iconographical Study," *Burlington Magazine* 86 (April 1910): 99-109, DGC. On Underhill's technique of describing a specific art work to clarify or highlight a point that she wanted to emphasize, see Mary Brian Durkin, "Evelyn Underhill Anchored in God," *Christianity and the Arts* (February-April 1997): 46-54. Cf. Karl Rahner, "Art against the Horizon of Theology and Piety" and "The Theology of the Religious Meaning of Images," *TI* 23, 149-168.

For Underhill's understanding of grace, see Grace Adolphsen Brame, "Divine Grace and Human Will in the Writing of Evelyn Underhill" (Ph.D. Diss., Temple University, 1988). For a classical understanding of grace, see, for example, Jean-Marc Laporte, *Patience and Power: Grace for the First World* (New York: Paulist, 1988). For a contemporary understanding of grace, see, for example, Anne E. Carr, *Transforming Grace: Christian Tradition and Women's Experience* (San Francisco: Harper & Row, 1988); and Stephen J. Duffy, *The*

Dynamics of Grace: Perspectives in Theological Anthropology (Collegeville, Mn.: Liturgical Press, a Michael Glazier Book, 1993).

4. On this point, see, for example, Annice Callahan, *Karl Rahner's Spirituality of the Pierced Heart* (Lanham, Md.: University Press of America, 1985), 130. For an excellent contemporary overview of Christian spirituality, see Michael Downey, *Understanding Christian Spirituality* (New York: Paulist, 1997), esp. 108-109, where Downey insists that the cross is the vital center of Christian spirituality for reflection and discernment, and the paschal mystery its touchstone and norm.

5. For information in the last three paragraphs, see Cropper, pp. 115,137-194, 224. On her contribution as a spiritual director to the general religious public, see Henry Bodgener, "Evelyn Underhill: A Spiritual Director to Her Generation," *London Quarterly and Holborn Review,* January 1958, 45-50, DGC.

6. See *Eucharistic Prayers from the Ancient Liturgies,* chosen and arranged by Evelyn Underhill (London: Longmans, Green & Co., 1939), 14-16. See also Nicolas Zernov with Miltza Zernov, *The Fellowship of St. Alban and St. Sergius: A Historical Memoir* (Oxford: The Fellowship of St. Alban and St. Sergius, 1979).

7. Cf. Cropper 205, 214-215, 222-232.

8. For contemporary theological reflection on mystics' experiences and images, see Annice Callahan, ed., *Spiritualities of the Heart: Approaches to Personal Wholeness in Christian Tradition* (New York: Paulist, 1990). Cf. Susan Bergman, ed., *Martyrs: Contemporary Writers on Modern Lives of Faith* (San Francisco: HarperSanFrancisco, 1996).

For a thematic approach to Underhill's writings, see Anniee Callahan, "Evelyn Underhill (1875-1941): Pathfinder for Our Way to God," *Spiritual Guides for Today* (New York: Crossroad, 1992), 25-42, 141-47.

Part One

Influences on Her Life

Evelyn Underhill

Introduction

This first part discusses the influences on Evelyn Underhill's life which affected her growth, her writings on spirituality for daily living, and her ministry of spiritual guidance. The first chapter reflects on experiences and images in her life.

The second chapter discusses her interest in the writings of the mystics as revelations of their mystical life with God. By presenting us with powerful images of the self, God, Christ, the church, and the world, the mystics gave us clues about their vision of God and their view of the world. Underhill's reflection on their experiences and images revealed her to be in control of the material and able to use it with originality and insight.

Chapter Three discusses her work with spiritual guides both by receiving spiritual direction from Baron Friedrich von Hügel, and by reading letters of spiritual direction by other spiritual writers with whom she was familiar and who may have had an influence on the way she wrote hers, namely, those of Jean-Pierre de Caussade, Henri de Tourville, and Dom John Chapman. By being open to spiritual direction herself, she was better able to name and deepen her experience of the life of the Spirit within her and in her midst.

Chapter 1

Experiences and Images in Her Life

Evelyn Underhill lived her Christian life in the world under the guidance of the Spirit. She did not grow up with a regular practice of Sunday church worship since neither of her parents was a practicing Anglican. She was a dutiful daughter but not particularly close to either of her parents who never understood or appreciated her love of the mystics or of religion. Her mother was a proper woman who trained Evelyn in etiquette; her father was a successful barrister who loved yachting. Evelyn and her parents enjoyed their social life in London and holidays on the sea. In their later years, she had them for lunch everyday and often took her mother on trips to the Continent.

This chapter considers her experiences and images of the self, God, Christ, the church, and the world. Her own religious experience is viewed as the foundation for and personal expression of her spirituality for daily living.

Evelyn Underhill's Experiences and Images of the Self

An image of her self is revealed in Evelyn Underhill's early desire to write as a way to reach and touch people: "When I grow up I should like to be an author because you can influence people more widely by books than by pictures" (12/6/1892, Cropper, 6). Her keen desire to influence people was supported and transformed by her desire to work for the glory of God.

When Evelyn was eighteen, she considered openness and compassion based on a sense of oneness to be the most important womanly attitudes of heart, as she wrote in an article called, "How Should a Girl Prepare Herself for a Worthy Womanhood:"

> In order to become widely and generally sympathetic, a girl should try to cultivate a habit of observation and interest in everything, not only in her fellow-creatures but in all the beauties of nature and art. . . If she gets no further than this she will at any rate have made herself a pleasant and sociable companion; but she must, if she wishes her life to be good and beautiful, acquire what Watson called a sense of oneness with our kind, which helps us to remember that A may be stupid and B tiresome, yet they are just as worthy of our tact and consideration as other more brilliant or pleasing people.[1]

This sense of oneness is an apt image of spirituality for today when our postmodern paradigm is one of interconnectedness. She went on to say:

> A girl who can converse on every subject from metaphysics to penny novelettes but cannot darn a stocking or boil a potato, is not, in my opinion, a worthy specimen of womanhood. Nothing fosters helplessness so much as an education which gives all its attention to the brain but utterly neglects the hands.[2]

She described as well an image of the self as a balance between the abstract and the concrete, an insistence on our embodied way of knowing, or what might be called the incarnational principle which marked all her life and thought. When she was nineteen, she revealed another image of herself not as restless and pessimistic but as an earnest, unassuming student, contented even in an atmosphere of agnosticism.[3]

Evelyn Underhill was influenced by the sea and Europe. In her youth she was familiar with her father's yacht; she with her parents, and later with Hubert, her husband, took yachting holidays. Evelyn accompanied her mother to Switzerland and Italy in 1898, the first of many such trips to the Continent. For her Europe was like a homecoming, a mirror experience of her self. She remarked: "Italy, the holy land of Europe, the only place left, I suppose, that is really medicinal to the soul. There is a type of mind which must go there to find itself" (Cropper, 13).

Underhill studied history and botany at King's College, London. She also took lessons in art, bookbinding, and cookery. These classes enabled her to develop nondevotional interests (Armstrong, 4-23; Cropper, 1-15).

Her ability to integrate the practical and spiritual, and even to view the practical as spiritual, was evident in her first novel, *The Grey World*. Her ability to combine the common sense of realism with the idealism of her convictions was a lifelong trait. A New York reviewer observed: "The most striking characteristic of the book is found in the fact that the writer has one eye constantly fixed on the most concrete matters and incidents, while the other is as constantly engaged in exploring the spiritual depths."[4]

Integration marked her ideal self-image and the search for integration characterized her life, for example, the three years during which she wrote *Mysticism.* As Dana Greene has observed: "The quiet support of Hubert, the regularity of leisure, her social commitments, the cats and garden, were all essential to keep her romantic spirit on course" (*Artist,* 47). This aspect of balance, while it characterized her pastoral advice to others, was always a difficult lesson for her to learn.

As growing demands for addresses and writing conflicted with family duties and her work with the poor, she felt in need of direction. In October 1922, she claimed she heard an inner voice after which she felt "called out and settled" *(Fragments,* 43; *Artist,* 85, 98-119).

Underhill knew intuitively the healing power of learning the stories and symbols of heroes, in her case, the mystics like Francis of Assisi, Ruysbroeck, and Richard Rolle. She also had her heroines like Julian of Norwich and Teresa of Avila.[5]

According to her 1923-1924 journal, called the Green Notebook, Underhill was increasingly conscious of her unredeemed self as healed more by adoration than by mortification. Her Lent 1923 resolutions reflected her tendency to dwell on discipline more than on dependence on God. Her preoccupation with her faults, temptation to desolation, and doubts about her experience would be a lifelong struggle, recurring in times of nervous exhaustion (*Fragments,* 35-37, 44, 46, 53, 64).

Keenly aware of herself, she realized that the hidden peace springing up when the mind is rested and free from anxiety is probably what the medieval mystics meant by the "ground of the soul." For example, her illnesses were times of such quiet which allowed for a deepening of her prayer. In a December 1923 entry, she used the image of the house of the soul on which she later based a set of retreat addresses. Peace and joy characterized the strength and balance she felt (*Fragments,* 54-56, 66).

She frequently advised different kinds of people: Daphne Martin-Hurst, a medical social worker who became an Anglican nun; Lucy Menzies, a Presbyterian author of religious books who joined the Anglican church in 1923 and became warden of the Retreat House at Pleshey for a decade; Agatha Norman, a theological student; Margaret Robinson, a single laywoman; Mrs. Laura Rose, a widow with children in the North Kensington slums; Clara Smith, her secretary; and Margaret Smith, an Islamic scholar and teacher at Girton. She called them forth to be their true selves before God. Through her, some of them got to know one another. She helped her friends to empower themselves and one another to be mystics.[6]

Evelyn Underhill had a marvelous sense of humor which must have saved her on many occasions. In a 1924 letter from Assisi, she wrote about being at a sunrise Mass on the Feast of the Stigmata: "The lay congregation consisted of half a dozen peasants, a few mosquitoes, and myself" (*Lt,* 159). She thought nothing of referring to her mother as "the Missis" in letters to Hubert and to the Baron as "my Old Man" to Laura Rose (*Lt,* 117; 160). In describing the movement from consolations to the dark night, Underhill used a homey metaphor: "The transition when the jam-jar is removed from the nursery table and only the loaf is left--is very bitter to our babyish spirits but *must* happen if we are to grow up" (1/10/34, *Lt,* 231). At a retreat at Liverpool, one of the women retreatants said that while she was watering their souls, she hoped that Evelyn would get a few drops for herself, and Evelyn replied: "Well, I have to give most of my attention to holding on to the can" (10/31/28, *Lt,* 334)!

The death of her mother in the spring of 1924 and the death of Baron von Hügel at the beginning of 1925 took their toll on Evelyn, and she was ill for most of 1925. The loss of these two significant people only mirrored the stripping that was going on within her, which Grace Adolphsen Brame has called a crucifixion of the ego (*Ways,* 16).

At her father's death in 1939, Evelyn must have felt the barrenness of what had been her relationship with him and the loss of what might have been. She had tried to win her father's attention and affection by writing *A Bar Lamb's Ballad* about his world of law, dedicating a book of her poems to him, and then being faithful to the dutiful visits and lunches and vacations on the yacht.[7] Perhaps she was never able to embody his positive masculine traits.

Experiences and Images of God

What were Evelyn's experiences and images of God? She was confirmed at sixteen and shortly afterwards expressed her own credo:

> I believe in God and think it is better to love and help the poor people around me than to go on saying that I love an abstract spirit whom I have never seen. If I can do both, all the better, but it is best to begin with the nearest. I do not think anything is gained by being orthodox, and a great deal of beauty and sweetness of things is lost by being bigoted and dogmatic. If we are to see God at all it must be through nature and our fellow men.

> I don't believe in worrying God with prayers for things we want. If he is
> omnipotent he knows we want them, and if he isn't, He can't give them to
> us. I think it is an insult to Him to repeat the same prayers every day. It is as
> much as to say He is deaf, or very slow of comprehension.
>   I do not believe the Bible is inspired, but I think nevertheless that it is one
> of the best and wisest books the world has ever seen (Cropper, 5).

In this entry she claimed that she experienced God's self-revelation in
nature, people, especially poor people, and beauty, not in the Judeo-
Christian scriptures. Her image of God's omnipotence forestalls nagging
God about our needs.

One of her earliest essays about experiencing God in beauty and nature
appeared in "A Woman's Thoughts about Silence:"

> Go out under the solemn stars and strive to think of the Infinite Love which
> guides and governs them in their courses from the least to the greatest,
> which is also guiding these poor human lives of ours, each to fulfil a
> Divinely appointed purpose.[8]

This advice seems timely in light of the new cosmology taught by
Thomas Berry and Brian Swimme and the way this is influencing our
contemporary spirituality and challenging us to shift from an
anthropocentric to a cosmocentric spirituality: instead of focusing only
on our relationship with God, we are invited to ponder as well the
universe and its relationship with God and with us.[9]

In "A Green Mass," (1904), Underhill's love of nature is coupled with
a strong sense of the liturgy of the woods ritualized in the worship
offered by the daily living of even the smallest forest animals, and by the
need for the healing of creation. In this short story, she seemed to be
giving the Roman liturgy its context in nature and the creatures on the
earth, as if inviting its readers to ponder and celebrate the canticle of the
cosmos sung by birds, animals, plants, and trees.[10]

In a revealing letter in 1911, Underhill recalled that she believed
herself to be an atheist for about eight or nine years. Then philosophy
brought her to a theism which was not long-lived. After frequenting both
Anglican and Roman churches at the time, she was finally drawn to stay
for a few days at a convent after which she was convinced by a vision
that Catholicism was the true religion and her ultimate home. Painfully
aware of the narrow exclusiveness of Rome made so clear in its
resistance to Modernism, she nevertheless granted that Roman
Catholicism had kept its mysteries intact: "There I can touch--see--feel
Reality: and--speaking for myself only--nowhere else. . . to join any
other communion is simply an impossible thought."(*Lt*, 126).

When she was twenty-three, her first of sixteen trips to Italy and the
rest of the continent showed her forcibly that beauty was a way to God.

This beauty was not only in nature and art, but also in religious ritual, that is, in the Roman Catholic ritual of the medieval world as well as of the late nineteenth-early twentieth centuries. Her appreciation of European architecture as a medium of God's revelation is expressed in her book on *Shrines and Cities of France and Italy*.[11]

Her deep need and desire for intimacy can be understood in light of her lonely youth, her parents' emotional distance from her, and her dispassionate marriage. As Dana Greene has perceptively observed:

> What dominates in her twenties and thirties is a desire for intimacy that she found neither with her parents nor with Hubert. In the mystic's relationship with God, however, she saw both intimacy and freedom from self; this became the paradigmatic relationship not only for herself but for all humanity (*Artist*, 107).

Later on she adopted in her own spirituality three attitudes of heart that characterized the French School of Spirituality: adoration, adherence or communion, and cooperation with God.[12] She was drawn to focus on God not on herself, and invited others to do likewise.

In December 1923, she recorded in her Green Notebook that for a few minutes of prayer, she knew the ocean of love immersing her and all in one love, even though she would fall into separateness again. Later on, she expanded on this image, writing of sea waters passing through a shell fish, of being plunged in a formless joy, and of submerging desire in the ocean of charity (*Fragments*, 55, 60, 85).

One dominant image in Underhill's spiritual life was the image of God as the ocean or the sea. For her it was a compelling image that combined strength and tenderness, power and protection, surrender and union. She offered it to others in her writings, quoting from the mystics. This is an example of how her spiritual guidance showed her integration of her experience and her knowledge of the mystics.

In 1925, Evelyn Underhill described the experience of God as a call to service: "Now the experience of God . . . is, I believe, in the long run always a vocational experience. It always impels to some sort of service: always awakens an energetic love. It never leaves the self where it found it."[13] This call had certainly been her experience when she began giving retreats and spiritual direction within the Anglican communion.

Experiences and Images of Christ

At Ascensiontide in 1922, Evelyn Underhill made her first retreat at the Anglican Retreat House at Pleshey. The silent support and prayer of her fellow retreatants helped her feel she belonged to the Christian family. She realized how beautiful and real the Christian life is and her experience of Christ in Holy Communion seemed to be particularly significant to her. This felt presence of God in tranquil surrender marked a turning point in her conversion.[14]

One Sunday morning in February 1923, Underhill sick in bed was given an experience of Christ, a sheer gift in spite of her irritability later that same day. In June a sense of the self-outpouring of Christ's whole life came to her at Communion *(Fragments,* 37-38, 47-48).

In a letter of 1927, Underhill confided how Baron von Hügel had helped her receive a personal experience of Christ:

Somehow by his prayers or something he compelled me to experience Christ. He never said anything more about it--but I know humanly speaking he did it. It took about four months--it was like watching the sun rise very slowly--and then suddenly one knew what it was *(Lt,* 26).

She went on to indicate that her life of prayer had become increasingly Christocentric. For one thing, "that sort of quasi-involuntary prayer which springs up of itself at odd moments is always now directed to Him. I seem to have to try as it were to live more and more towards Him only-- and it's all this which makes it so utterly heartbreaking when one is horrid" *(Lt,* 26). The New Testament also came alive for her, and Holy Communion which she once did out of duty became delightful to her.

In 1932, she wrote: "I came to Christ through God, whereas quite obviously lots of people came to God through Christ. But I can't show them how to do that -- all I know about is the reverse route" *(Lt,* 205-206). Clearly her spirituality continued to be basically theocentric but grounded in the concreteness of the Incarnation.

Experiences and Images of the Church

In her adolescence, Evelyn Underhill considered institutional religion to be narrow and exclusive, falsely self-exalting. Visits to the Continent, and in particular a visit to San Marco in Venice on Easter Sunday in 1905, however, showed her the Roman Catholic Church as a great spiritual household that communicated strength, order, and coherence to its members.[15]

In February 1907, she made a retreat at a Franciscan convent after which she experienced the truth of the Catholic religion. Torn between her commitment to intellectual honesty and her mystical quest in the Catholic church, she began a correspondence with Robert Hugh Benson, an ordained convert from Anglicanism to Roman Catholicism and a writer on mysticism, who helped her clarify her choices *(Lt* 13, 36, 56).[16]

When she married the Anglican barrister Hubert Stuart Moore in July 1907, she had hoped to become a Roman Catholic but decided to wait. Her husband's chief objection was that her confessor would make a third in their marriage with rights of possession over her. The Vatican condemnation of Modernism that same year confirmed her decision to wait. She and Hubert went to the Anglican church only for weddings and funerals. For about fourteen years, then, she was a nominal Anglican.[17]

In March 1910, Evelyn went to Rome with her mother. Her audience with Pius X left her with a favorable impression of his kindness, holiness, and simplicity. She recognized his spiritual leadership even though she did not agree with him intellectually or politically (4/1910, *Lt,* 113-14).

Evelyn's closest friend, Ethel Ross Barker, who became a Roman Catholic and accompanied Evelyn to liturgies, died in 1921. After losing this faith-companion, Evelyn joined the Anglican communion in which she had been baptized and confirmed, and sought spiritual direction from Baron Friedrich von Hügel.[18]

As a prominent Anglican woman lecturer and spiritual writer, she was often the only woman on Anglican church commissions. She was a member of the commission on the 1929 *Prayer Book* of the Church of England, the revision of which was never adopted by Parliament. Her retreat work and books on spiritual direction and the spiritual life made a significant contribution. She offered retreats at Pleshey, Cumbrae, Glastonbury, Leiston Abbey, Moreton, and Water Millock (Cropper, 119,141-43).

Her sense of the oneness of humanity in Christ was based on her personal experience of communion in the Body of Christ. In a February 1923 letter she wrote: "Yesterday I *saw and felt* how it actually is that we are in Christ and He in us--the interpenetration of Spirit--and all of us merged together in Him actually, and so fully described as His Body. The way to full intercessory power must, I think, be along this path" (*Lt,* 28; *Fragments,* 35-36). This vision of the life of the Spirit in us all marked her entire life of faith and her service in the Anglican Church (*Artist,* 100).

When Underhill rejoined the Anglican communion in 1921, she made it plain that she was an Anglo-Catholic who valued the place of sacramental worship. It was appropriate, then, that she be asked to write reviews of books about the Anglo-Catholic revival. She was extremely interested in and committed to efforts at reunion among Protestant churches like the Lambeth Conference, and intercommunion between the free churches and Anglicans.[19]

Underhill allied with Anglo-Catholicism and did everything she could to strengthen the influence of this tradition. Her growing confidence in her call to be in the Anglican church led her to make her retreats at Anglican retreat houses and to seek counsel from Anglicans (*Artist*, 102).

In April 1924, she further developed her imagery of the body of Christ writing about a cell in a boundless living web linked with others involved in redeeming work. She connected Communion with Christ's self-giving, not being rescued but being part of his rescuing body (*Fragments*, 37-38, 47, 61, 63).

In a February 8, 1935 letter, Underhill confided that she had just joined the Anglo-Russian confraternity out of her interest in the Orthodox Church, an interest might have been fostered by her director, Walter Howard Frere, who was himself very drawn to the Russian Church. In a June 27, 1935 letter, she indicated that she had attended the Anglo-Russian Conference and had loved the Orthodox services and a few days later, she described a Russian Liturgy she had attended. In a January 23, 1937 letter, she claimed that the Russian Orthodox sense of Christ's presence in the liturgy and refusal to venerate the reserved sacrament except for the sick influenced her later inability to consider veneration of the reserved sacrament as a theologically sound practice, although it was still very meaningful to her personally (*Lt*, 243, 248, 249, 255).

In her introduction to *Mysticism and the Eastern Church* by Nicholas Arseniev, she underscored the contribution of the Eastern Church to Christian mysticism with its emphasis on the centrality of the resurrection and its focus on the Eucharist. Its awareness of the inward in the outward allowed the West to view the visible world as a manifestation of God's glory and to extend the Christian message of hope beyond human beings to the whole universe which is destined to be transformed by the Spirit. In this perspective, the Eucharist takes on cosmic meaning by witnessing to this ultimate transfiguration of the material order. Underhill defended the profound nature of the Orthodox doctrine of icons against the suspicion regarding the use of images in worship.[20]

Over the years, Underhill became more and more strongly committed to ecumenism. Familiar with and favorable toward the efforts of the Benedictine Monks of Union in Belgium to foster ecumenical dialogue with members of the Roman, Orthodox, and Anglican communion, she welcomed efforts toward building Christian unity such as the January octave for unity. Joining the Confraternity of the Spiritual Entente, founded by Sorella Maria in Italy, Underhill wrote a pamphlet in 1923 describing the confraternity as an invisible fellowship of prayer for Christian unity which acted like leaven. She encouraged Maisie Spens who formed a communion of praise whereby Christians would pray together for Christian unity and build union in adoration, and promoted Maisie's efforts by publicizing them to her correspondents.[21]

Underhill supported the Anglican-Roman Catholic dialogue. She felt that the Conversations at Malines 1921-1925 between Anglicans and Roman Catholics, including Cardinal Mercier and Dr. Frere, later Underhill's spiritual director, were an important step to improve sympathy and shed prejudice.[22]

She was also increasingly open to interreligious dialogue. Her familiarity with and respect for Sufi mystics is reflected in her help with the translation of the poems of Kabir. In reviewing a book about early mysticism in the Near and Middle East, she acknowledged the early contacts between Christianity and Islam when Moslem conquerors were dependent on Christian educators and an existent Christian culture. In reviewing a book about Rabi'a, a Moslem woman mystic, Underhill observed that mortification and prayer remain the twofold mystic way to loving union with God in Christianity and in Islam. While she saw similarities, she was also aware of differences between the spiritual life and experience of East and West.[23]

In an essay on "Christianity and the Claims of Other Religions," she acknowledged that union with God is possible outside of Christianity on the one hand, while on the other hand, she asserted that Christianity's claim to uniqueness as a world religion must demonstrate the life-enhancing power of its vision of God, its experience of God, and its obligation toward God. Unlike the non-Christian theism of Buddhism, Hinduism, and the religious philosophies of China, the Christian revelation is of a God incarnate in Christ who is both infinite and personal, transcendent and immanent. The Incarnation implies a sacramental view of the world. For Underhill, Christianity cuts across other forms of theism without dismissing them or regarding them as imperfect revelations of God. Its view of God is superior regarding holiness, redemption, and grace, that is, the reality of the universe is basically ethical, God works within the world to redeem it from sin, and grace is God's love active in our lives. Christianity is both personal and social; it involves the penetration of every moment by the Spirit of Christ. Its full claim to be God's peculiar self-revelation to people must reflect a balance between expansion and inwardness, orthodoxy and initiative, zeal and quietude, the application of the Christian ethic to private life and its application to public life. While granting the value of non-Christian religions and of dialogue with them, Underhill underscored Christianity's uniqueness.[24]

Underhill made a particular study of Jewish mysticism. Her review of two books on Jewish mysticism revealed her familiarity with the Zobar, the sacred book of one branch of mystical Judaism.[25]

In the end, what kind of Christian was Evelyn Underhill? Certainly she was committed to the Anglican communion of worship and service. At the same time, she was strongly drawn to the mystical and sacramental aspects of Roman Catholicism. She entered into ecumenical dialogue with the Russian Orthodox Church and participated in their liturgies. She joined other Christians in consciously praying for Christian unity. And she engaged in interfaith dialogue with mystics who were affiliated with other world religions such as Jewish mysics and Sufi writers.

Experiences and Images of the World

Underhill valued natural beauty tremendously. Her experiences of travel in England and on the Continent, the sea, mountains, and gardening brought her close to nature, the seasons, and the cycles of the earth. She invoked her own mystical experience of having seen God's beauty in the world's ugliness: "The first thing I found out was exalted and indescribable beauty in the most squalid places. I still remember walking down the Notting Hill main road and observing the (extremely sordid) landscape with joy and astonishment" (7/29/1908, *Lt*, 80). She did not find the ugly beautiful but she found something beautiful in the ugly. It was perhaps her ability to find God in squalor that enabled her to connect her love of the poor with her love of God.

For many years, the world in which Evelyn lived and worked was a safe place, an interesting place, a sacred place wherein she sought God. World War I drove a wedge in this haven, when a home on her block was bombed and the place where her husband worked was destroyed. When the war began, she visited the families of soldiers and sailors, and in 1916 worked in the African section of naval intelligence at the Admiralty where she wrote guide books (*Artist*, 67-68).

Underhill almost postponed the publication of *Practical Mysticism: A Little Book for Normal People*, 1914. The outbreak of World War I in England made it difficult to reconcile the mystical attitude of self-surrender with the struggle and sacrifice called for; a contemplative attitude calling for quietness of mind with conflict; and a conviction about the immanence of the Divine Spirit with the horror of human history. Refusal to accept the compatibility of the principles of mysticism and the duties of national life meant reducing mysticism to the status of a spiritual toy. Suffering and hardship could often, in fact, throw into relief a spiritual vision which would otherwise lose stability and certitude in time of distress. This did not mean that a mystical consciousness isolated people from the pain and toil of daily life in some sort of separate peace; instead it could renew vitality, give people a perspective from which to discern the real from the illusory, and a capacity for practical judgment. Those practicing the spiritual life did not abstract from the world of things. They were not a whole human being unless and until they owned and exercised their spiritual gifts. Practical mysticism increased efficiency, wisdom, and perseverance, helping us enter into the life of the group to which we belonged, teaching us to see the world in relationship to the eternal, educating us to love in a steadfast not sentimental way (*Practical,* vii-xi). Her sense of the interconnectedness of the universe, God, and us is conveyed in the following passage:

> Whether you realise it in its personal or impersonal manifestation, the universe is now friendly to you; and as he is a suspicious and unworthy lover who asks every day for renewed demonstrations of love, so you do not demand from it perpetual reassurances. It is enough, that once it showed you its heart. A link of love now binds you to it for evermore: in spite of derelictions, in spite of darkness and suffering, your will is harmonised with the Will that informs the Whole *(Practical,* 167-68).

In 1915 and 1916 she published a pamphlet and several articles which urged the necessity of mysticism in a time of war. She showed the value of mysticism in providing detachment from war's violence and heroic action. She dispelled certain misunderstandings, namely, that concrete patriotic action takes the place of contemplative prayer, that a mystic is necessarily a pacifist in the sense of standing aloof from conflict, and that the mystical outlook contradicts the facts of war. War can provide new opportunities for service, love, loyalty, corporate life, the displacement of selfishness, and individualism, but spiritual destruction is the real horror of war. The consecration of England means the cultivation of a spirit of faith, hope, and love, which implies interior warfare that in the Spirit must accompany the battle for deliverance from outward forces of evil. In the fight for right one uses visible and invisible weapons to defeat cruelty and injustice, risking death in the service of humankind. Her plea for no non-combatants in World War I was a far cry from her pacifist stance in World War II.[26]

In 1918, she worked on a book on Jacopone da Todi, an Italian medieval Franciscan lay-brother and poet, in whom "she saw the world-denying tendency of the Neoplatonic overcome by the world-affirming orientation of the Franciscan. The link between these two disparate positions was Jacopone's profound sense of poverty which led him from a life of asceticism to one of an ecstatic poet" (*Jacopone*, 26; *Artist*, 71). This experience of studying Jacopone da Todi had something to do with the shift in Underhill from denial of the world of shadow to affirmation of the world of the real. It inaugurated her shift away from Neoplatonism, its "flight of the alone to the Alone" and its detached pursuit of the transcendent, to Christianity, its creative way to deal with sin and evil, and its commitment of love for the world. It marked a step for her away from the dualism of Neoplatonic idealism to the duality of what was then called "critical realism."[27]

Around 1921, she began to move toward an institutional affiliation with the Anglican church. At the same time, Underhill began to prepare a series of lectures she was to give at the Manchester College of Oxford University as the first woman lecturer in religion on the university list. These lectures published in 1922 as *The Life of the Spirit and the Life of Today* represented a corresponding shift in her focus: they were not about mysticism but rather about the spiritual life, talking about people's relationship to God viewed as the life of the Spirit and the life of today. These lectures challenged religion's tendency to reduce the religious response to the social gospel, stressing instead the centrality of God expressed in a commitment to prayer and inclusive love (*Artist*, 71-76).

Characteristic of all her work was the care she gave others, responding instantly to whomever sought her help and being interested in the tiny details of their lives such as their hobbies, their amusements, and their animal friends. She took the trouble to become a friend to so many. And she counted on her friends, begging their prayer for each retreat she gave and reading out their names at the retreat as members of a kind of prayer support team, a *palanca (Light*, 22).

Underhill valued work. Workaholism might be attributable to her since she undertook the writing of so many books and articles, in spite of her fragile health, commitments as a barrister's wife in London, care for aging parents, and lack of the technological helps that we take for granted in our day. She believed that work was valuable and purposeful for all since she found work for herself was so. She must have experienced work as co-creative. Perhaps because she was a trailblazer for women in undertaking research on mysticism and reflections on the spiritual life, it may not have occurred to her to write much about the value of meaningful work as such, especially for women. Yet she was aware of the tendencies of workaholics to aggravate anxiety hysteria through nervous exhaustion.[28] In 1923 she gave an address on "The Spiritual Aspect of Work among Young Girls" in which she hammered home her point about finding the spiritual aspect of the practical, the transcendent in the homey, the divine mystery in the human problem. She compared the mysterious quiet of a night sky of stars with the atmosphere of an average committee room in order to bewail the lack of spiritual substance in much social work:

> Yet only this will keep us aware of the underlying unity of all life's effort; and will defend us both from the depressing effect of small failures and the self-satisfaction born of small success. There must be a touch of contemplation in our action, if it is to be right.[29]

Later in one of her essays, she asked whether we know many people who work and will in quiet love, thus participating in eternal life: "Willed work, not grudging toil. Quiet love, not feverish emotionalism" (*Spirit, 26).* I would call this the basis of her spirituality of work: the freedom to choose in faith, the fidelity to persevere without feeling. Willed work means focused energy not frenetic energy that is dissipated. What would it have been like if Underhill herself had incorporated into her spiritual dictums something about the co-creative value of work for women in particular? She herself could easily have identified with the following passage written by the Benedictine Joan Chittister in her chapter on "Work: Participation in Creation:"

> Work is my gift to the world. It is my social fruitfulness. It ties me to my neighbor and binds me to the future. It lights up that spark in me that is most like the God of Genesis. I tidy the garden and plant the garden and distribute the goods of the garden and know that it is good.[30]

In her work, Underhill discovered that working faithfully involves a struggle to see a connection between what we do and a broader sense of purpose. For Underhill, this perspective was contained in adoration, adherence or communion, and cooperation with God, the threefold doctrine of the French School of Spirituality. Second, working faithfully involves an inner effort. For Underhill, this meant the discipline of integrating her retreat work and writing with her commitments as wife and daughter. Working faithfully implies valuing the process as well as the product. Underhill learned to honor the process of gardening and scriptwriting as well as the products she published. Lastly, working faithfully has to do with overcoming the false duality between the sacred and the secular. Underhill committed herself to a serious Christian life in the world; she did not have the safeguards of cloistered life. She had to oversee domestic tasks each morning before she sat down to her desk.

Her outer work on mysticism and her inner work on her own spiritual life came together in her commitment to absolute pacifism before World War II: the peace for which she was striving was not only inner peace but world peace.[31]

Her experience of the world at war and a deepened understanding of the spiritual life led to her pacifist stance. She indicated in a letter of May 1936 that she had read Aldous Huxley's peace pamphlet, *What are you going to do about it?* Underhill was convinced that Christianity meant living ordinary life as the medium of the Incarnation. She was also deeply convinced of the meaning of the Cross as loving abandonment to the worst that might come. From December 1939 on, she identified herself in her letters as a pacifist. She wrote her prayer group of women that had to disband at the beginning of World War II in England to pray for those causing the war and those suffering from it; they were also to pray for themselves to be delivered from the spirit of hatred and bitterness. Her commitment to nonviolence led her to join the Anglican Pacifist Fellowship in 1939 and to publish several articles on peace and how to live the Christian life in a world at war. She advocated living peacefully with warlike people and behaving toward them with compassion and gentleness. Her 1939 pamphlet on *The Spiritual Life in War-Time* emphasized the need for love, joy, peace, time for formal prayer, dealing with the facts and tensions of human life in our prayer, and the redemptive acceptance of suffering. In "A Meditation on Peace," published in 1939 by the Fellowship of Reconciliation, Underhill reflected on peace as a supernatural attitude borne of abandonment to God and sacrifice, not a natural feeling. It is tranquility in anxiety and conflict inseparable from joy. In a 1940 review of a book about the Catholic church, Underhill noted that aerial warfare was considered in certain circumstances as compatible with Christian life, even though divorce and contraception were not. She reviewed two books about Pastor M. Niemöller, a Prussian officer in World War I, who was in a concentration camp during World War II for having spoken out against what was happening in Germany. In *The Church and War,* a 1940 pamphlet written for the Anglican Pacifist Fellowship, Underhill challenged Christianity to make a commitment to peace so that the work of the Spirit could be done. In a 1940 book review, she marveled that a church committed to control of mind, heart, and will by love and truth should not be completely pacifist. In a letter to the editor of *The Challenge,* she criticized church leaders for not making a pronouncement about the war, one which she herself had asked them to do. Her essay called "Postscript," 1941, called pacifism one expression of complete confidence in divine power and urged pacifists to create an atmosphere of tranquillity in a world at war, to witness to God's love by offering and living a message of peace. Increasingly strengthened in her commitment to pacifism, she did not leave her busy, everyday life in the world during World War II, even though she was advised to do so, in order to seek peace. She was not convinced that military victory is a victory of the Spirit. She was convinced that God's purposes are worked out through the disasters of history, even in the apparent defeat of the good.[32]

The realism of her faith led her to commit herself to reconciliation and communion. She took a pacifist stance toward a world sorely in need of God's compassion.

Conclusion

Evelyn Underhill's spiritual life was characterized by a developmental sense of herself as an author and spiritual mentor, a sense of God's beauty and glory in people and in art, of Christ in the gospels and in the concrete details of daily life, of the church as a communal form of worship and service, and of the world as a place of peace. She lived quietly her own trust in God and unpretentious service of the poor.

Underhill's commitment to pacifism at the end of her life established in her an attitude of peace that had individual, social, and political implications. For Underhill, pacifism came to mean an abiding abandonment to God, complete confidence in divine power, and tranquility in anxiety, conflict, and war. Her articles on peace challenged Christians to commit themselves to peace as a way of cooperating with the Spirit. Her pacifism can be viewed as the outgrowth of her lifelong sensitivity to the cause of social justice.[33] One must note the developmental process of her commitment to pacifism: "Underhill's vision of peace was ahead of its time . . . She shows that mature people can reverse earlier positions and remain models of responsible citizenship and ethical sensitivity."[34]

Underhill was granted the breadth of mind and depth of heart for which she had longed as a young girl. After her death, *The Times Literary Supplement* claimed that she had been given "an insight into the meaning both of the culture and of the individual gropings of the soul that was unmatched by any of the professional teachers of her day."[35]

Underhill's books can be divided into two types: her books on mysticism and her books on the spiritual life. It is significant that after World War I when she had achieved prestige, success, and fame with her books on mysticism, she was able to move in a different direction and write books on the spiritual life. This shift probably represented a shift in her self-understanding and values at the time. For years, she had sought, perhaps unconsciously, masculine approval, attention, affirmation through the writing of her scholarly works. These works relied on information about and validation by external authorities. I believe that her decision to write practical works on living the spiritual life in the world symbolized her ability to claim at last her authority, to be her own authority for others, and to help them claim the authority of their religious experience. She found her own voice and invited others, especially other women who attended her retreats and sought her out for spiritual direction, to do likewise.

Underhill valued her own relationship with God and valued helping others to deepen theirs. The only daughter of a well-to-do couple neither of whom understood her, a spouse in a childless marriage, Evelyn turned to the mystics, perhaps because she could not join the Roman Catholic Church. She felt nourished by her study of the mystics and then found ways to nourish others. She discovered the mystics as friends and companions of her spiritual journey. Her familiarity with their works reflected her ease in their company. Her eagerness to make them accessible to a wider public sprang from her sense of others' spiritual hunger for a real and personal relationship with God. In this way, she discovered the truth of the Anglican Frederick Buechner's words about vocation: "Neither the hair shirt nor the soft berth will do. The place God calls you is the place where your deep gladness and the world's deep hunger meet."[36] Let us see how she communicated her simple message in her study of the mystics.

Suggestions for Prayerful Reflection

Annice Callahan, R.S.C.J.

Get in a comfortable position preferably at night and breathe deeply for a few minutes. Ponder this passage written by Evelyn Underhill:

> Go out under the solemn stars and strive to think of the infinite love which guides and governs them in their courses from the least to the greatest, which is also guiding these poor human lives of ours, each to fulfil a Divinely appointed purpose.[37]

1. What helps you try to develop the habit of observation of and interest in creatures and in the beauties of nature and art? What keeps you from doing so?

2. What helps you develop a sense of oneness with everything and with everyone, regardless of whether they are to your liking or not? What keeps you from doing so?

3. What helps you see God in nature and other people? What keeps you from doing so?

4. What image would you use to describe the infinite love which guides and governs the stars as well as our lives?

5. How would you describe the divinely appointed purpose of Underhill's life? of your own life?

Readings

For an excellent contemporary biography of Evelyn Underhill, see Dana Greene, *Evelyn Underhill: Artist of the Infinite Life* (New York: Crossroad, 1990). For an insight into Evelyn's spiritual journey in the years 1923-24 and 1926-1937, with an introduction and annotated entries, see *Fragments from an Inner Life: The Notebooks of Evelyn Underhill,* ed. Dana Greene (Harrisburg, Pa.: Morehouse, 1993).

Notes

1. Evelyn Underhill, "How Should a Girl Prepare Herself for a Worthy Womanhood," *Hearth and Home* (July 27, 1893), EUC, folder 19, DGC, and quoted in D. Greene, *Artist,* 11, n. 14. Emphasis mine.

2. Ibid., n. 15.

3. See E. Underhill under the pseudonym of Shirley, "Are Modern Women as Contented as Their Grandmothers?" *Hearth and Home* (April 5, 1894): 7, DGC.

4. In Lucy Menzies, Biography of Evelyn Underhill, TS unfinished, Underhill Collection, Archives, St. Andrews University Library, St. Andrews, Scotland, III.4, DGC.

5. I am not sure she made the heroine's journey in her quest for wholeness, as Maureen Murdock puts it. See Maureen Murdock, *The Heroine's Journey: Woman's Quest for Wholeness* (Boston: Shambhala, 1990).

6. See, for example, E. Underhill, *Lt* 154, 159, 161, 341; and letters to Daphne Martin-Hurst in "Letters to a Novice," *Evelyn Underhill Anglican Mystic* (Oxford: SLG Press, 1996), 35-47. Cf. D. Greene, *Artist,* 112.

7. *Artist,* 130-31. Today one might call her a typical father's daughter who, by not wanting to be like her mother, ended up emulating her father's values of hard work, dedication, success, and efficiency. I am not sure she ever really left her father's house and made the journey to conscious femininity, as Marion Woodman phrases it. See Marion Woodman et al, *Leaving My Father's House: A Journey to Conscious Femininity* (Boston: Shambhala, 1993). Cf. Wilkie Au and Noreen Cannon, *Urgings of the Heart: A Spirituality of Integration* (New York: Paulist, 1995), esp. 64-77.

8. E. Underhill, "A Woman's Thoughts about Silence," 1892, EUC, folder 19, DGC, and quoted in D. Greene, *Artist,* 9, n. 6.

9. Brian Swimme and Thomas Berry, *The Universe Story* (San Francisco: HarperSan Francisco, 1992).

10. See Underhill, "A Green Mass," *Horlick's Magazine* (1904): 445-448, DGC.

11. See E. Underhill, *Shrines and Cities of France and Italy,* ed. Lucy Menzies (London: Longmans, Green & Co., 1949).

12. On the French School of Spirituality, see William M. Thompson, ed., *Bérulle and the French (School* New York: Paulist Press, 1989); and Raymond Deville, *The French School of Spirituality: An Introduction and Reader*, trans. Agnes Cunningham (Pittsburgh, Pa.: Duquesne University Press, 1994).

13.   Evelyn Underhill,"The Authority of Personal Religious Experience," *Theology* 10, no. 55 (January 1925):13, in *Guide,* 125.

14. See E. Underhill to F. von Hügel, midsummer, 1922, von Hügel-Underhill Collection; and *Fragments,* 111-20. Cf. M. Avery, *Pleshey: The Village and Retreat House* (Bishop's Stortfod: Ellis and Phillips Ltd., 1981); Fay Campbell, "Evelyn Underhill: Conversion at Pleshey," *The Living Church,* 1 March 1987, 11-13.

15. See Lucy Menzies, Biography of Evelyn Underhill, TS unfinished, St. Andrews University Archives, St. Andrews, Scotland, II.10, and III.8, DGC. Cf. D. Greene, *Artist*, 10, n. 10.

16. See E. Underhill, *Lt*, 125. Also in February 4, 1907 diary entry now lost. See Lucy Menzies, "Biography of Evelyn Underhill." Underhill Collection Archives, St. Andrews University Library, St. Andrews, Scotland, DGC, IV.3.

17. See E. Underhill, Letter to Mrs. Meyrick Heath of 5/14/11, *Lt,* 125-26; Pius X, *Lamentabili Sane: Syllabus Condemning the Errors of the Modernists and Pascendi Dominici Gregis in The Papal Encyclicals 1903-1934* ed. Claudia Carlen (Salem, N.H.: McGrath, 1981), 71-97, and Anne Freemantle, *The Papal Encyclicals in their historical context* (New York: Mentor Omega 1963), 197-201, 202-207; and Michael Ramsey;, "Evelyn Underhill," *Evelyn Underhill: Two Centenary Essays* (Oxford: S.L.G. Press, 1977), 16. See also Grace Adolphsen Brame, "Evelyn Underhill and Vatican II: A Comparison of the Catholic Church of Her Time and Ours," *The Evelyn Underhill Association Newsletter* 3 (November 1992): 1-3; and "Evelyn Underhill: The Integrity of Personal Intellect and Individual Religious Experience as Related to Ecclesiastical Authority," *Worship* 68, no. 1 (January 1994): 23-45.
          Cf. Todd Johnson, "In Spirit and Truth: Pneumatology, Modernism and Their Relation to Symbols and Sacraments in the Writings of Evelyn Underhill," (Ph.D. diss.: University of Notre Dame, 1996), 81-89. On p. 82, Johnson claims that "Underhill's reluctance to convert to Catholicism was primarily intellectual." Later on pp. 88-89, he indicates his position that her concession not to join the Roman Catholic church for sake of marriage was influenced by John of the Cross's emphasis on sacrifice.

18. See Armstrong, 30, 200-209; and Michael Ramsey, "Evelyn Underhill," *Religious Studies* 12 (September 1976): 273-79.

19. See, for example, E. Underhill, "Quo Vadis?" review of *A Century of Anglo-Catholicism* by H.L. Stewart, *The Spectator*, 21 September 1929, 374-75, DGC; "Looking Forward," review of *My Hopes and Fears for the Church* by H.R.L. Sheppard, *The Spectator*, 10 May 1930, 788, DGC; and "Ecclesia Anglicana," review of *The History of the Anglo-Catholic Revival from 1845* by W.J. Sparrow Simpson, *The Spectator*, 8 October 1932, 449, DGC. Cf. Delroy Oberg, "Head vs. Heart: Mysticism and Theology in the Life and Writings of Evelyn Underhill," *St. Mark's Review* 149 (1992): 7-14; and Todd E. Johnson, "Evelyn Underhill: Middle-Way within the Via Media?" *The Evelyn Underhill Association Newsletter* 4 (November 1993): 3-4.

20. See E. Underhill, 1926 introduction to *Mysticism and the Eastern Church* by Nicholas Arseniev, tr. Arthur Chambers (Crestwood, N.Y.: St. Vladimir's Seminary Press, 1979), 13-15; her favorable evaluation of Arseniev's "Grace in Christian Mysticism" in "Recent Theology," review of *The Doctrine of Grace*, ed. W.T. Whitley, *The Spectator* (September 10, 1932): 317, DGC; and "Religion and Religions," review of *Holy Images* by Edwyn Bevan, *Time and Tide*, 18 May 1940, 537-58, DGC. Cf. Louis Bouyer, *Orthodox Spirituality and Protestant and Anglican Spirituality* (New York: Seabury, 1969); and Vladimir Lossky, *The Mystical Theology of the Eastern Church* (Crestwood, N.Y.: St. Vladimir's Seminary Press, 1976).

21. See E. Underhill, *The Spiritual Entente*, 1923, in Lucy Menzies, Biography of Evelyn Underhill, VIII.9-10, DGC; "Ut Sint Unum," review of *Irénikon: Bulletin Mensuel des Moines de l"union des Eglises, Avril-Dec., 1926, The Spectator* 19 February 1927, 292, DGC; "Una Sancta," review of *Divided Christendom* by M.J. Congar, *Time and Tide*, 10 June 1939, 762-63, DGC; and idem, 4/30/41, *Lt*, 305-6; 5/5/41, *Lt*, 307; 5/41, *Lt*, 309. See also Margaret O'Gara, "Understanding 'A Certain, though Imperfect ' Communion between Anglicans and Roman Catholics," *The Ecumenical Gift Exchange* (Collegeville, Mn.: Liturgical Press, 1998). Cf. K. Rahner, "Part Two. Ecumenism," *TI* 22: 67-93; and George A. Tavard, *Church: Community of Salvation* (Collegeville, Mn.: Liturgical Press, 1992).

22. See E. Underhill, "The Spirit of Malines," review of *The Conversations at Malines 1921-1925 and Notes on the Conversations at Malines 1921-1925* by Vicount Halifax, *The Spectator*, 28 January 1928, 121, DGC. On Cardinal Mercier, see also E. Underhill, " Cardinal Mercier, review of *Cardinal Mercier* by Georges Goyau, *The Spectator*, 4 December 1926, 1034, DGC; and "Le Grand Sympathique," review of *The Life of Cardinal Mercier* by Henry Louis Dubly, *The Spectator*, 5 May 1928, 685-86, DGC.

23. See E. Underhill, "East and West," review of *Rabi'a the Mystic and her Fellow-Saints in Islam* by Margaret Smith, *The Spectator* 29 December 1928, 995-96; idem, "Saints and Sufis," review of *Studies in Early Mysticism in the Near and Middle East* by Margaret Smith, *The Spectator*, 17 October 1931, 499, DGC; and idem, "Meeting in the Centre," review of *Mysticism East and West* by Rudolf Otto, *The Spectator*, 2 April 1932, 482, DGC. Cf. Margaret Smith, *Rabi'a the Mystic and her Fellow-Saints in Islam* (Cambridge: Cambridge University Press, 1928); *The Way of the Mystics: The Early Christian Mystics and the Rise of the Sufis* (London: Sheldon Press, 1976); and *An Introduction to Mysticism* (London: Sheldon Press, 1977).

24. See E. Underhill, "Christianity and the Claims of Other Religions," *Essays Catholic and Missionary*, ed. Edmund Robert Morgan (New York: Macmillan, 1928), 3-22. Cf. Kevin Hogan, "The Experience of Reality: Evelyn Underhill and Religious Pluralism," *Anglican Theological Review* 74, no. 3 (Summer 1992): 334-47. For an argument against Christianity's uniqueness and superiority, see Roger Haight,"Towards an Understanding of Christ in the Context of Other World Religions," *East Asian Pastoral Review* 26 (1989): 248-265. Cf. K. Rahner, "Jesus Christ in the Non-Christian Religions," and "The One Christ and the Universality of Salvation," *TI* 16: 39-50 and 199-224; and "Christianity's Absolute Claim," *TI* 21: 171-84.

25. E. Underhill, "Jewish Mysticism," review of *The Zobar in Moslem and Christian Spain* by Ariel Bension, and *The Messiah of Ismir Sabbatai Zevi* by Josef Kastein, *The Spectator*, 3 September 1932, 291, DGC.

26. See E. Underhill, "The Consecration of England," *For the Right: Essays and Addresses by Members of the Fight for Right Movement* (New York: G.P. Putnam's Sons, 1918), 232-42, DGC; *Mysticism and War* (London: John Watkins, 1915), DGC; "A Note on the Fight for Right Movement," *The Training of the Combatant* by Caroline F.E. Spurgeon (London: J.M. Dent and Sons, 1916), 21-28, DGC; and "Problems of Conflict," *Hibbert Journal* 13 (April 1915): 497-510, DGC. Cf. D. Greene, *Artist*, 68, n. 59.

27. The term "critical realism" is used here in the sense in which Baron von Hügel used it, that is, to refer to a philosophy based on the dual nature of reality, namely the temporal and the eternal: the finite is a sacrament of the infinite. See *Fragments*, 28. Later, when Underhill wrote the preface to the twelfth edition of *Mysticism* in 1930, she referred to philosophers who were bringing back into modern thought the "critical realism" of the scholastics. In this context, she was using the term in another sense, one which has been refined by twentieth-century cognitional theory. See Appendix: A Note on Critical Realism.

 For the view denying that she made the shift to a duality and for a critique of her basically dualistic account of the relationship between God and the world, see Terry Tastard, "Divine Presence and Human Freedom: The Spirituality of

Evelyn Underhill Reconsidered," *Theology* 104, no. 762 (Nov./Dec. 1991): 426-432.

28. Lucy Menzies, a Presbyterian author of religious books who became an Anglican, the warden at the House of Retreat, Pleshey, for ten years, and a close friend, attested to Evelyn's proneness to nervous and physical exhaustion. She remembered being on holiday with the Hubert Stuart Moores in Norway and climbing a mountain with Evelyn. They still had a small summit to reach. Even though Evelyn was tired, she could not resist pushing herself to reach it. Her original austerity yielded only when her health warranted that she choose care and comfort. According to Menzies, what saved Underhill was that she could avail herself of the lengthy holidays afforded to lawyers in her time since her husband was a lawyer: "But she arrived at those holidays drained to the last drop of her vitality." Lucy Menzies, *Light*, 16. Cf. Greene, *Artist*, 99. See also E. Underhill, "The Beauty of Holiness," review of *Mirrors of the Holy: Ten Studies in Sanctity* by Lucy Menzies, *The Spectator*, 10 November 1928, 703, DGC.

29. E. Underhill, "The Spiritual Aspect of Work among Young Girls," in Lucy Menzies, Biography of Evelyn Underhill, XI.23-24, DGC.

30. Joan Chittister, "Work: Participation in Creation," *Wisdom Distilled from the Daily: Living the Rule of St. Benedict Today* (San Francisco: HarperSan Francisco, 1990), 92-93.

31. For points in this paragraph about working faithfully, see Doris Donnelly, "To Work Faithfully," *Weavings: A Journal of the Christian Spiritual Life* 8, no. 1 (January/February 1993): 27-32. Cf. Eric Steven Dale, *Bringing Heaven Down to Earth: A Practical Spirituality of Work* (New York: Peter Lang, 1991); Elizabeth Dreyer, "Towards a Spirituality of Work," *Earth Crammed with Heaven: A Spirituality of Everyday Life* (New York: Paulist, 1994), 84-99; Joe Holland, *Creative Communion: Toward a Spirituality of Work* (New York: Paulist Press, 1989); Dorothee Sölle, *To Work and To Love: A Theology of Creation* (Philadelphia: Fortress, 1986), esp. 83-113; and Douglas Steere, *Work and Contemplation* (New York: Harper & Row, 1957).

32. On incarnational living, see E. Underhill, letter of 1937, *Lt*, 259. On her pacifism, see E. Underhill, letter of 12/39, *Lt*, 283-84; 1/40, *Lt*, 286; 5/20/40, *Lt*, 288; 4/27/41, *Lt*, 305; 5/12/41, *Lt*, 308; 6/41, *Lt*, 310; *Guide*, 197-217; id., "Men and Books," review of *Peace and Pacifism* by Humphrey Beevor, *Time and Tide*, 5 March 1938, 312-13, DGC; id., *Fruits*, 46-47; id., "Prayer in Wartime," in *G.D.A. Letter*, 1 November 1939, 2-5, DGC; id., *A Service of Prayer for Use in Wartime* (London: Christian Literature Association, 1939); id., *Spiritual Life in Wartime* (London: Christian Literature Association, 1939), DGC; id., "Martin Niemöller," review of *From U-boat to Concentration Camp and Pastor Niemöller and His Creed, Time and Tide*, 18 February 1939, 213;

id., *The Church and War* (London: Anglican Pacifist Fellowship, 1940); id., "Lenten Fare," review of *Readings in St. John's Gospel, 2nd Series* by William Temple, *The Love of God: an Essay in Analysis* by Aelred Graham, and *Christian Discourses* by Sören Kierkegaard, *Time and Tide,* 10 February 1940, 141-42, DGC; id., "Letter to the Editor," *Time and Tide,* 20 July 1940, DGC; id., "What about the Church?" review of *The Betrayal of Christ by the Churches* by J. Middleton Murry, *The Church of England* by Cecilia Ady, and *Catholic Design for Living* by G.B. Bentley, *Time and Tide,* 30 November 1940, 1162-1164, DGC; and id., letter to the editor, *The Challenge,* n.d. Cf. James R. Horne, "A Moral Mystic--Evelyn Underhill," *The Moral Mystic* (Waterloo, Ontario: Wilfrid Laurier University Press, 1983), 77-84; D. Greene, "Evelyn Underhill and Her Response to War," *The Historical Magazine of the Protestant Episcopal Church* (June 1986): 127-35; and *Artist,* 142, n.48. On the advice of Sister Mary, a Carmelite prioress, that Evelyn retreat from the world's suffering to gain more peace, see Sister Mary of St. John to Evelyn Underhill, Christmas 1940, EUC, folder 45, in *Artist,* 142.

33. See Reginald Cant, "Evelyn Underhill," *Dictionary of Christian Spirituality,* ed. Gordon Wakefield (London: SCM Press, 1983), 381-82.

34. Robert Gail Woods, "'The Future We Shan't See': Evelyn Underhill's Pacifism," *Christian Century* (May 16, 1979): 555. Cf. Martin Ceadel, "Christian Pacifism in the Era of Two World Wars," *Studies in Church Life,* ed. W.J. Sheils, Vol. 20: The Church and War (London: Blackwell, 1983), 391-408.

35. In Lumsden Barkway, introduction to *An Anthology of the Love of God from the Writings of Evelyn Underhill,* ed. Lumsden Barkway and Lucy Menzies (Toronto: Anglican Book Centre, 1976), 17.

36. Frederick Buechner, *Wishful Thinking: A Theological ABC* (New York: Harper & Row, 1973), 95.

37. E. Underhill, "A Woman's Thoughts about Silence," 1892, EUC, folder 19, quoted in D. Greene, *Artist,* 9, n. 6.

Chapter 2

Study of the Mystics

Evelyn Underhill is perhaps best known for her writings on the mystics beginning with the first edition of *Mysticism* in 1911. In this classic on the subject, she described mysticism as "the expression of the innate tendency of the human spirit towards complete harmony with the transcendental order" *(Mysticism,* xiv). She was not interested in naming the end of mysticism but the means to it, insisting that mysticism entailed an authentic life process rather than intellectual speculation. Mystics claim to seek the one whom they have found; they know the reality of God insofar as they themselves are real. By analogy she called mysticism an organic process leading to the love of God and the art of establishing our conscious relationship with God, thereby distinguishing it from a philosophy or the pursuit of occult knowledge on the one hand, and the mere power of contemplating eternity or religious oddness on the other. For her, all its elements refer to natural, organic growth, although accompanying each stage is a specific kind of activity.[1]

Ecumenical and interfaith perspectives mark her study of mysticism. She quoted mystics from different religious traditions even in the same passage, for example, Plato, Rabi'a, the Mohammedan contemplative, the evangelist John, Augustine, Catherine of Genoa, and the Hindu Kabir. And she was familiar with Christian mystics of different denominations, such as Paul, Bernard, Francis of Assisi, Teresa of Avila, John of the Cross, John Wesley, Elizabeth Fry, the Curé d'Ars, George Fox,

Ruysbroeck. She valued mysticism as a human experience and studied Christian mysticism within the cross-cultural and interreligious context of mysticism in general.[2]

What was important for Underhill was the mystics' Christian lives rather than their extraordinary religious experiences. She turned to the mystics as spiritual guides at a time in her life when she had no spiritual director.[3] She trusted the experience of the mystics, although she always found it difficult to trust her own. Since these spiritual geniuses offer a rich storehouse of images about themselves, God, Christ, the church, and the world, let us gather those images which Underhill observed in her study.

The Ground of the Soul

Underhill noticed that the mystics imagined the self in relation to God, for example, as the ground of the soul. She observed that in Western Christian mystics, divine union impels the self to active not passive life. She represented that mystics move from a consciousnesss of the ego, as a center of self-activity, to modes of the divine consciousness and a life of oneness with all that is as an organ revealing universal being. For example, Underhill pointed out that in her description of the Seventh Mansion, Teresa of Avila emphasized divine fecundity not spiritual marriage, turning with greater ease and ardor than before to the service of God.[4]

Underhill conveyed the dignity and depth of the true self in a metaphor. She observed that we treat the ground of our soul, that gathering point of our selfhood, as busy citizens treat a national monument: they never have time to go in, although it gives dignity to their existence. She wrote of our having a capacity for the infinite (*Practical*, 44, 114, 134).

In "The Mystic as Creative Artist," 1913, Underhill developed the point that mystics see infinite reality and convey it to others with imaginative appeal through the use of artistic language. They draw on symbols from all the arts, in particular, music, poetry, and dancing (*Essentials*, 64-85).

Underhill called the mystic a creative artist using the arts to convey a sense of God's presence. In this way, I believe, she conveyed her insight into the likeness between creative intuition and contemplative intuition. At the same time, she was aware that not every mystical poet was a mystic in the technical sense; the mystical poet's urge is to express not to discover. This attraction for self-expression can outweigh the attraction to linger before beauty letting it reveal itself.[5]

For Ruysbroeck, as Underhill reported, we achieve reality through three stages, namely, the active, the interior, and the superessential life. They are symbolized at times by the conditions of servant, friend, and hidden child of God. The active life consists of self-discipline and service. The interior life includes illumination, emotional unrest, union, and contemplation or introversion. The superessential life is the life of glory, unity, and simplicity. Underhill cautioned against drawing parallels between these three stages and the traditional stages of purgation, illumination, and union.[6]

Meister Eckhart called the true self "the spark of the soul" and "the ground of the soul;" Johannes Tauler and Jacob Boehme called it the "ground." Other mystics called it "the apex of the soul," the point where it touches the divine. Sometimes this image meant the transcendental self in contact with God; other times it referred to the divine Spirit present in the cosmos as well as in the human heart.[7]

Underhill described Francis of Assisi as a spiritual realist who wanted his inner and outer life to be one. This "little brother of the birds" called himself a penitent of Assisi. This bridegroom of lady poverty and troubadour of Christ asked of God in the middle of the night "Who are you? and who am I?" In other words, Underhill chose to portray his craving for the infinite and for the austere (*Mystics,* 90-94). In her lecture on "St. Francis and Franciscan Spirituality," 1933, Underhill explored the unconverted life of Francis of Assisi in order to establish that grace builds on nature, that saints are flesh and blood people with a particular psycho-socio-historical context that shapes their holiness. What stands out is that Francis was at home in both the visible and the invisible world, and lived in both at once with reverence and delight. He had a sense of the realness and sacredness of both. He was indifferent to class and convention, stripping off his clothes in the streets of Assisi, friendly with all classes and types of people. He loved music and nature intensely. He had a strong sense of God and of his own creatureliness.[8]

Catherine of Siena emphasized her notion of the cell of self-knowledge in which we are to dwell. By it she implied not only a literal cell in which we dwell in solitude, but also a spiritual cell wherein we dwell in the world. It includes knowledge of self and knowledge of God. Underhill reflected on the meaning of this self-knowledge:

> It is not a niggling introspection, but that clear view of human nothingness matched against the perfection of God which is the sovereign remedy against pride and self-love; the only foundation of that charity which she calls in one of her jeweled phrases "a continual prayer" (*Mystics,* 161).

Toward the end of her life, Catherine of Genoa perceived that she only knew who she was in God. She realized that her being was God, by transformation not only by participation. God became her being, her self, her strength. Underhill's theological reflection on this mystic led her to write:

> In the development which was crowned by such convictions as these, we have an almost classical example of spiritual growth; moving out from the limitations of a selfish and unsatisfied naturalism, through purifying self-discipline and service, to the levels of full, creative personality (*Mystics*, 165).

In mid-life, Teresa founded the reformed Convent of St. Joseph in Avila where her mystical experiences illuminated and supported her undertakings. Underhill remarked on the balance between contemplative prayer and work in the life of Teresa:

> The spiritual and practical sides of her nature were completely harmonized. She could turn from directions about the finances of the community or the right sweeping down of the house to deal in a manner equally wise and precise with the most delicate problems of the soul (*Mystics*, 176).

This insight reflects Underhill's ideal of balance between the spiritual and the practical to the point where one can see the spiritual side of practical things, and where one can exercise wisdom and precision in both realms.

The author of *The Mirror of Simple Souls,* considered today to be Marguerite Porete, emphasized the search for the freedom of love rather than the servitude of love. By freedom, Underhill observed, the author meant the liberation of our will from finite desires that it may rejoin the will of the infinite.[9]

The Cloud of Unknowing described the art of contemplative prayer as a single-minded intent stretching to God, who is known and felt through humility and love. Walter Hilton, Underhill observed, condemned a spirituality that neglected practical tasks in order to indulge in contemplation. His scale of perfection demanded both adoring vision and devoted service. And Lucie-Christine as a devoted wife and mother of five children proved that the mystic vocation includes involvement in ordinary duties and relationships. The Christian Sadhu Sundar Singh lived a balanced life of prayer and work, communicating to others his intense consciousness of God. With all these examples, Underhill underlined how practical mysticism really can be. This position stands in marked contrast with that of Quietism, a religious movement at the end of the seventeenth century in France which stressed the passive element of mysticism to the apparent neglect of the humanity of Christ.[10]

Underhill's essay on "Walter Hilton" revealed her belief in the interaction of divine initiative and human subjectivity when she wrote of Hilton as a teacher of the double movement of docility to the working of grace and the need of a vigorous use of will. She reinforced this conviction when she wrote of his emphasis on the practice of self-oblivious love replacing all self-occupied scruples and struggles with adherence to God in Christ. Her introduction to his book *The Scale of Perfection* described his approach to the mystical life as the flowering of an interior life of love and prayer to which every Christian is called lived in the experiences and duties of daily life in the world, not an abnormal condition of consciousness nor the prerogative of a few elect.[11]

In "What Is Mysticism?" 1936, Underhill described the mystic as a religious realist, one for whom God is the one reality of life and the supreme object of love. A mystic is ruled by a thirst for God with a first-hand experience and knowledge of God through love and an openness to God's gift, not a person who has unusual experiences. This experience of God is purely gratuitous. It is God's free gift; a person cannot induce it or demand it (*Papers* 122-39).

One's abandonment to God can be captured in the image of one's self as a fish in the sea; the sense of life as a spiritual journey is aptly represented in the image of one's self as a mountain-climber shown a precipice to which one can be led by God's Spirit alone. One self-image a mystic may have is that of living in the ocean of God like a fish in the sea, meaning, a life of union and abiding in God. Based on her experiences in the Alps, Underhill also called the mystic a mountain-climber, willing to weather fog, storm, fatigue, cold, darkness, rough paths, and heights, driven by a mysterious love to let go of the hotel-life level of religion with its conveniences and comforts (*Papers* 122-39).

Underhill reflected in various ways on mystics' experiences and images of themselves. Catherine of Siena's cell of self-knowledge was a sense of God's greatness and our nothingness before God, not introspection. Catherine of Genoa's sense of herself being in God was a sign of the flowering of her personality. The German Dominican mystics referred to the true self in terms of the spark of the soul, the ground or apex of the soul. Teresa of Avila's integration of the practical and the spiritual enabled her to exercise wisdom and precision in both areas of her life. With these examples and many others, Underhill hammered home her point that mysticism is practical: a sense of God's presence is lived in the way we go about the duties and details of our state of life.[12]

Personal and Impersonal Symbols of God

Underhill perceived that the mystics used both personal and impersonal symbols of God. One impersonal symbol of God which Underhill used was Augustine's image of the country of the soul. Another impersonal symbol of God already referred to is that of the ocean, the sea, with which we are one like a fish in the sea.[13]

Underhill underlined the interpersonal mystery of the Trinity. Julian of Norwich was for her the poet of the Trinity who wrote about the trinitarian mystery of the human soul as well as of God. Ruysbroeck called the Father the living ground and the Son wisdom. Catherine of Siena experienced the Son as the bridge. Meister Eckhart wrote of the mystic birth of the Son in our hearts. The Spirit is the dweller in the innermost self.[14]

Some mystics combine personal and impersonal symbols of God. For Julian of Norwich, God is father, mother, and lord, as well as light, life, and love (*Essentials,* 196).

Underhill affirmed the oneness of God by quoting a wide range of mystics including Heraclitus, Plotinus, the Hindu author of the *Katha Upanishad,* the Sufi poet Jelalu'ddin, the author of the Epistle to the Ephesians, and Rabindranath Tagore. This God is one with the world (*Way,* 15-16).

She affirmed the transcendence of God but criticized Plotinus' Neoplatonic idealism for setting up an artificial system of ecstatic union rather than supporting the organic life process. Deification in this worldview means a transitory experience of being alone with the alone, not an ongoing gift of self to others. It focuses on being not on becoming. Its goal is a state of static knowledge rather than a state of abundant life. It makes an end of a means leading to Quietism. Dionysius' Neoplatonism reduced a practical science that had been worked out in life to intellectual terms. The Christian mystic, on the other hand, integrates the principle of contemplation with the principle of growth; aims at being not just knowing; and moves toward identification with the Spirit not simply clearer vision. The Christian mystic aims at a living, abiding union with God through penance and prayer, that is, purification and communion (*Way,* 291, 294, 302, 306-7).

In *Practical Mysticism,* she used impersonal images of God as the ocean of being, unifying cosmic energy, indrawing love, as well as personal images of God as the divine artist, a personal and friendly presence counseling and entreating us, lover, friend, companion, bridegroom, hound of heaven. Her God is immanent and transcendent, calling us to a union for which the symbols of food, touch, marriage, and immersion falter (*Practical,* 112, 129, 137, 139-41, 146, 158, 167).

John Ruysbroeck was one of the few mystics in Underhill's view who experienced God as both personal and impersonal, infinite and intimate, generative creativity and fruition. The superessence of God is the dark and nameless essence of the divine without activity in eternal rest and infinite bliss (*Ruysbroeck,* 52-65, 89).

In her 1915 introduction to a set of poems thought to be by Kabir which she had helped Rabindranath Tagore to translate, Underhill classified Kabir with Augustine, Ruysbroeck, and the Sufi poet Jalalu'ddin Rumi, claiming these mystics had a synthetic vision of God which merged the personal and impersonal, the immanent and the transcendent, the dynamic and static aspects of God. She insisted on the necessity for a sane mysticism to hold the union-in-separateness of God and the soul.[15]

In her 1916 introduction to the autobiography of Maharishi Devendranath Tagore, father of Rabindranath Tagore, Underhill reiterated this synthetic mysticism based on a balanced attitude toward the intimate and infinite, immanent and transcendental reality of God which characterized both Rabindranath and his father. She then proceeded to trace in the father's life the stages of the mystic way, regarding Devendranath Tagore an exception to characteristic Eastern mysticism because his union with God did not end in a life of pure contemplation but rather spurred him on to radiate light from his heart to the world. Leaving his two-year retreat in the holy land of the Himalayas, he began forty-six years of an active career of religious reform borne of the divine fecundity within him (*Tagore,* ix-xlii).

Underhill considered Plotinus a philosopher who was also a practical mystic. Plotinus described the absolute one in an impersonal way, whereas he described his ecstasy of being possessed by love and desire in a passionate way. His Neoplatonism lacked a sense of a response to God in terms of self-giving, and it lacked the social side of religion. It looked at but did not solve the problem of evil. Its influence can be seen in such mystics as Augustine, Dionysius, Julian of Norwich, Ruysbroeck, and Jacob Boehme (*Essentials,* 6, 116-40).

According to Underhill, Richard Rolle's image for God as the fire of love referred to the divine energy's action of purification. It includes three states or phases: the "heat" of God's passion and warmth, the "sweetness" of peace, and the "song" of adoring contemplation. Like other English medieval mystics, Rolle blended the personal and impersonal aspects of the ineffable God.[16]

In "Richard the Hermit," 1928, Underhill wrote of the spiritual genius Richard Rolle and his experience of God as heat, sweetness, and song. Granting that this is a psycho-physical automatism and that the form of a religious experience is always conditioned by traditional symbols, Underhill added that there is an element present which defies psychological analysis. On the other hand, she was quick to observe that Rolle's status as a mystic has been overestimated; his works belong to the literature of sensible devotion. Rolle considered heavenly song to be the highest devotion; Ruysbroeck considered it the lowest mode of the contemplative life. Although she would rank Rolle behind Julian of Norwich and Walter Hilton, Underhill recognized the primacy of joy to be his contribution to English mystical life.[17]

Underhill noted that Hildegard of Bingen's image for God was that of living light and her consciousness of God she called the shade of the living light. Underhill wondered if this image was the germ of Ruysbroeck's distinction between the sudden light of God blazing from the face of divine love and the everlasting light in which we see God (*Mystics*, 76-77).

For Jacob Boehme, God is fire, light, and life. In other words, out of the divine will come the light-world of wisdom, the dark-world of conflict, and the giver of life. In platonic terms, from the absolute come the *nous* of wisdom and the *psyche* or soul of the world. His doctrine of God, then, reveals several points of contact with Neoplatonism, as Underhill observed.[18]

In her study of the mystics, Underhill realized that they use impersonal and personal symbols of God; some, in fact, use both. For Augustine, God is the soul's country, for Hildegard of Bingen, God is the living light. For Catherine of Siena God is father. For Julian, God is triune: father, mother, and lord, as well as light, life, and love. For Ruysbroeck, God is both infinite and intimate.

Underhill was adept at quoting from what we call today apophatic and kataphatic mystics. On the prayer of quiet, she quoted from the author of *The Cloud of Unknowing* and then quoted Teresa of Avila. The former is considered an apophatic mystic who does not use images while the latter is called a kataphatic mystic because Teresa does employ images on her way to God. Underhill was very aware that a mystic is usually both apophatic and kataphatic. One example she gave was Ruysbroeck's synthetic experience of the personal and the impersonal transcendent, the bridegroom and the abyss. She could not resist adding her own metaphor for these different methods of approach to God, as the difference between preparing for a wedding and preparing for an expedition to the Arctic Seas. She signaled her adeptness in working with this material when she wrote that Dionysius the Areopagite is "of course" the classic example of imageless contemplation of the transcendent. Her familiarity with the sources of mystical theology was evident, for example, in her note recommending the study of Rudolf Otto's *The Idea of the Holy* in its treatment of the contemplation of reality. One helpful clarification that she added was that mystics' descriptions of their experiences are impressionistic rather than scientific. Apophatic images like darkness and kataphatic images like the beloved's embrace represent one's relation with God rather than God, one's felt impression rather than the observation of an object.[19]

Jesus the First and Greatest Christian Mystic

Underhill also observed that mystics use both impersonal and personal symbols of Christ. Catherine of Siena experienced Christ as the truth and the bridegroom. Ruysbroeck described Christ as wisdom and bridegroom. Underhill described Christ as a mystic following the mystic way, entering into the cell of self-knowledge in the wilderness and integrating prayer and action during his public life, an illuminative phase. Mystics' union with his paschal mystery throws into relief the social value of Christian mysticism.

Underhill presented Jesus as a mystic in her books on the mystics. In her 1911 classic *Mysticism,* Underhill referred to several traditional images for Christ in Ruysbroeck's experience: the impersonal images of wisdom and word of God, and the personal image of the bridegroom and the son of the eternal light (*Mysticism,* 116-19, 345).

In *The Mystic Way,* Underhill portrayed Jesus as the first and greatest Christian mystic; his historical life is the classic expression of the mystic way. Jesus entered into his cell of self-knowledge during the forty days in the wilderness. The three years of Jesus' public life were his experience of the illuminative way in a unity of prayer and action. The transfiguration of Jesus was a public ecstasy for the three apostles. Jesus experienced the dark night of the soul in his passion and death. He experienced the unitive life in his resurrection and ascension. The mystical doctrine of the Incarnation is, then, the cornerstone of the mystic life *(Way,* 71-154).

In *The Mystic Way,* Underhill wrote about other mystics following Jesus. She believed that Paul of Tarsus lived through all the stages of the mystic way. He put on the mind of Christ and so entered into the mystery of loving knowledge of God. Paul experienced the risen Christ empowering him by what Underhill called the organic process of transcendence to bear fruit in missionary work and sending him to preach the good news to the Gentiles. The mystical author of the Gospel of John experienced Christ as the indwelling Logos or Word incarnate, the principle of life, light, and love. He is the vine empowering us to give life to others. Paul and Catherine of Siena spent three years in solitude, each seeking a unification around the center of life. Underhill also saw Jesus' dual experience of solitary prayer and social action in the lives of the mystics. Francis of Assisi combined active love with the solitary experience of La Verna. Catherine of Siena was an ecstatic and a wise politician. Catherine of Genoa balanced solitary contemplations with her ministry of serving in hospital and slum. Jesus' transfiguration was a revelation of his divine person. A transformation of personality characterized the lives of mystics like Francis of Assisi, Teresa of Avila, and Catherine of Genoa.[20]

In "Mysticism and the Doctrine of Atonement," 1914, Underhill explored subjective and objective aspects of redemption: that we are saved by effort and growth, and that we are saved as members of a group. She cited Paul as emphasizing the mystical view of individual and corporate union with God in the body of Christ based on the mystical act of Jesus' self-donation of love in death. The Christian mystics' search for God is not a solitary quest because the church is a mystical body. It is a process of individualization and also interpenetration whereby mystics mediate for others in the communion of saints by their self-donation of love. Therefore, the doctrine of the atonement throws into relief the social value of the mystics (*Essentials,* 44-63). In this essay, Underhill seemed to be searching for the mystical value of Christianity as well as the social value of Christian mysticism. She reflected on the cross as an historical event and as the mystical process.

One of Catherine of Siena's favorite names for Christ was the truth. Her gauge of spiritual health was one's capacity to see things as they really are. To see with a true and perfect light is the fruit of living in the cell of self-knowledge (*Mystics,* 161).

The Corporate Life of the Church

In her analysis of the mystic life of the early church, Underhill discussed four streams of development: the inspirational form taken by the prophets and martyrs, the contemplative form taught and practiced by the early church writers in the desert, the ascetic form of monasticism, and the sacramental form. The goal of early church mystics like the Egyptians Anthony and Macarius was deification, the new birth of the new creature, whose growth depended on being fed by reality, that is, strengthened and refreshed by the presence of God (*Way*, 263-330).

In her essay on "The Mystic and the Corporate Life," 1915, Underhill explored the mutual benefits a mystic and a church can be to one another. She disagreed that a mystic is a religious individualist. The church can give the mystic a favorable environment and a social group that believes in spiritual values, since we cannot live alone. It provides a self-merging in the common life which is an education for self-mergence in eternal life. It offers a conservation of values in its tradition which is a rich legacy. By the same token, mystics contribute heroic and unselfish service to the church. Their heightened spiritual consciousness is caught, not taught. Their intercessory prayer and action are vital to the communion of saints. This is an interesting comment when one realizes that Underhill wrote it outside any church affiliation of her own.[21]

Later, in her preface to *The Mystics of the Church*, 1925, Underhill chose to emphasize the mystics' dependence on and contribution to the life of the household of faith. Skipping mystical philosophers and spiritual individualists, she selected several mystics whose experience of God had an impact on their fellow Christians, who deepened the corporate spiritual consciousness. In so doing, she portrayed them as representatives of a type of religion conducive to ceremonial worship and downplayed the extraordinary features of their mystical experience. By this time Evelyn's experience of the Anglican church enabled her to underline the relationship between individual mystics and their corporate life in the church. Her own image of the church was positive and so she was able to see the benefits which mystics drew from it and vice versa.[22]

An outstanding example of a mystic's contribution to the church was Catherine of Siena, for whom the pope was Christ on earth. Catherine was instrumental in bringing the pope back to Rome from Avignon in order to foster Christian life and restore the spiritual authority of the church. Underhill observed that Catherine always used her power with humility for the good of others and that her sense of Christian unity included the mystery of vicarious suffering for others (*Mystics*, 158-60).

Underhill delineated some of the mutual benefits that the mystic and the church give each other. The church provides a legacy and an environment of shared faith, shared prayer, and shared concern for others. The mystic contributes to the communal awareness of God and the betterment of the household of the faith by prayer, service, and suffering for others.

The corporate dimension of mysticism is one which Underhill came to appreciate only gradually. Through her study of mysticism, she began to realize that mystics do not live in isolation from a community of shared faith, a religious tradition of worship and service. She ended up regarding the faith community as a litmus test for the authenticity of mystical experience: is the mystic impelled to serve others? does that mystic's faith community accept the experiences reported?

The Web of the Whole Universe

Underhill was aware of a cosmic consciousness which gave the mystics an illuminated vision of the world. Paul of Tarsus saw the universe as soaked through by God's presence. At the same time, the whole creation groans to be delivered into the liberty of the children of God *(Mysticism,* 254-65; *Way,* 193-209).

Francis of Assisi's love of sister birds, brother sun, mother earth, and sister water, was coupled with his love of poverty, a detachment from all that is not God. Underhill also quoted a dying Hindu ascetic: "Oh Mother Earth, Father Sky, Brother Wind, Friend Light, Sweetheart Water, here take my last salutation with folded hands" *(Mysticism,* 208)!

Underhill believed that to be a mystic is to participate fully and deeply in eternal life here and now:

It is to share as a free and conscious agent in the joyous travail of the universe, its mighty, onward sweep through pain and glory to its home in God. . . The mystic act of union, that joyous loss of the transfigured self in God . . . is the contribution of the individual to this, the destiny of the Cosmos.[23]

For Underhill, then, the mystics kept a broadening and unitive view of the universe as the place of God's presence. This cosmic dimension of spirituality was developed by Pierre Teilhard de Chardin. For him, mind is the interiority of matter and the planet earth is a living organism.[24] This approach corresponds with the Gaia hypothesis of planetary biologists that the entire planet is a living, unified system.[25] Thomas Berry and Brian Swimme, proponents of the new cosmology, are exploring the implications of cosmocentric spirituality.[26]

In true mysticism, world-denial is combined with world-renewal. The mystic way is a life process of growth that issues in a new creation not a new creed. Its real achievements are more tangibly indicated in the deeds of mystics to better the quality of Christian life for others in the world by regenerating their cities and countries, or founding congregations and societies, than in the austerities and ecstasies of the early desert writers. Angela of Foligno delighted in the vineyards of Assisi since she perceived in them God's creation. Brother Lawrence saw God's providence in a leafless tree. The Sufi 'Attar was given a transformed view of the world as a garden of flowers (*Way*, 32-33, 46, 51, 66).

Underhill was conscious of our interconnectedness with the universe in God: "the secret of life, the urgent, suffering, forward-moving life of God, latent in the web of the whole universe, shining in the twice-born soul" (*Way*, 363). She repeated this image of the web to contradict the notion of union with God as the alone with the alone: "divine love is not a single thread that links creature and creator; but rather a web that knits up the many with the one" (*Way*, 365-66). Our union with God is made fruitful in our Christian life in the world, "true to that central principle of the spiritual life, that law of divine fecundity, which runs through the history of Christian mysticism and receives in the liturgy its most perfect symbolic expression" (*Way*, 367).

In *Practical Mysticism,* Underhill defined mysticism as the art of union with reality, a science of love. By union is meant a loving knowledge by assimilation, by the interpenetration of something and ourselves, like the knowledge of an artist or a lover. This art turns our attention to new levels of awareness of our universe. It is a union with the process of life and with the whole. In this work also, Underhill spoke of "the web of things." [27]

Underhill recounted that one image which the Indian mystics have of the universe is *Lila* or sport of God, in which we are all invited to play. Our comrades in nature include the birds and animals, the lakes and trees. Our comrades in human nature are the poor and the rich, the young and the aged. If we look on them with the loving gaze of contemplation, we will experience communion between ourselves and them creating an interpenetration of our spirit with their spirit. Julian of Norwich found in the hazelnut an image of the energy of divine love. [28]

The mystics' interconnectedness with the earth is like a web binding all, one to another. This metaphor of the web of life has been precious in native North American spirituality and has become prominent in contemporary feminist and ecofeminist literature as an image of interconnectedness. In his letter about the sacredness of tribal lands, the native North American Indian Chief Seattle used the image of the web of life to write about a sense of human interdependence with animals, the dead, the land, the seasons, and the earth. Carol Christ, an ecofeminist theologian, has written about our profound connection to all beings in the web of life, and the ecofeminist Charlene Spretnak has described women weaving the earth into a new human being. [29]

This healthy web of life needs to be sustained personally,

institutionally, economically, globally, and cosmically. And strategies need to be developed to undo the pollution of natural environmental communities like air, soils, and water by human abuse.[30]

Introducing the poems of Kabir in 1915, Underhill stated her underlying convicton that the common trait of mystics is their acceptance of the here-and-now to represent the divine. All aspects of the universe are sacramental affirmations of God's presence with no fences between the natural and supernatural: "everything is a part of the creative play of God, and therefore--even in its humblest details--capable of revealing the player's mind" *(Kabir,* 20).

In "The Future of Mysticism," 1918, Underhill described mysticism as the practical education of the spirit leading to the unitive life, as well as the mystics' vision of the spiritual world behind the sensible world. Its future depends on the appearance of one or more explorers of the infinite and a hunger of the heart creating a receptivity to their revelations. Its future also depends on some institutional expression without which it can be reduced to strangeness, vagueness, or sentimentality. As the soul of religion, mysticism's destiny is social as well as individual (*Guide,* 63-66).

In her 1928 introduction to a translation of Nicholas of Cusa's *The Vision of God,* Underhill was still intent on the practicality of mysticism for helping us live our Christian life in the world. She observed the consonance between Nicholas of Cusa's inner vision and his busy but beatified outer life: "These are not the agreeable meditations of a leisured piety; but the support of a man weighed down by responsibility, whose varied and exacting duties were performed under that 'gaze of God' of which he writes."[31]

Conclusion

Underhill understood that mysticism is eminently practical. It gives us a faith perspective and a capacity for perseverance in the face of opposition. It does not remove us from responsibility nor isolate us from world events. As the art of union with reality, it is not sentimental, vague, or lazy. It leads to a practical education of the whole person for a life of union with God. And it underlies authentic social reform. Its communal dimension strengthens discipleship and counteracts individualism. The mystics' lives of prayer inform their lives of service. Their generativity leads them to start spiritual families. They accept everyday details and duties in faith.

Underhill affirmed that mystics are practical: they write to describe

Suggestions for Prayerful Reflection
Annice Callahan, R.S.C.J.

Consider the following passage written by Evelyn Underhill and apply it to your own life:

Mysticism is the art of union with Reality. The mystic is a person who has attained that union in greater or less degree; or who aims at and believes in such attainment. . .

Contemplation, even at its highest, dearest, and most intimate, is not to be for you an end in itself. It shall only be truly yours when it impels you to action: when the double movement of Transcendent Love, drawing inwards to unity and fruition, and rushing out again to creative acts, is realised in you. You are to be a living, ardent tool with which the Supreme Artist works. . . .It is your business to actualize within the world of time and space--perhaps by great endeavors in the field of heroic action, perhaps only by small ones in field and market, tram and tube, office and drawing-room, in the perpetual give-and-take of the common life--that more real life, that holy creative energy, which this world manifests as a whole. . . Do your hours of contemplation and of action harmonise? . . . Mystics are asked to think celestially; and this, not when considering the things usually called spiritual, but when dealing with the concrete accidents, the evil and sadness, the cruelty, failure, and degeneration of life. . . . We said, at the beginning of this discussion, that mysticism was the art of union with Reality: that it was, above all else, a science of Love. Hence, the condition to which it looks forward and towards which the soul of the contemplative has been stretching out, is a condition of *being,* not of *seeing (Practical,* 3, 158, 163-65, 168).

1. What does Evelyn Underhill mean by mysticism? How would you describe mysticism in your own words?

2. How does Underhill view the relationship between contemplation and action? How do you view it?

3. How can a Christian spirituality be lived in the field and market, the office and the drawing-room? What is that like for you in the circumstances of your daily life? Do your hours of contemplation and of action harmonize?

their experience because of its significance to humanity, not to hand o⌐
a philosophical scheme. Underhill's assessment is that John of th⌐
Cross's commentary upon the dark night of the soul is one of the fine⌐
and most subtle descriptions of the psychology of contemplation. It ca⌐
help us identify dark nights in our lives of prayer.[32]

What did Evelyn Underhill's study of the mystics contribute to her lif⌐
For one thing, I believe it was a catalyst for her intellectual conversi⌐
from Neoplatonic idealism to a critical realism. For another, it led her⌐
see the value of the communal, sacramental, institutional dimension⌐
the spiritual life, which for many years she did not feel was importa⌐
Third, it convinced her that relating to God is not a matter of "flight of ⌐
alone with the alone," but rather a loving engagement with one's daily ⌐
and with others. She realized that the mystics lived their lives for ⌐
with God, by living gospel values but in a practical way not i⌐
perfectionistic way. Fourth, it provided her with a valuable source for⌐
spirituality for daily living, a source rooted in Christian traditio⌐
foundation from which to draw nourishment not only for herself bu⌐
her spiritual directees, and a way to ease the gap between the spiri⌐
life and theology.[33]

Evelyn Underhill used the mystics as a source for her reflections o⌐
spiritual life. Discussing Underhill in relation to English mys⌐
theologians writing in her day, Christopher Armstrong wrote:

> Neither Inge nor von Hügel was greatly interested in the writings of ⌐
> mystics as documentary evidence for mystical *lives,* considering them mu⌐
> more in the light of medieval and, indeed, contemporary metaphysics, eth⌐
> and theology. . . She was without doubt Great Britain's leading pionee⌐
> this field."[34]

Her exploration of the mystics shed light on her understanding ⌐
advice for Christian life in the world. The centrality of her pastoral ⌐
has been spelled out most clearly by Armstrong: "Mystical writin⌐
for her a document of lived experience or it was nothing. It is impro⌐
that she ever in her life turned over a scholastic manual of so-⌐
'mystical theology'" (Armstrong, 184). She made a valuable contri⌐
to the study of the mystics.

Underhill lived what she wrote, namely, that spiritual valu⌐
caught, not taught. Her study of the mystics was very much a firs⌐
study of their lives and writings. Toward the end of her life, she ex⌐
the social implications of mysticism in terms of the contribution⌐
spiritual life to church life and to society, as we shall see in the fol⌐
chapters.

4. What does she mean by writing that the mystics think celestially in the concrete details of life? How would you put that in your own words?

5. What does she mean when she writes that the condition of the soul of the contemplative is a condition of *being* not of *seeing?* How would you spell this out in the context of your spirituality for daily living?

Readings

The classic of Evelyn Underhill's scholarly work on mysticism is *Mysticism: The Preeminent Study in the Nature and Development of Spiritual Consciousness* (New York: Doubleday Image, 1990), first published in 1911 and now in its thirteenth edition. It was followed by *The Mystic Way: A Psychological Study in Christian Origins* (Folcroft, Pa.: Folcroft Library Editions, 1975), first published in 1913.

Notes

1. See E. Underhill,, 23, 97, 298-99.

2. See E. Underhill, *Papers,* 131, 133-34. On the importance of studying Christian mysticism within the cross-cultural and interreligious discussion of mysticism as a human experience, see Sandra Schneiders, "Spirituality in the Academy," *Theological Studies* 50 (December 1989): 641-62.

      Protestant traditions in general have had a hesitation about the role of the imagination in mysticism. The doctrine of original sin implies for them that the human imagination after the Fall is not a reliable place to look for revelation. Roman Catholics, especially with Thomas Aquinas, have taught that human nature has been "marred" by the Fall, but not fully corrupted, and that grace comes to "perfect" human nature. Protestants generally have taught that grace ultimately "transforms" a corrupted human nature. With the exception of the doctrine of sanctification in Methodist and other holiness traditions, most Protestants have held that this transformation is not fully effective in this life. Anglicans have generally been closer to the Catholics in this matter, and trust a disciplined, not naively uncritical, use of the imagination, even more than Roman Catholics who trust more to systematic theological thinking. Methodists have generally been wary of mysticism due to their doctrine of sanctification. Lutherans and Presbyterians are more suspicious of mysticism. They shy away from talking about the touch of God, an expression which Underhill herself used in *Worship,* 170. See Robert G. Tuttle, Jr., *Mysticism in the Wesleyan Tradition* (Grand Rapids, Mich.: Francis Asbury Press, 1989), for an understanding of Wesley's critical appreciation of mysticism. For this insight about the Protestant distrust of imagination and for this reference, I am indebted to Dale Cannon, philosophy professor at Western Oregon State College, in a conversation at the Ecumenical Institute on April 15, 1993.

3. For an excellent treatment of this topic, see Joy Milos, "Chapter II: The Mystic as Guide," in "The Role of the Spiritual Guide in the Life and Writings of Evelyn Underhill," (Ph.D. diss., The Catholic University of America, 1988), 63-101.

4. Her sources included Catherine of Siena, Teresa of Avila, Delacroix' studies on mysticism, and Starbuck's research on the psychology of religion. See E. Underhill, *Mysticism,* 172-73; and "The Philosophic Temperament," review of *The Psychology of Philosophers* by Alexander Hersberg, *Spectator Times Supplement,* 4 May 1929, 699-700, DGC. Cf. Joan M. Nuth, *Wisdom's Daughter: The Theology of Julian of Norwich* (New York: Crossroad, 1991), 138 and 201, n. 53.

5. See E. Underhill, "A Franciscan Poet--Jacopone da Todi," *Essays by Divers Hands Being the Transactions of the Royal Society of Literature of the United Kingdom,* NS, Vol. 6, ed. G.K. Chesterton (London: Oxford University Press, 1926), 43-75, esp. 64, DGC. On poetry and mysticism, see also E. Underhill, "The Alchemy of Poetry," review of *Road to Xanadu: A Study in the Ways of Imagination* by Lavington Lowes, *The Spectator,* 27 September 1927, 321; id., "Spiritual Songs," review of *Lyra Mystica: An Anthology of Mystical Verse,* ed. C.C. Albertson, *The Spectator,* 2 July 1932, DGC; id., "A Poet's Theology," review of *God without Thunder: An Unorthodox Defense of Orthodoxy* by John Crowe Ransom, *The Spectator,* 15 October 1932, 485-86; id., "Men and Books," review of *Illustrations of the Book of Job, Time and Tide,* 8 January 1938, 46-47; and id., "Spiritual Song,"review of *The Oxford Book of Christian Verse,* ed. David Cecil, *Time and Tide,* 29 June 1940, 691-92, DGC. Cf. Annice Callahan, "Creative Intuition and Contemplative Intuition," *RSCJ: A Journal of Reflection* 2, no. 2 (1980):77-88.

6. See E. Underhill, *Ruysbroeck* 66-185; and introduction to *The Adornment of the Spiritual Marriage, The Sparkling Stone, and The Book of Supreme Truth,* tr. C.A. Wynschenk Dom, ed. E. Underhill (London: John M. Watkins, 1951), xi-xxxii.

7. On spark of the soul, see E. Underhill, *Cloud,* 22; *Mysticism,* 41, 54, 74, 93, 99, 100, 117, 121, 132, 145, 230, 259, 298, 304, 352, 366, 390, 396, 402, 445; *Mystics,* 137; *Practical,* 41, 58, 91, 117, 156; *Ruysbroeck,* 63, 66, 68, 131; *Way,* 6, 38, 50, 95, 105-6, 109, 168, 370; idem, "Discussions: Theology and the Subconscious," *Hibbert Journal* 9, no. 8 (April 1911): 645, DGC; idem, "The Hope of Glory," review of *The Testament of Immortality: an Anthology, Time and Tide,* 19 October 1940, 1028, DGC.

On ground of the soul, see *Essentials,* 193; *Guide,* 38, 185; Lt, 199; *Mysticism,* 54, 102, 105, 109, 259, 303-4, 312, 320, 339, 343-45, 349, 390, 401; *Practical,* 43; *Ruysbroeck,* 67, 146, 157, 172.

On apex of the soul, see *Essentials,* 9, 122, 126; *Mysticism,* 54, 366; *Practical,* 43, 117; *Ruysbroeck,* 94.

8. See E. Underhill, *Mixed,* 147-68; "A Franciscan Hermitage," *The Spectator,*11 February 1928, 183-84, DGC; id., "The Human Francis," review of *The life of St. Francis of Assisi* by Luigi Salvatorelli, *The Spectator,* 19 May 1928, 771-72, DGC; id., "The Unchanging Path," review of *Franciscan Mysticism* by Boniface Macs, *The Spectator* (August 18, 1928): 220, DGC; id., "The Franciscan Reform," review of *The Capuchins: a Contribution to the History of the Counter-Reformation* by Cuthbert, *The Spectator,* 19 January 1929, 90-91, DGC; id., "Followers of St. Francis,' review of *Among the Franciscan Tertiaries* by Nesta de Robeck, *The Spectator,* 22 February 1930, 280, DGC; and id., "Giotto and St. Francis," *The Spectator,* 26 December 1931, 873-74, DGC.

9. See E. Underhill, introduction, *The Mirror of Simple Souls*, extracts, *The Porch*, Series 1, no. 8, 2-4; and "The Mirror of Simple Souls," review of English translation of *The Mirror of Simple Souls*, *Fortnightly Review*, no. 78 (February 1911): 345-54, DGC, reprinted in *Essentials of Mysticism*. Cf. *A Mirror for Simple Souls: The Mystical Works of Marguerite Porete*, ed. and trans. Charles Crawford (New York: Crossroad, 1990); Marguerite Porete, *The Mirror of Simple Souls*, trans. Ellen L. Babinsky (New York: Paulist, 1993); and *Meister Eckhart and the Beguine Mystics: Hadewijch of Brabant, Mechtild of Magdeburg, and Marguerite Porete*, ed. Bernard McGinn (New York: Continuum, 1994).

10. See E. Underhill, *Mystics*, 126, 243, 253-56; introduction to *A Book of Contemplation the Which Is Called the Cloud of Unknowing, in the Which a Soul is Oned with God*, 7th ed., ed. E. Underhill (London: John M. Watkins, 1970), 5-31; introduction to *The Scale of Perfection* by Walter Hilton, ed. E. Underhill (London: John M. Watkins, 1948), v-liv; and introduction *to A Simple Method of Raising the Soul to Contemplation in the Form of a Dialogue* by François Malaval, trans. Lucy Menzies (London: J.M. Dent & Sons, Ltd, 1931), v-xx. Cf. David Knowles, "Quietism," *What is Mysticism?* (London: The Catholic Book Club, 1968), 116-21.

11. See E. Underhill, *Mixed*, 188-208; and introduction to *The Scale of Perfection* (London: John M. Watkins, 1948), v-liv.

12. These images of our center remind me of what Thomas Merton called *le point vierge*, inspired by Louis Massignon. By this is meant that point within us that belongs solely to God and lies beyond the fantasies of the imagination or the brutalities of the will. It is there that we surrender all we are, have, and do to God not only in our formal prayer but also in our everyday lives. On *le point vierge*, see Thomas Merton, *Conjectures of a Guilty Bystander* (Garden City, N.Y.: Doubleday Image, 1966), 131-32, 151, 158, 160, 271. He borrowed this phrase from Louis Massignon. Cf. M. Madeleine Abdelnour, "'*Le point vierge*' in Thomas Merton," *Cistercian Studies* 6 (1971): 153-71; and Sidney H. Griffith, "Thomas Merton, Louis Massignon, and the Challenge of Islam," paper presented at the First International Thomas Merton Society General Meeting, Louisville, Kentucky, May 26, 1989.

13. On God as country, see E. Underhill, *Mysticism* 110, 126, 140, 337, 404, 420; *Way* 107; idem, "The Great Divide," review of *Christianity and Classical Culture. A Study of Thought and Action from Augustus to Augustine* by Charles Norris Cochrane, *Time and Tide* (August 24, 1940): 869-70, DGC.

      On God as the ocean, see E. Underhill, *Mysticism* 36-37, 125, 132, 401-406; *Guide* 59; *Way* 19-20.

      On Underhill's use of country and ocean as images of God, see E. Underhill, *Mysticism* 199, 379, 417; *Tagore* xi.

14. Underhill, *Mysticism,* pp. 63, 112, 116-20, 122, 127, 145, 231, 233. For Underhill's doctrinal reflections on the Trinity, see Kevin Hogan, "The Proximity of Doctrine: Underhill and Sayers on the Trinity," *Anglican Theological Review* 78/2 (Spring 1996): 275-289, esp. 277-282. Had Hogan reflected on *The Golden Sequence* as well as *The School of Charity,* he might have expanded on her emphasis on the Spirit.

For contemporary theological reflection on the Trinity, see, for example, Elizabeth A. Johnson, *She Who Is: The Mystery of God in Feminist Theological Discourse* (New York: Crossroad, 1992); Catherine Mowry LaCugna, *God for Us: The Trinity and Christian Life* (San Francisco: Harper, 1991); and Thomas Marsh, *The Triune God: A Biblical, Historical, and Theological Study* (Mystic, Ct.: Twenty-Third, 1994).

15. See E. Underhill, *Ruysbroeck,* 166, 178; *Kabir,* 22, 28; "Kabir, the Weaver Mystic," *The Contemporary Review,* no. 598 (February 1914), 193-200. Cf. Armstrong, 133-46; and D. Greene, *Artist,* 57. On her difficulties with the actual publication of this book of poems, see *Imperfect Encounter: Letters of William Rothenstein and Rabindranath Tagore 1911-1941,* ed. Mary M. Lago (Cambridge, Mass.: Harvard University Press, 1972), 124, 156-60. On her favorable assessment of R. Tagore's work, see, for example, "An Indian Mystic," review of *Gitanjali* by R. Tagore, *The Nation,* 12 November 1912, 321; and "The Circle and the Centre," review of *Sadhana: The Realization of Life* and *The Crescent Moon* by R. Tagore, *The Nation* (December 13, 1913): 499-500, DGC.

16. See E. Underhill, introduction to *The Fire of Love or Melody of Love and the Mending of Life or Rule of Living* by Richard Rolle, ed. Frances M.M. Comper (London: Methuen & Co., Ltd., 1914), vii-xxv; idem, "East and West," review of *The Life of Richard Rolle, together with an Edition of his English Lyrics* by Frances M.M. Comper, *The Spectator* (December 29, 1928): 995-96, DGC.

17. See E. Underhill, *Dublin Review,* no. 367 (October 1928): 176-87, reprinted in *Mixed,* 169-87; idem, "Richard the Hermit," review of *Writings ascribed to Richard Rolle* by Hope Emily Allen, *The Spectator,* 7 April 1928, 538-39, DGC.

18. See E. Underhill, introduction to *Confessions of Jacob Boehme,* tr. W. Scott Palmer (London: Methuen, 1920), xi-xxxi.

19. E. Underhill, *Mysticism,* 319-21, 335, 345-48; idem, "Theism: Theoretical and Practical," review of new edition of *Western Mysticism* by Cuthbert Butler, *The Spectator,* 26 March 1927, 564, DGC; idem, "Outward and Inward," review of an English translation of vol. 1 of *Studies in the Psychology of the Mystics* by Joseph Maréchal, *The Spectator* 19 November 1927, 889-90, DGC. Cf. Harvey

D. Egan, "Christian Apophatic and Kataphatic Mysticisms," *Theological Studies,* 39 (1978): 399-426; and David Granfield, "The Kataphatic Prelude" and "The Apophatic Venture," *Heightened Consciousness: The Mystical Difference* (New York: Paulist, 1991), 56-118.

Around 1923, Underhill began to read Rudolf Otto's books on mysticism and was influenced by them. She referred to two of his works in her book *Mysticism.* See Rudolf Otto, *The Idea of the Holy* (London: Macmillan, 1923). Cf. Underhill, *Mysticism* (New York: New American Library, 1974), 340 and 348. In the Bibliographical Note to the Thirteenth Edition, she added an entry on "Otto, Rudolf. *Mysticism East and West* (Sankara and Eckhart). Translated by B.L. Bracey and R.C. Paine, London, 1932" in *Mysticism,* 507.

See also E. Underhill, "The Numinous," review of *The Holy and the Living God* by M.D.R. Willink, and an English translation of *Religious Essays: a sequel to The Idea of the Holy* by Rudolf Otto, *The Spectator,* 19 December 1931, 854, DGC; id., "Meeting in the Centre," review of *Mysticism East and West* by Rudolf Otto, *The Spectator,* 2 April 1932, 482, DGC; and id., "Men and Books," review of *The Kingdom of God and the Son of Man: A Study in the History of Religion* by Rudolf Otto, *Time and Tide,* 5 March 1938, 312-313, DGC.

20. See E. Underhill, *Way,* 155-257, esp. 120, 123, 170, 175, 192, 214, 229. Cf. id., "St. Paul and the Mystic Way. A Psychological Study," *Contemporary Review,* 99 (June 1911): 694-706, DGC; id., "Men and Books," review of *Spirit and Reality* by Nicolas Berdyaev and *St. Paul and the Church of the Gentiles* by Wilfred L. Knox, *Time and Tide,* 8 April 1939, 448, DGC. Along with other critics of her time, Underhill questioned the authenticity of the epistles to Timothy and Titus, as well as the authorship of the Gospel of John. See *Way,* 159, n. 1; 217, n. 1.

One can argue the lack of scriptural depth in her works on mysticism and on the spiritual life. For this view, I am indebted to Karlfried Froehlich, Professor Emeritus of Ecclesiastical History at Princeton Theological Seminary, in a conversation at the Ecumenical Institute, Collegeville, Minnesota, on May 13, 1993.

21. See E. Underhill, *Essentials,* 25-43.

As examples of how the corporate life affects the mystic, Underhill noted that institutional, sacramental religion saved Lucie-Christine from individualism. It invited Charles Péguy to make a pilgrimage to pray for the life of his sick child. See E. Underhill, *Essentials,* 225, 232.

22. See E. Underhill, *Mystics,* 8; idem, "Medieval Mysticism," *Cambridge Medieval History* 7 (1932), 777-812, DGC. Cf. Regina Marie Bechtle, "The Mystic and the Church in the Writings of Evelyn Underhill," (Ph.D. diss., Fordham University, 1979), esp. 169-182, 213, 215, 279-285.

23. E. Underhill, *Mysticism*, 447. Cf. Margaret Brennan, "'. . . It's Like Looking at God,'" *The Way* 32 (October 1992): 281-291.

24. See, for example, Pierre Teilhard de Chardin, *The Divine Milieu* (New York: Harper & Row, 1968), *Hymn of the Universe* (New York: Harper & Row, 1965); and *The Phenomenon of Man* (New York: Harper and Brothers, 1959). Cf. Annice Callahan, "Teilhard de Chardin: Toward a Theology of Presence," *The Barat Review* 1 (1966): 141-160; and Robert Faricy, *The Spirituality of Teilhard de Chardin* (Minneapolis: Winston Press, 1981).

25. See, for example, James Lovelock, *Gaia: A New Look at Life on Earth* (Oxford: Oxford University Press, 1979); and id., *The Ages of Gaia: A Biography of Our Living Earth* (New York: Norton, 1988); and William Irwin Thompson, *Gaia: A Way of Knowing: Political Implications of the New Biology* (Great Barrington, Ma.: Lindisfarne Press, 1987).

26. See, for example, Thomas M. Berry, *The Dream of the Earth* (San Francisco: Sierre Club Books, 1988); and Brian Swimme and Thomas M. Berry, *The Universe Story* (San Francisco: HarperSan Francisco, 1992).

27. See E. Underhill, *Practical*, 3-4, 11, 30, 32-33, 45, 49, 60, 67, 75, 78, 88, 91, 103, 124-25, 131-32, 161. On the web, see E. Underhill, *Practical*, 108.

28. See E. Underhill, *Practical*, 42, 91-104. See also E. Underhill, "Lila, the Play of God," in *Theophanies: A Book of Verses* (New York: E.P. Dutton & Co., 1916), 34-36.

29. See Chief Seattle, letter about the land, according to Joseph Campbell, *The Power of Myth* with Bill Moyers, ed. Betty Sue Flowers (New York: Doubleday, 1988), 32, 34-35; and according to Dr. Henry A. Smith in the *Seattle Sunday Star*, 29 October 1877, in Clarence B. Bagley, "Chief Seattle and Angeline," *The Washington Historical Quarterly* 22, no. 4 (Oct. 1931): 243-274, esp. 251-255. Cf. Eva Greenslit Anderson, *Chief Seattle* (Cantwell, Idaho: Caxton Printers, 1950).
    See also Carol P. Christ, "Rethinking Theology and Nature," in Judith Plaskow and Carol P. Christ, eds., *Weaving the Visions: New Patterns in Feminist Spirituality* (San Francisco: Harper & Row, 1989), 314-325, esp. 314, 321, and 323; and Charlene Spretnak in Brian Swimme, "How to Heal a Lobotomy," *Reweaving the World: The Emergence of Feminism*, eds. Irene Diamond and Gloria Feman Orenstein (San Francisco: Sierra Club Books, 1990), 15-22. Cf. Maureen Murdock, feminist psychologist, who has written about women as weavers intertwining with men, children and each other to protect the web of life, in *The Heroine's Journey: Woman's Quest for Wholeness*

(Shambhala: Boston, 1990), 185; and Catherine Rettger, "Web of Life," *Womenpsalms,* ed. Julia Ahlers, Rosemary Broughton, and Carl Koch (Winona, Minnesota: Saint Mary's Press, 1992), 129.

30. See Rosemary Radford Ruether, *Gaia and God: An Ecofeminist Theology of Earth Healing* (San Francisco: Harper & Row, 1992), esp. 1-2, 250.

31. E. Underhill, introduction *to The Vision of God* by Nicholas of Cusa, tr. Emma Gurney Salter (New York: E.P. Dutton, 1960), x. See idem, "Types of Holiness," including a review of *Nicholas of Cusa* by Henry Bett, *The Spectator,* 25 June 1932, 903, DGC.

32. See E. Underhill, *Mysticism,* 347-48, 353-54; id., "In Caligine," review of *The Dark* by Archibald Weir, *The Spectator,* 5 July 1930: 21-22, DGC; id., "Martha and Mary," review of *Christian Mysticism: a Critique* by Paul Elmer More, *The Spectator,* 13 August 1932, 198-99, DGC, in which Underhill corrected More's appraisal of John of the Cross as a "mixed type" by recommending the reading of Allison Peers, *St. John of the Cross.* Cf. id., "Lux in Tenebris," review of *Light: a Philosophy of Consciousness* by Archibald Weir, *The Spectator,* 16 July 1932, 85, DGC.

33. K. Rahner would concur that mystical experiences can inform theological reflection and thus help to bridge the rift between lived piety and abstract theology. See "Faith, Rationality, and Emotion, *TI* 16: 72, n. 12. Cf. Joan M. Nuth, *Wisdom's Daughter: The Theology of Julian of Norwich* (New York: Crossroad, 1991); and "Two Medieval Soteriologies: Anselm of Canterbury and Julian of Norwich," *TS* 53 (1992): 611-45.
     On critical realism, see Appendix: A Note on Critical Realism.
     On Teresa of Avila's influence on Underhill's writings, see Mary Brian Durkin, "Teresian Wisdom in Selected Writings of Evelyn Underhill," *Spiritual Life* 41 (Spring 1995): 20-31.

34. Armstrong 181. The other theologians he named were William Inge who had published *Christian Mysticism* in 1899, and Friedrich von Hügel who had published *The Mystical Element of Religion in* 1908.

Chapter 3

Work with Spiritual Guides

This section introduces us to Underhill's experience of spiritual guides. It explores her relationship with Baron Friedrich von Hügel. And it includes a brief description of other letters of spiritual direction written by three spiritual guides whose writings influenced her spirituality: the French Jesuit Jean Pierre de Caussade, the Abbé Henri de Tourville, and the English Benedictine abbot Dom John Chapman.

Evelyn Underhill became a spiritual guide for others, but she herself felt the need for spiritual guidance. The term "spiritual guidance" suggests an interchange in which one gives what one has received with another. She certainly offered this sharing of her faith, hope, and love with those who sought her out by writing her, listening to her retreats, reading her books, and coming to speak with her. The term does not convey, however, an interaction in which one person becomes directive and offers advice that may be construed as expecting blind obedience. The latter is one interpretation of what is called "spiritual direction." At the same time, the term "spiritual accompaniment" implies a listening presence that is more of a sounding board than a spiritual resource. In light of these clarifications, Evelyn's work with von Hügel can be described as that of a spiritual directee who sought out and welcomed his advice, taking it very much to heart.

Her work with others, however, was more in the order of a spiritual mentoring.[1] She was an excellent listener and walked with others in their spiritual journey. But she did more than that. She helped them sort out a viable devotional program, encouraged them to balance their spiritual lives with other interests, brought her study of mysticism to bear on their problems and difficulties in helpful and sometimes humorous ways, and proclaimed the good news of God's presence in an idiom with which they could readily identify in their own practical lives.

A Spiritual Directee

One of the most significant relationships of her life was working with Baron Friedrich von Hügel as her spiritual director. He was a Roman Catholic Modernist, a married layman, and like her one of the leading authorities on mysticism in England at that time, known especially for his work on *The Mystical Element of Religion, as studied in St. Catherine of Genoa and her Friends.*[2]

He helped to stabilize several transitions in Evelyn Underhill's worldview. She confided to him that during World War I she had gone to pieces but then afterwards had been given peace, stability, and a sense of forgiveness, of having been dealt with personally by God. Her growth in a personal relationship with Christ depended, in part, on the Baron's invitation to a Christocentric focus in her prayer as a corrective to her tendency to what he called pure mysticism. Her shift from a Neoplatonic spirituality to an incarnational spirituality was supported by von Hügel's own incarnational spirituality. Her commitment to sacramental religion which was apparent in her Manchester College, Oxford lectures delivered in 1921 and published as *The Life of the Spirit and the Life of Today,* 1922, was reinforced by the value he placed on religion. His encouragement of her volunteer work with the poor which later developed into friendship with the poor was not the first time she had thought of it. In fact, she had suggested it years earlier to one of her directees. His advice about developing some nondevotional interests in times of nervous exhaustion and spiritual dryness was an aspect of incarnational spirituality which she embodied and passed on to others because it proposed a sane way to balance the lofty ideals of a devotional life with the real needs of the body and psyche for beauty, leisure, and rest.[3]

In addition to giving advice, Baron von Hügel functioned as a "sounding board," a confidante, and a medium for Evelyn's self-revelation. This is an aspect of spiritual direction which frees a person to listen and relate to God after feeling heard and received. For example, in a 1922 midsummer letter to Baron von Hügel, Underhill described a retreat she had made that spring at Pleshey. She had the feeling of belonging to the Christian family and lost her last bit of separateness. The simple regime of daily Communion and four services a day with silent times in between left her with a new sense of the beauty and realness of the Christian life. Her impressions of this retreat are recorded nowhere else. In this same letter to von Hügel Evelyn confided that her practice of visiting the poor had taken her out of herself and made her grateful, peaceful, and nearer to God. Seeing their trials and hearing their troubles, she felt religiously pampered and realized what a spiritual luxury her devotional life was. She enjoyed feeding chocolates to little children, especially since she had had no children of her own. A third instance of her letters to him as mediating her self-revelation was her June 1923 description of having heard a voice in prayer after which she felt "called out and settled." Apprehensive about the voice, she could not doubt the fruit and sensed it was for her a turning to trust from remorse and worry.[4]

A third way in which her relationship with von Hügel was significant was the way it gave her space to explore and establish her values and priorities. Her plea to lengthen the half-hour he had allowed her for personal prayer showed her experience and affirmation of the value of recollection, all the time it takes to become present to God, and the value of contemplative prayer which is more than the recitation of vocal prayers or personal concerns to God. Her desire to spend more time in intercession reflected her choice to make her devotional life redemptive and fruitful for others.[5]

Her willingness to submit to his directives was a dependent part of their transaction. In an early letter, for example, she felt she had to explain why she had made a retreat at Pleshey without having consulted him, and part of her explanation was her promise to the warden at the Pleshey retreat house to go before von Hügel took charge of her! In a later letter, her grateful acknowledgement that the happiness and joy of a Christocentric dimension she owed entirely to the Baron seems overstated. And she actually did ask his permission to make two three-day retreats a year instead of a week-long one.[6]

His letters of reply seem overbearing in parts. He wrote that he would have prevented her from having made a General Confession and that he did not recognize her right to go to Pleshey without having consulted him![7]

Apart from this dimension, they experienced an adult relationship, a spiritual friendship. It was an oasis for Evelyn and a life-giving incentive for both of them. Both married laypeople committed to living a serious

Christian life in the world, they strengthened each other, keenly aware of their priorities regarding their spouses, families, and home duties. When Evelyn wrote von Hügel that her aging parents were jealous of the claims on her life and wanted her to spend more time with them, he wrote back advising her not to lengthen her visits but to increase their quality by showing interest in the tiniest details out of love for them.[8]

At the same time, Underhill and von Hügel were intellectual colleagues. Both had published significant studies on mysticism. On this level, they could offer one another mutual support and challenge. For example, von Hügel wrote a critique of her *Mysticism* and suggested she await his detailed analysis before reprinting it. This she did not do. Likewise, Underhill pointed out to the Baron a mistranslation from *Jacopone da Todi* which he corrected in the second edition of his *Mystical Element of Religion*. He mentioned three of her books in the revised preface to this book.[9]

Underhill and von Hügel were kindred spirits. They were both Modernist Christians, open to the dialogue between religion and science, which archeological excavations, theories of biblical criticism, and the theory of evolution sought to renew.

She was cautioned by von Hügel to avoid belonging to prayer guilds. Warning her that she should look for a group of solid, simple, sober people who would steady rather than entrap her, he was not opposed to her joining the Order of the Holy Dove. Evelyn belonged to this lay order of contemplatives living in the world until the order dissolved.[10]

Von Hügel's death in January 1925 was a profound loss for Evelyn. He had been her spiritual father, her intellectual sparring partner, and her soul friend. In "Finite and Infinite: A Study of the Philosophy of Baron Friedrich von Hügel," Underhill revealed the mirror experience of their relationship by emphasizing aspects of his doctrine which were aspects of her own: the homey and the transcendent, our double orientation to the finite and the infinite, critical realism, the double relatedness of all we do as grounded in the twofold nature of reality and reflected in our twofold nature, the interpenetration of realities, the church as the interconnection of souls, and a synthesis of the transcendental, the incarnational, and the institutional. In "Additional Note: Baron von Hügel as a Spiritual Teacher," Underhill dubbed him the most influential religious personality of her time. In "The Essence of von Hügel," she praised his consistent refusal to dilute the truth.[11]

This relationship satisfied some of Evelyn's most basic emotional needs for attention, affirmation, and understanding. At the time of her mother's death, von Hügel wrote that the difference of outlook between her and her mother must have added to the trial and given a special discomfort to it. He understood how emotionally starved she had been all her life. He also understood how hard she was on herself and cautioned her to focus her attention on God, Christ, and the poor, rather than on the state of her soul, especially when she felt irritated or confused. He recognized that the way she was built, with such an active inner critic, what she needed was self-abandonment to divine providence, not self-analysis.[12]

On the other hand, a yearly reply to a yearly letter over a three-year period could not have been very satisfying. True, Underhill had visited von Hügel several times during the time she was writing and revising *Mysticism*. But if there were letters, then there were no or fewer visits during the time when she worked with him in spiritual direction. He met her need for a father, a spiritual father, someone she could admire and emulate. He was not aware of being for her a soul-friend in a mutuality of ministry to one another. They kept their emotional distance according to the culture of Edwardian England.

In fact, what Underhill considered her difficulty with attachments to some of her women friends, her jealousy, possessiveness, what she called her claimfulness, must be seen in the context of her tremendous capacity for intimacy, a need that was not met during her life except by God. Her search for a soul-friend in Ethel Ross Barker, Lucy Menzies, and Clara Smith opened her to her own emotional vulnerability, a side she rarely showed anyone. Von Hügel was very astute in being gentle with her in this regard, inviting her to turn to God, not to dwell on getting rid of these attachments, lest she throw out the roots of her own passionate nature along with the weeds.[13]

That Evelyn condemned herself for attachments to some of her women friends, was another indication of how emotionally starved she was. Von Hügel's gentleness with her in this regard was probably redemptive. The barrenness of her emotional life in the context of her husband and parents was filled by her ministry of spiritual direction and retreat work, as well as her service to the poor.

Underhill did not really need to give Friedrich von Hügel as much power as she did over her life, in particular, her devotional life. She completed her formal study of mysticism and realized that her own mysticism lacked a communal dimension. She then rejoined the Anglican Church of her youth. She also ended her academic presentation of mysticism. The devastation and disillusionment of World War I led her to take seriously people's pastoral concerns and pleas for advice about making mysticism practical in their daily lives. In particular, she listened to those who turned to her for spiritual direction and retreat work. Her response signaled a shift from a concentration on mysticism to a concentration on the spiritual life. That is to say, she began to explore in earnest the pastoral dimensions of mysticism and to articulate the practical mysticism of living the Christian life in the world. She needed courage and confidence. She needed to trust the wisdom of her own inner resources. She needed to integrate focus and discipline inside herself with receptivity and spontaneity. It is not surprising, then, that she sought a man much older than herself, a father figure, whose protection and care could carry her until she felt strengthened and enlightened. Providentially, even though von Hügel was patriarchal in his giving and refusal of permissions, he did not foster her dependence on him. A yearly report was all he wanted and a yearly reply was all he gave.

From her books and retreats we can assume that Evelyn Underhill was a perfectionist with a propensity for detail. Possibly some of what looks like an overdependence on von Hügel might have been her tendency to list points and questions in an organized way. Perhaps her need to be perfect prevented her from letting herself feel loved by God unconditionally.[14]

One can speculate that Underhill's scrupulously asking permission and seeking advice of von Hügel was her rhetoric of femininity in the face of his chauvinistic tendencies. Teresa of Avila called herself a weak and foolish woman. It may have been not only to acknowledge her creatureliness but also to appease the pride of her male spiritual directors and confessors who had never tasted the kinds of mystical experiences she was given. On the other hand, she had no duplicity. Evelyn Underhill berated herself with von Hügel not only because she believed herself to be a permanent beginner in the spiritual life but also because she had a tendency toward self-scrutiny. She must have known, if only unconsciously, how delicate it was working with a man who was her intellectual equal, not recognizing that she herself was also one of England's leading authorities on mysticism at the time.[15]

Her humble self-effacement and appreciation of von Hügel's help is found in her letter to J.A. Herbert: "I have become the friend (or rather, disciple and adorer) of von Hügel. . . I feel very safe and happy sitting in his shadow, and he has been most awfully kind to me" (9/16/11, *Lt,* 129).I wonder if she overstated von Hügel's influence on her in a letter to Dom John Chapman: "Under God, I owe him my whole spiritual life" (*Lt,* 196). It was, in any event, under his spiritual guidance that she found the balance and strength to guide others.

Underhill expressed her debt of gratitude to Friedrich von Hügel in her book on *Man and the Supernatural,* published two years after his death. Her insight into the twofold nature of the human being that seeks the eternal in the concrete matched his. Her conviction about the place of historical, sacramental, institutional religion in a committed Christian life had been reinforced by his own. Her emphasis on the incarnational principle of divine self-giving in this book underlined the central place of the Incarnation in the Baron's spirituality. She quoted him often in this book on God, mysticism, the relationship between historical and eternal life, the sacramentality of matter, Catherine of Genoa's transforming union with God, the integration of the natural and the supernatural. She noted his realization that neither experience nor awareness can be isolated as mystical; what matters is the divine influence on our action and thought.[16]

Underhill's spirituality can be misunderstood to mean that one is to draw close to God by distancing oneself from others. Grace Jantzen has called it "disengaged" and has looked in vain for Underhill's attempt to analyze either the class structure of Edwardian England or the poverty therein. As Dana Greene has pointed out, however, while it it true that Underhill did not make a social analysis of the institutions of her day and did not like causes, she did foster the development of the life of the spirit that must underlie a life of service in faith and she did take the courageous position of pacifism at a time when the Anglican church had not done so.[17]

Underhill's relationships with men to whom she grew close have been severely criticized. Grace Jantzen has taken issue with Evelyn's decision to postpone becoming a Roman Catholic, not only because of Evelyn's willingness to sacrifice taking the next step in her spiritual journey for the sake of a man and of a marriage, but also with her attitude toward Hubert, calling herself his nurse and him her boy, and choosing not to put her fads before his real interests.[18]

Even before reading Jantzen's criticism, I perceived certain difficulties in Underhill's relationships with Hubert and with von Hügel. One must take into account, however, that her decision to delay becoming a Roman Catholic was based not only on Hubert's anti-clerical bias but also, and perhaps more importantly, on her intellectual reservations about joining a church that seemed closed to scientific progress. It seems inappropriate to name her main motivation for this postponement her willingness to sacrifice self for a man. In fact, she had hoped that when she married him, she would be able to convince him.

Since there is, however, a prevalence of parental interaction in many adult relationships, I am not entirely uncomfortable with the mother-son aspect of her relationship with her fiancé since it is a historical, acceptable convention, and other aspects loomed larger in their marriage: their companionship, their common interests in nature and church architecture, their social life, and Hubert's efforts to support her work.

Jantzen has claimed that Underhill wanted von Hügel's authoritativeness and patronage in choosing him to be her spiritual director (Jantzen, "Legacy," 18-20). Yet Underhill seemed able to take von Hügel's chauvinism along with the healing draught of his gentle advice and support at a time when his spiritual guidance freed her to get back in touch with her own center.

Instead of finding her own voice more clearly and emphasizing themes of women's spirituality such as interconnectedness, God's indwelling presence, spaciousness of thought and love, Underhill, Jantzen has asserted, became a voice of the male institutional church (Jantzen, "Legacy," 20-21). Especially in her letters, retreat addresses, and works on the spiritual life, Underhill found her own voice. As the following chapters show, she wrote on themes of women's spirituality: embodiment, honoring our bodies and psyches, interconnectedness, the web of life, being grounded in nature and the cycles of the earth, and the empowerment of others. She was not, in my opinion, a voice for the male institutional church; she spent years of her adult life outside of it. She was a voice proclaiming gospel values according to Christian tradition within her English Edwardian culture. If anything, she challenged the institutional Church of England to speak out and denounce World War II publically. Her pacifist stance set her against the church's claim to a just war theory.

In Jantzen's view, Underhill's accounts to von Hügel of her visits to the poor revealed her lack of social analysis. She seemed satisfied with individual charity that does not work against unjust structures.[19]

Her private reflections about her visits to the poor revealed, to my mind, her needs for such emotional connectedness. If by social analysis is meant the challenging of unjust structures in society, one must concede that her spirituality lacked social analysis and this would today be a glaring lack. If by social analysis is meant a diagnosis of society's need for a spiritual outlook on daily life based on the individual's orientation to the transcendent, one can say that her spirituality was based on such a social analysis and this is a notable contribution of her life and work.

According to Jantzen, Underhill's avoidance of the feminist agenda for social justice can be supported by her lack of appreciation for the work of Suffragists and Suffragettes who made it possible for her to vote in the General Election of 1918. She also took for granted their successful campaigning for women's rights to education and access to professions in teaching at every level which enabled her to study at and become a Fellow of King's College. For years not wanting to ally with any one movement or party within the church, she was inconsistent since she did promote the elimination of conditions hostile to spiritualization, and as a committed pacifist publically denounced World War II (Jantzen, "Legacy," 22-27). Underhill chose not to be a feminist although feminism was an option. A woman who was as literate, as published, and as traveled as she, would have had to be aware of the feminist movement burgeoning in England in her day. If she had wanted to be feminist, there were other women around with whom she could have connected, women who were speaking and writing in favor of child protection and women's rights, against prostitution and pornography. Being the prolific writer that she was, she could have engaged with them but chose not to do so. Instead of characterizing her attitude as one of indifference or rejection, one can argue that she placed an intentional emphasis on promoting mysticism and the spiritual life without alienating people. In her search for guides and companions, she looked to women of the past not her contemporaries like Maude Petre (1863-1942).[20]

For her times Evelyn Underhill was, in many respects, a liberated woman who did claim her own voice in her later works. She wrote prolifically and well, spoke in distinguished gatherings of clergy and scholars as well as in devotional gatherings of retreatants. She established herself as a self-taught scholar of mysticism, and was a pioneer breaking ground for women to give retreats and spiritual direction, to lecture at Oxford and receive honorary degrees.

A Reader of Letters of Spiritual Direction

In order to gauge the originality of Underhill's method and content of spiritual mentoring in her letters, one might study other letters of spiritual direction with which she was familiar, namely, those of Jean Pierre de Caussade, the Abbé Henri de Tourville, and Dom John Chapman.

Jean Pierre de Caussade was a remarkable French Jesuit spiritual writer in the eighteenth century who wrote letters of direction for the Sisters of the Visitation at Nancy. An English translation of these letters as well as of his classic treatise on abandonment to divine providence was made available in 1921. Frequently quoting Francis de Sales, the co-founder of the Visitation Order, de Caussade based his spiritual direction on two key insights: abandonment to divine providence and the sacrament of the present moment. Based on the gospel attitude of *fiat*, his twofold conviction was as follows: nothing happens that is not ordained or permitted by God, and everything that happens turns to the advantage of those who submit to God's will. He wrote often about one's *attrait* for solitude, for prayer, for a particular vocation.[21]

In her letters, Underhill mentioned de Caussade's book called *Abandonment* at least three times and quoted in fact, his twofold conviction. Like him, she advocated surrender to God's purpose and openness to receive the sacrament of the present moment, that is, in her words, seeing the transcendent in the simple details of each day. Like him, she advised those in dryness to proceed quietly without effort, not repeating formal acts. Unlike his seeming insistence on fidelity to the ordinary duties of piety, however, she counseled those in dryness or desolation to shorten their exercises of formal prayer in favor of developing broader interests. Unlike his authoritarian style of direction which allowed him to forbid his directees to have scruples regarding their religious obligations, she urged her directees to claim their own authority about which of her suggestions would be helpful. De Caussade's doctrine can be summarized in this way: trusting providence, living in faith, and honoring the will of God. Underhill's approach can be described thus: trusting our religious experience, living the disciplines of prayer, service, and worship, and honoring our body and our psyche. Particularly toward the end of her life, as was seen in her advice about Lent, she realized that confidence in God is a better focus than offering up things painful to nature, while de Caussade emphasized both. If de Caussade's strength was his call to the surrender necessary for real conversion, Underhill's strength was her call to the autonomy necessary for real surrender.[22]

Underhill's use of de Caussade's doctrine of abandonment to divine providence and the sacrament of the present moment revealed her self-taught aptitude as a spiritual guide. In one passage, she developed a whole section on creation in which she quoted de Caussade's vision of the divine action bathing the whole universe and penetrating all creatures. Her doctrine of seeking and revealing the divine in the human was, in fact, her original adaptation of such a mainstream aspect of Christian spirituality (*House*, 27; *School*, 12, 108; *Abba*, 19, 46).

It is above all in Underhill's call to affective conversion that she marked herself as an outstanding spiritual director. She was very conscious that conversion is a human experience, that God acts with, not in spite of our selfishness, and that conversion is a lifelong process including the integration and acceptance of our gifts and limits, strengths and weaknesses, desires and disordered affections.[23]

Abbé Henri de Tourville, who lived in late nineteenth-century France, wrote his letters of direction during the last twenty years of his life as an invalid. He was convinced that the goal of spiritual direction is not conforming oneself to some prescribed or imported model of the spiritual life, but directing one's unique God-given powers and impulses, drawing out one's goodness. He urged his directees to be true to themselves and their own path, to believe in God's love for them, and to cherish the ministry of suffering which he had learned to do himself.[24]

Evelyn Underhill was familiar with these letters. She would have agreed with his emphasis on living in the truth of one's own way to God and of God's loving way with each one. She wrote the introduction to Lucy Menzies' translation of these letters. She considered his method of direction, which also characterized that of Francis de Sales and Friedrich von Hügel, appropriate for her times. Her description of it also applies to her own: "a robust common sense, a touch which is firm yet delicate, a wise tolerance of human weakness, a perpetual recourse to facts, a hatred of moral and devotional pettiness."[25]

In her introduction to Lucy Menzies' translation of Henri de Tourville's *Letters of Direction,* Underhill emphasized his practical mysticism which she called his twofold realism. This consists of a strong sense of God's presence and transcendence, and, at the same time, an acceptance of the human condition as it is finding the raw material for sanctification in the details of everyday life.[26]

Dom John Chapman, a former Anglican and an English Benedictine monk who was the fourth abbot of Downside Abbey in the early twentieth century, gave retreats and spiritual direction to laypeople and religious, and wrote a collection of spiritual letters. In the last decade of his life, he discovered the writings of de Caussade whose insights into *abandon* and the sacrament of the present moment deeply influenced him. John of the Cross's doctrine of the dark night also had a significant impact on him. He was very opposed to over-direction. Instead of assuming the role of a professional "director" to anyone, he preferred giving occasional advice and answering letters. He did not pretend to have special knowledge. Chapman's two favorite maxims were: "Pray as you can, and don't try to pray as you can't!" and "The less you pray, the worse it goes."[27]

Evelyn Underhill knew Chapman personally and corresponded with him for a time. In explaining her position as a practising Anglo-Catholic to him, she acknowledged her deep appreciation of Roman Catholicism, and added, however, that she believed it was God's will for her to remain Anglican and to care for Anglican souls. Although she often recommended the *Spiritual Letters* by Dom Chapman, she, a married Anglican laywoman living in the heart of London, wrote from a different vantage point than he.[28]

Underhill seemed to prefer giving occasional advice and answering letters as he did. There was always something informal and unassuming about her ministry of spiritual direction. She considered him a safe guide with a calm, matter-of-fact manner and a reassuring sense of the fundamental mystery of existence. She valued his advice in dryness since he, too, considered it a normal experience in spiritual growth. While they agreed about the attitude to have in dryness, it was she who went on to suggest a set of helpful guidelines for those in dryness. She noticed that he abhorred distinctions about types of prayer and stressed what was conducive to simple contemplation. She felt he knew more about prayer than anyone she had ever met.[29]

Conclusion

Did von Hügel shape the main lines of her spirituality or confirm them? He confirmed the main lines of her spirituality, empowering her to deepen and develop them in appropriate ways. She adhered to the principle of the Incarnation, seeing and seeking the divine in the human. Von Hügel invited her to develop a personal relationship with Christ which reinforced that. He also strongly supported her commitment to institutional, sacramental religion, which was ratified by her Manchester lectures written just before she began to work with him. She came to the decision on her own to rejoin the Anglican communion. In fact, von Hügel never encouraged her to join the Catholic Church unless it became clear that this was God's will for her. She had urged Margaret Robinson to get involved with the poor. Seventeen years later von Hügel urged Underhill to get involved with the poor. He ratified her commitment to volunteer work with the poor. He advised her to develop some nonreligious interests. She continued her gardening and began to do scriptwriting. Was it that he influenced her to start something new? I think he encouraged her to continue building in leisure activities which she had always done, such as bookbinding. The notion of cultivating broader interests in periods of spiritual dryness instead of dwelling on the misery of one's plight was again not something which von Hügel taught her. As early as 1911, Underhill had written Margaret Robinson to let the dry time pass like a storm, resting in God.[30]

After the Baron's death in January 1925, she worked with two Anglican spiritual directors, namely, Bishop Walter Howard Frere, a founding member of the Community of the Resurrection and a prominent liturgist through whom she came in touch with the Russian Orthodox Church, and then Reginald Somerset Ward, a married Anglican priest and spiritual director. From time to time, she also consulted Dom John Chapman, Father Bede Frost, a spiritual writer, and Father Edward Talbot, a member of the Community of the Resurrection who had been greatly influenced by von Hügel.[31]

The Green and Flowered Notebooks, 1926-1937, begin by recording her work with Bishop Frere, 1926-1933, which focused on her tendency to berate herself for petty faults, her domestic concerns, and her low point in the summer of 1929 when she was most discouraged by what she called her claimfulness of others' affections. Reginald Somerset Ward, who became her spiritual director in 1933, ushered in a regime of gentleness that she was to cultivate with herself and others based on her experience of Christ's gentleness and a positive image of herself from God's point of view as beautiful, robed in divine beauty *(Fragments,* 75-104).

Evelyn Underhill had been deeply wounded by her father's benign neglect and projected her positive masculine self on significant men in her life. It is understandable, then, that she always chose a man as spiritual director in her endless search to connect with this part of herself: von Hügel, Frere, Chapman, and Ward. It is understandable that she engaged in such strenuous work, since her research and publications were a way for her to connect with the masculine part of herself that gave her focus and discipline. It is also understandable that she turned to von Hügel for more than a "sounding board:" she projected on to him her unconnectedness with a positive masculine energy that could have helped her with decision-making. Torn between trying to be a strong, dutiful daughter and yet feeling inside the vulnerability of having been emotionally orphaned, she did the best she could with the resources she had.[32]

Underhill was influenced by the letters of spiritual direction which she read. Her emphasis on abandonment to divine providence can be traced to her reading of de Caussade's letters. Her conviction about approaching each individual directee uniquely and suggesting only what might be helpful to this person must have been strengthened by de Tourville's conviction about this approach. Her fear of giving too much advice must have been reinforced by Chapman's abhorrence of over-direction.[33]

Christopher Armstrong, one of Underhill's biographers, has called it a fundamental axiom of Evelyn Underhill that "all of life was sacred. That, after all, was what Incarnation was all about" (Armstrong, 95). He aptly summarized the pastoral impact of her Christian life by stating that Underhill would have been the first to welcome contemporary spiritual guides who may without knowing it be indebted to her since she stood for a contemplative viewpoint that she not only accepted theoretically but embodied (Armstrong, 292). In 1946 the Dean of St. Paul's called her a modern mystic: "In a quiet and unobtrusive manner Evelyn Underhill was one of the religious forces of our time."[34]

Suggestions for Prayerful Reflection
                                        Annice Callahan, R.S.C.J.

Read prayerfully the following excerpt from a letter that Underhill wrote in 1927:

Until about five years ago I never had *any* personal experience of our Lord. I didn't know what it meant. I was a convinced Theocentric, and thought Christocentric language and practice sentimental and superstitious. . . I had from time to time what seemed to be vivid experience of God, from the time of my conversion from agnosticism (about twenty years ago now). This position I thought to be that of a broadminded intelligent Christian, but when I went to the Baron he said I wasn't much better than a Unitarian. Somehow by his prayers or something, he compelled me to experience Christ. He never said anything more about it--but I know humanly speaking he did it. It took about four months--it was like watching the sun rise very slowly--and then suddenly one knew what it was.

Now for some months after that I remained predominantly Theocentric. But for the next two or three years, and especially lately, more and more my whole religious life and experience seem to centre with increasing vivideness on our Lord--that sort of quasi-involuntary prayer which springs up of itself at odd moments is always now directed to Him. I seem to have to try as it were to live more and more towards Him only--and it is this that makes it so utterly heartbreaking when one is horrid. The New Testament, which once I couldn't make much of, or meditate on, now seems full of things never noticed--all gets more and more alive and compellingly beautiful. . . . Holy Communion which at first I did simply under obedience, gets more and more wonderful too. It is in that world and atmosphere one lives (Cropper, 98).

1. Who have been spiritual guides for you? Perhaps you can take time to thank for them and the gift they have mediated to you.

2. For whom have you been a spiritual guide? Perhaps you can take time to thank for each person entrusted to you.

3. Have you been given a personal experience of God, Christ, or the Spirit? If so, perhaps you can take time to thank for this gift in your life. If not, perhaps you can take time to beg for the gift. Has spiritual direction helped you to deepen and develop your personal relationship with God, Christ, and/or the Spirit?

4. Do you find it helpful to pray with Scripture? with the New Testament in particular? Is your spirituality biblical? Does spiritual direction help you discover creative ways to let Scripture come alive for you?

5. Do you find it helpful to celebrate the Eucharist regularly or to worship with a group from time to time? Is your spirituality liturgical? Does spiritual direction help you worship more meaningfully?

6. Do you value spiritual direction? If so, perhaps you can take time to thank for the gift of it in your life. If not, are you willing to try it for a time?

Readings

For a sense of her work with spiritual guides and their influence on her, see her introductions to the following spiritual writings: *The Adornment of the Spiritual Marriage: The Book of Supreme Truth* by John Ruysbroeck, trans. C.A. Wynschenck Dom, ed. Evelyn Underhill (London: J.M. Dent and Sons, 1916), xi-xxxii; *The Autobiography of Maharishi Devendranath Tagore* (London: Macmillan and Co., 1916), xi-xliii; *Cloud of Unknowing,* ed. Evelyn Underhill, 7th ed. (London: Stuart & Watkins 1970), 5-31; *Confessions of Jacob Boehme,* ed. W. Scott Palmer (London: Methuen and Co., 1920), xi-xxv; *The Fire of Love or Melody of Love and the Mending of Life or Rule of Living* by Richard Rolle, trans. Richard Misyn, ed. Frances M.M. Comper

(London: Methuen and Co., 1914), vii-xxv; *Letters of Direction: Thoughts on the Spiritual Life* by Abbé Henri de Tourville, trans. Lucy Menzies (Wilton, Ct.: Morehouse-Barlow, 1939), 1-4; *The Mirror of Simple Souls in Fortnightly Review* 78 (Feb. 1911): 345-354; *Mysticism and the Eastern Church* by Nicholas Arseniev, trans. Arthur Chambers (Creatwood, N.Y.: St. Vladimir's Seminary Press, 1979), 13-15; *One Hundred Poems of Kabir*, trans. Rabindranath Tagore assisted by Evelyn Underhill (London: Macmillan & Co., Ltd., 1915), v-xliv; *The Scale of Perfection* by Walter Hilton (London: John M. Watkins, 1948), v-liv; *A Simple Method of Raising the Soul to Contemplation in the Form of a Dialogue*, by François Malaval, trans. Lucy Menzies (London: J.M. Dent and Sons, 1931), v-xx; *Songs of Kabir*, trans. Rabindranath Tagore assisted by Evelyn Underhill (London: Macmillan, 1914), 1-18; *The Vision of God* by Nicholas of Cusa, trans. Emma Gurney Saltet (N.Y.: E.P. Dutton & Co., 1960), vii-xvii.

For a current, readable collection of passages from her works, see *Given to God: Daily Readings with Evelyn Underhill,* selected and arranged by Delroy Oberg (London: Darton Longman and Todd, 1992). It has also been published under the title *Daily Readings with a Modern Mystic,* ed. Delroy Oberg (Mystic, Ct.: Twenty-Third, 1993). See also *An Anthology of the Love of God from the Writings of Evelyn Underhill,* ed. Lumsden Barkway and Lucy Menzies (Toronto: Anglican Book Centre, 1976; Harrisburg, Pa.: Morehouse, 1983); and *Heaven a Dance: An Evelyn Underhill Anthology,* eds. Brenda and Stuart Branch (London: SPCK, 1992).

Notes

1. On the use of the term "mentoring" in this context, see, for example, Edward Sellner, *Mentoring: The Ministry of Spiritual Kinship* (Notre Dame: Ave Maria Press, 1990).

2. See Maurice Nédoncelle, *Baron Friedrich von Hügel: a Study of his Life and Thought* (London: Longmans Green, 1937); and Hans Rollmann, "Baron Friedrich von Hügel and the Conveyance of German Protestant Biblical Criticism on Roman Catholic Modernism," *Biblical Studies and the Shifting of Paradigms, 1850-1914*, eds. Henning Graf Reventlow and William Farmer (Sheffield: Sheffield Academic Press, 1995), 197-222.
    Cf. Ellen Leonard, "Friedrich von Hügel's Spirituality of Empowerment," *Horizons* 21, no. 2 (1994): 270-287. On 284-287, Leonard discusses von Hügel's lay spirituality of scholarship, certainly an aspect of Underhill's as well.

3. On traditional religion and developing some nondevotional interests, see his letters to her of Oct. 29, 1921, Nov. 5, 1921, and Sept. 1922, 1-3, 40-41. On the peace she felt after having gone to pieces in World War I, see her letter to him of Dec. 21, 1921, 4-5, von Hügel-Underhill Collection. Cf. Cropper, 69; and *Fragments*, 108-110.

4. E. Underhill, Midsummer 1922 letter to Baron von Hügel, 24-27; and her June 1923 letter to von Hügel, 44-45, von Hügel-Underhill Collection. Cf. Cropper, 85-93;; and *Fragments*, 113-115, 122-123.

5. E. Underhill, Midsummer 1922 letter to Baron von Hügel, 29-30; and June 1923 letter to Baron von Hügel, 46, von Hügel-Underhill Collection. Cf. Cropper, 85-93; and *Fragments*, 123, 125-26.

6. E. Underhill, Midsummer 1922 letter to F. von Hügel, 24; and her June 1923 letter to the Baron, 43 and 49 , von Hügel-Underhill Collection. Cf. Cropper, 85-93, 105-10; and *Fragments*, 126.

7. Von Hügel, July 21, 1922 letter to Underhill, 33-34, von Hügel-Underhill Collection. Cf. Cropper, 93-96

8. E. Underhill, letter of June 1923 to von Hügel, von Hügel-Underhill Collection, 49-50; and von Hügel, letter of July 12, 1923, to Underhill, von Hügel-Underhill Collection, 53-54. Cf. Cropper, 105-113; Milos, 145-66; and *Fragments*, 127.

9. Baron von Hügel, February 10, 1923 letter to E. Underhill, in von Hügel-Underhill Collection, 42. Cf. Friedrich von Hügel, "Preface to the Second Edition," *The Mystical Element of Religion as Studied in Saint Catherine of Genoa and Her Friends* (N.Y.: E.P. Dutton & Co., 1923), xiv, xviii-xix, where he acknowledged her correction of his translation.

10. F. von Hügel, July 17, 1923 letter to E. Underhill, von Hügel-Underhill Collection, 55. Cf. Cropper, 114.

11. E. Underhill, *Pasture*, 209-33; "Baron Friedrich von Hügel," review of *Essays and Addresses on the Philosophy of Religion* by Baron von Hügel, *The Spectator*, 18 November 1926, 862; "Baron von Hügel's Essays," review of *Essays and Addresses on the Philosophy of Religion* by Baron Friedrich von Hügel, *Theology* 14 (February 1927): 102-106; "The Scholar Saint," review of *Selected Letters* by Baron von Hügel, *The Spectator*, 30 April 1927, 766; and "The Essence of von Hügel," *The Spectator*, 1 December 1928, 822.

      Cf. Ellen Leonard, "Traditions of Spiritual Guidance: Friedrich von Hügel as Spiritual Guide," *The Way* 31 (July 1991), 248-58; and Thomas Michael Loome, "The Enigma of Baron Friedrich von Hügel--as Modernist, I, II, III," *Downside Review*, 92, no. 302 (Jan. 1973): 13-34; 92, no. 303 (Apr. 1973):123-40; 92, no. 304 (July 1973): 204-30. For the view that von Hügel was the major influence on Underhill's spiritual and intellectual development, see Susan J. Smalley, "Evelyn Underhill and the Mystical Tradition," in Richard Bauckham and Benjamin Drewery, eds., *Scripture Tradition and Reason: A Study in the Criteria of Christian Doctrine* (Edinburgh: T & T Clark, 1988), 266-287. On von Hügel's spiritual direction relationship with Underhill, see also Todd Johnson, "In Spirit and Truth"(Ph.D. diss: University of Notre Dame, 1996), 116-138.

12. F. von Hügel, May 30, 1924 letter to E. Underhill, p. 55; August 9, 1924 letter to E. Underhill, p. 57, von Hügel-Underhill Collection.

13. See F. von Hügel, letter with no date to E. Underhill, von Hügel-Underhill Collection, 10. On detachment as nonclinging rather than renunciation, see William Johnston, *Christian Mysticism Today* (San Francisco: Harper & Row, 1984), 90.

14. Terry Coutret faults von Hügel for having neglected the one thing that she most needed, to know she was forgiven and loved by God and could therefore forgive herself. See Terry Coutret, "The Life of Evelyn Underhill," Paper presented at St. Paul's Episcopal Church, Washington, D.C., February 24, 1988, 32-33.

15. See Alison Weber, *Teresa of Avila and the Rhetoric of Femininity* (Princeton, N.J.: Princeton University Press, 1990), esp. 42-76.

16. See E. Underhill, *Man,* 16, 27, 35, 39, 56, 75, 93, 106, 159, 167, 182, 221, and 252; and "Man and the Supernatural," letter to the editor, *The Spectator,* 15 October 1927, DGC, in which she defended positions she took in her book, such as the need for a balance of mystical experience with historical, sensible, and intellectual elements, of intuition and reason, in the face of one critic's scathing review of it.

17. Grace Jantzen, review of *Evelyn Underhill: Artist of the Infinite Life* by Dana Greene in *Theology,* 94 (1991): 468-69; and Dana Greene, unpublished letter to the editor of *Theology,* August 10, 1991, DGC.

18. See Grace Jantzen, "The Legacy of Evelyn Underhill," paper presented at King's College, London, June 15, 1991, DGC, esp. 15-18.

19. Jantzen, "Legacy," pp. 21-22. For a view which held that Underhill noted the role of social action, see Richard Woods, Introduction, *Understanding Mysticism,* ed. Richard Woods (Garden City, N.Y.: Doubleday Image, 1980), 5.

20. For example, in eighteenth-century England, Mary Wollstonecraft began to demand women's right to vote, to be joined later by others, ten of whom are notable enough to be discussed individually in the book listed below. Florence Nightingale described the reality of women's oppression. Her first cousin, Barbara Bodichon, can be considered a major force behind the founding of the nineteenth-century women's movement in England. George Eliot pieced together some of the written fragments of women's experience and tried to construct a meaningful pattern for women's lives in a male-dominated society. In the early part of the twentieth century, Virginia Woolf wrote feminist literature, using in one lecture the image of "a room of one's own" to portray women's need for economic independence and freedom from emotional availability. See Dale Spender, *Women of Ideas and What Men Have Done to Them: From Aphra Behn to Adrienne Rich* (London: Routledge & Kegan Paul, 1982), esp. 3-355, 483-89. For this source I am indebted to Margaret Guider in a conversation, Cambridge, Massachusetts, August 18, 1993.

    See also Mary Wollestonecraft Godwin, *A Vindication of the Rights of Women* (1792; repr. New York: E.P. Dutton, 1929). Cf. Donna Alberta Behnke, "Created in God's Image: Religious Issues in the Woman's Right Movement of the Nineteenth Century," (Ph.D. diss., Northwestern University, 1975).

    On Maude Petre, see also Ellen Leonard, *Unresting Transformation: The Theology and Spirituality of Maude Petre* (New York: University Press of America, 1991).

21. See J.P. de Caussade, *Abandonment to Divine Providence,* ed. J. Ramière, 3rd Eng. ed., trans. from the 10th complete Fr. ed. by E.J. Strickland (Exeter: Sydney Lee, Ltd., 1921), esp. the "Letters of Direction," 107-377, in particular,

on his twofold conviction, 118, 127, 141, 219, and 248; *Self-Abandonment to Divine Providence*, rev. ed. P.H. Ramière, trans. Algar Thorold (London: Bruns Oates & Washbourne, Ltd., 1933); *The Spiritual Letters of Father P.J. de Caussade, S.J.: On the Practice of Self-Abandonment to Divine Providence*, trans. Algar Thorold (London: Burns Oates & Washbourne Ltd., 1934). Cf. J.P. de Caussade, *L'Abandon a la Providence divine* (Paris: Desclee de Brouwer, 1966); and *The Sacrament of the Present Moment*, trans. Kitty Muggeridge (San Francisco: Harper & Row, 1966).

22. See E. Underhill, *Lt, 212*, 291, 298; "Père de Caussade," review of English translation of *Prayer: Spiritual Instructions on the Various States of Prayer* by Jean Pierre de Caussade, *The Spectator*, 25 July, 1931, 133, DGC; and "The Ignatian Tradition," review of English translation of the tenth French edition of *Abandonment to Divine Providence* by J.P. de Caussade, *The Spectator*, 28 November, 1931, 737-738, DGC. On accepting dryness in peace, gentleness, and without effort, allowing the storm to pass, as Francis de Sales had advised, see de Caussade, *Abandonment to Divine Providence*, 142, 185, 291. On forbidding scruples, see de Caussade, *Abandonment*, 243. On confidence in God and things painful to nature as good for the soul, see de Caussade, *Abandonment*, 256 and 264.

23. On the development of his point about affective conversion, see Paul Robb, "Conversion as a Human Experience," *Studies in the Spirituality of Jesuits* 14, No. 3 (May 1982): 1-50; and Donald Gelpi, "The Converting Jesuit," *Studies in the Spirituality of Jesuits*, 18 (January 1986):1-38. On affective conversion, see also Walter Conn, *Christian Conversion: A Developmental Interpretation of Autonomy and Surrender* (New York: Paulist, 1986), 316-17, n. 59.

24. See Abbé Henri de Tourville, *Letters of Direction: Thoughts on the Spiritual Life*, trans. Lucy Menzies (Wilton, Ct.: Morehouse-Barlow, 1939), esp. 27, 33, 37, 43, 75, 87-94.

25. E. Underhill, Introduction, *Letters of Direction* by Abbé de Tourville, 1. Cf. *Artist*, 131, 139, 140.

26. See E. Underhill, introduction to *Letters of Direction: Thoughts on the Spiritual Life from the Letters of the Abbé de Tourville* by Henri de Tourville, trans. Lucy Menzies (Westminster: Dacre Press, 1939), 7-10.

27. *The Spiritual Letters of Dom John Chapman O.S.B. Fourth Abbot of Downside*, ed. Roger Hudleston (New York: Sheed & Ward, 1935), 25. On *abandon*, see 325. On de Caussade, see 325. On John of the Cross, see 327. On night of the senses and night of the spirit, see 328. On spiritual direction, see 326.

28. See John Chapman, "To a Married Lady," and "To My Dear -----," 27 Nov. 1911 in Roger Hudleston, ed., *The Spiritual Letters of Dom John Chapman, O.S.B.*, 2nd ed. (London: Sheed & Ward, 1944), 103-107, 244. Cf. Cropper, 69-100, 105-113; *Artist,* 77-94; and *Fragments,* 69.

On Underhill's correspondence with Chapman, see *Lt* 195, 196, and 198, esp. letter of 6/9/31, *Lt,* 196. Cf. idem, review of *The Spiritual Letters of Dom John Chapman, Fourth Abbot of Downside,* ed. Roger Hudleston, *Theology* (June 1935): 369-73, DGC; and review of *The Spiritual Letters of Dom John Chapman, Criterion* 14 (July 1935): 641-44; and Armstrong, 251.

29. On Underhill's references to him in her letters, see *Lt,* 220, 225, 244-47, 335, 337.

30. E. Underhill, *Lt,* 120-21. For an opposite view which holds that von Hügel shaped Underhill's spirituality, see von Hügel, *Letters to a Niece,* ed. Gwendolen Greene (London: Dent, 1950), 174-75; Douglas Steere, Introduction, *The Very Thought of Thee,* ed. Douglas Steere and J. Minton Batten (Nashville, Tenn.: The Upper Room, 1953), 61-65; and "Baron von Hügel as a Spiritual Director," *Spiritual Counsel and Letters of Baron Friedrich von Hügel,* ed. Douglas Steere (New York: Harper & Row, 1964), 1-34, esp. 13-21 in which Steere discusses von Hügel's work with Evelyn Underhill as "A Case Study in Spiritual Direction." Cf. Joseph Whelan, *The Spirituality of Friedrich von Hügel* (London: William Collins, 1971), esp. Index references to Underhill.

For the view which holds that von Hügel confirmed Underhill's spirituality, see A.M. Allchin, "Evelyn Underhill, and the Unity in the Love of God," in A.M. Allchin and Michael Ramsey, *Evelyn Underhill: Two Centenary Essays* (Oxford: S.L.G. Press, 1977), 1-13; Armstrong, 198-237; Susan Smalley, "The Relationship between Friedrich von Hügel and Evelyn Underhill," Paper presented at the London Institute for the Study of Religion, London, June 1975; and id., "Evelyn Underhill and the Mystical Tradition," in Richard Bauckham and Benjamin Drewery, eds., *Scripture Tradition and Reason: A Study in the Criteria of Christian Doctrine* (Edinburgh: T & T Clark, 1988), 266-287, esp. 281. In both essays, Smalley concludes that von Hügel's influence on Underhill was not as deep, permanent, or profound as he had hoped and she had thought.

31. On Frere's influence on Underhill in her work with him, 1926-1932, see E. Underhill, "Spiritual Life and Influence," *Walter Howard Frere, Bishop of Truro: A Memoir,* ed. C.S. Phillips (London: Fabre and Fabre, 1947), 175-82; and *Worship* (New York: Crossroad, 1985), xiii. Cf. Todd Johnson, "In Spirit and Truth" (Ph.D. diss.: University of Notre Dame, 1996), 41-43, 155-164, 175-178, 180-185. On the correspondence between Underhill and Frere, see Johnson, 156, n. 148.

See also Reginald Somerset Ward, *A Guide for Spiritual Directors* (London: Mowbray, 1957); and *To Jerusalem: Devotional Studies in Mystical Religion* (Harrisburg, Pa.: Morehouse, 1994).

32. See Linda Schierse Leonard, *The Wounded Woman: Healing the Father-Daughter Relationship* (Boulder, Co.: Shambhala, 1982), esp. 16 which describes qualities a positive father can help a woman develop: "consciousness, discipline, courage, decision-making, self-valuation, direction."

33. See Evelyn Underhill's letters to Daphne Martin-Hurst in "Letters to a Novice," *Evelyn Underhill Anglican Mystic* (Oxford: SLG Press, 1996), 35-47, esp. 39, 41-42, which mention Chapman, de Caussade, and de Tourville. See also A.M. Allchin, "Evelyn Underhill and Anglican Spirituality," *Evelyn Underhill Anglican Mystic,* 15-34. Cf. Maureen Conroy, *Looking into the Well: Supervision of Spiritual Directors* (Chicago: Loyola University Press, 1995).

34. Dean of St. Paul's, "A Modern Mystic," review of *Collected Papers* ed. Lucy Menzies, *Sunday Times,* 19 May 1946, 59, DGC.

Part Two

Writings on Spirituality for Daily Living

Introduction

This second part of the book presents Evelyn Underhill's spirituality for daily living according to her letters, her retreat addresses, and her other works on the spiritual life. The first chapter discusses her letters of spiritual guidance. The chapter on her retreat addresses and clergy conferences discusses the possible influence of Ignatian spirituality on her own. The chapter on her other works dealing with the spiritual life includes not only books but also random essays she wrote which have implications for deepening the spiritual life.

Underhill was a practical mystic committed to the education of the human person for the enjoyment of life with God in the world for others. Her writing was based on the praxis of her own life of union with God for others and of her spiritual mentoring of others. She fostered the development and deepening of the life of the Spirit lived in the world.

Underhill incorporated the incarnational principle by bridging the gap between the transcendent and what she loved to call the "homely" or what we might call the "homey," that is, the simple details of our everyday lives lived in faith. She encouraged the integration of life and prayer.

Chapter 4

Letters

Evelyn Underhill gave spiritual direction in person and through correspondence, largely with women who sought her out. While Underhill cited the authorities in her books on mysticism, she claimed her own authority as she continued to write letters and articulate her own experience of how to live the Christian life in the world. It is in her letters that we find Underhill working out her original insights into relating with oneself, God, others, and the world. In particular, she brought to bear her frequent experience of overtaxed strength and how to pray from that place. Because she learned to trust her experience of God in dryness, she was able to help others accept their fatigue in faith, trusting that it, too, was an opening for God. Although Underhill visited several poor families, her letters focus on Laura Rose, a widow with six children who became her friend. I have chosen here to emphasize Underhill's correspondence with Margaret Robinson.[1]

Being our True Self

Underhill concentrated on the development of the true self as the integration of the inner and the outer, a discovery of the transcendent in the details of daily life. She wrote: "It is those who have a deep and real inner life who are best able to deal with the 'irritating details of outer life'" (12/33, *Lt,* 219; 1/6/35, *Lt,* 240-41).

Underhill also understood the integration of our psychological self and our spiritual self. Reviewing a book which treated of the human psychic drive, she felt it did not go far enough because it did not mention the transcendental spark in us which can be satisfied by God alone and which cannot be equated with libido. At the same time, she criticized this book's focusing on self-cultivation and leaving out the soul's thirst for God. She wrote: "It asks an immense self-giving and some real austerity to respond to the yet greater self-giving of God" (1/24/35, *Lt*, 242).

Underhill's emphasis on a harmony between our outer and inner life implied a detachment that was balanced and sane. It meant for her combining spiritual passion with an appreciation for the humdrum (7/8/29, *Lt*, 78-79). It enables us not to pour ourselves out too much in outward activities or relationships but to maintain a certain reserve, loving much but given totally to nothing but God, cultivating an inner stability by giving ourselves quiet time every day (1/6/35, *Lt*, 240-41). She was firm that detachment includes the simplicity to love all in God (5/3/41, *Lt*, 306-7).

Underhill's advice as a spiritual mentor about avoiding self-preoccupation by focusing on God does not seem to honor the psychological growth steps of the spiritual journey. She wrote to one directee that in all we do, think, or pray about, we are to throw the whole emphasis on God, God's work, God's call, God's creating us moment by moment: our whole purpose in life is to praise, reverence, and serve God (9/23/1929, *Lt*, 187). This is not entirely possible or even desirable before one has grown enough in a sense of self and self-esteem and self-worth. It can short-circuit some valuable inner work of self-affirmation.

She was convinced that we are meant to be at peace with ourselves (6/33, *Lt*, 336). Implied are the self-acceptance and integration which maintain that peace.

Adhering to God

Underhill's advice about adhering to God included three aspects. First, we are to trust our own religious experience, even in the face of standing up to our spiritual director. Second, we are called as Christians to live the disciplines of daily prayer, regular communal worship, service to others, and work with the poor. Third, as human beings on a spiritual journey, we are to honor our bodies and psyches, especially in the fatigue state known as dryness.

Trusting our Religious Experience

In the year of Underhill's wedding, 1907, she wrote to Margaret Robinson her insight into living deeply with God: "Self-surrender, an entire willingness to live in the dark, in pain, anything--this is the real secret. I think no one really finds the Great Companion till their love is of that kind that they long only to *give* and not to get"(5/12/1907, *Lt,* 64). Later that same year, she wrote Margaret her conviction about the primacy of experience for knowledge of the truth: "Direct spiritual experience is the only possible basis; and if you will trust yours absolutely you are safe" (10/9/1907, *Lt,* 69). This appeal to experience is the point of departure for contemporary spirituality and theology.[2]

In her continuing correspondence with Margaret Robinson, Underhill revealed that for her, realness of life depended on our consciousness of the presence of God in it: "Now it seems to me that one's life only attains reality in so far as it is *consciously* lived in the presence of God," helped by meditation "by which of course I do *not* mean thinking about a pious subject but the 'deep' meditation which tends to pass over into unitive prayer"(12/30/1907, *Lt,* 70-71). At the same time, she believed that trusting God in the dark was all that mattered: "The true attitude is to rest with entire trustfulness on the Love of God, and not care two straws what happens to one's self. If you are *there,* how little the question of whether you see you are there can matter" (1/22/1909, *Lt,* 90).

Not only did she trust her experience; she also expected her directee to trust her/his own experience and to let it be the gauge for assessing the value and relevance of the spiritual direction received. Rather than assuming that she had a superior point of view that was to be obeyed, Underhill preferred a style of mutuality in the quest for God. In a January 16, 1908 letter to Margaret Robinson, she wrote:

> I, in advising you, can only go on my own experience, which may not be a bit of use to you. So, I shall probably make mistakes, and you *must* exercise your own judgement in accepting what I say. We are both in a very confusing forest, and the fact that I say I think I have found a path in one direction is no valid reason for you to alter your course (*Lt,* 71).

This mutuality in ministry has come to the fore in our own era. It characterizes a feminist mode of relating that is cooperative rather than hierarchical.

We can benefit from the advice to trust our own experience. At the same time, we can understand how difficult it was for Underhill to trust her own experience. She would have periodic bouts of skepticism which she shared with her spiritual directors. Perhaps her own experience urged her to insist on this point for others.

Living the Disciplines of Prayer, Worship, Service, and Work with the Poor

A second aspect of Underhill's practical advice about adhering to God had to to with the disciplines of prayer, worship, service, and volunteer work with the poor. Her advice to Margaret Robinson about how to meditate included putting oneself in a natural position so one was not aware of one's body, closing one's eyes, turning a phrase, truth, or event over and over like fingering a precious possession, turning one's attention inward, and sinking into profound silence and peace. The simple method of turning a phrase over and over, focusing inward, and resting in peace resembles what we call today centering prayer.[3]

Her way to God was through simple acts of communion, as she put it: "Try, gently without strain, to turn your Psalms and your own thoughts and desires into prayers" (8/4/1929, *Lt*, 183). One of her images of prayer was resting quietly in the divine indwelling presence (2/7/31, *Lt*, 194; 4/8/35, *Lt*, 245). Her insistence on personal peace was based on her conviction that God holds our soul in tranquillity. She made a careful distinction, however, when she wrote: "The real equation is not Peace = satisfied feeling, but Peace = willed abandonment" (5/32, *Lt*, 204).

Part of her instinct for wholeness was that she perceived the integration between contemplative prayer and intercessory prayer whereby one could pray in deep peace for others and offer oneself for them (2/15/35, *Lt*, 244-45). And part of her instinct and need for wholeness showed itself in the gentle guidelines for a daily regime that she laid down for others: avoidance of strain, some vocal prayer, some reading, and a willingness to accept dryness or whatever is God's will (5/25/35, *Lt*, 247; 1940, *Lt*, 304).

Prayer for her was fundamentally a personal and living relationship that became simpler as one went on (4/12/39, *Lt*, 271). It included trust, a loving relationship with God in one's daily life, and a gentleness with oneself (2/7/27, *Lt*, 312-13; 5/3/41, *Lt*, 306; 5/41, *Lt*, 308).

As Underhill put it in one letter: "the hard and wholesome doctrine that the attitude of adoration and humility is what matters and that spiritual realization is secondary to this, and can only be prepared for, not obtained, by our deliberate conscious efforts" (1/7/1919, *Lt*, 149). Her own prayer life at this time seemed to be simplifying. She was convinced that the attitude of adoration is fostered by communal worship.

Even though she recommended a life of formal prayer and worship, she regarded it as only half one's job: "the other half is to love everything for and in God. . . to let faith issue in charity" (1/16/1908, *Lt*, 72). Prayer, then, was not complete without service to others. In fact, she counselled doing some volunteer work directly with the poor: "Half an hour spent with Christ's poor is worth far more than half a million spent on them" (8/29/1908, *Lt*, 81). Notice that Underhill urged being with the poor not servile work for the poor. I imagine her friendship with Laura Rose changed her perspective on this. Her practical advice about reaching out to the poor became a hallmark of her spirituality (*Light*, 89).

Underhill valued work with the poor and advised her directees to value it as well. This came from her own intuition about Margaret Robinson's need to get out of herself, and from her own experience of volunteering two afternoons a week to visit eight families in the North Kensington slums. Today spirituality is keenly aware of the challenge of the search for social justice to work in solidarity with the poor in their struggle for justice. Although she did not have the requisite social consciousness, she would have understood liberation theology's emphasis that the good news is for the poor and that the good news is from the poor for the rest of us.[4]

In addition to work with the poor, Underhill urged sacrificial love, an insight she gleaned from the mystics and gave to those who sought her counsel. Opposed to a rigorous asceticism, she was convinced that the personal experience of God's love leads us to a willingness to suffer. To Margaret Robinson she wrote that this insight:

> is not *mine* you know. You will find it all in Eckhardt, & the Imitation & lots of other places -- They all know, as Richard of St. Victor said, that the Fire of Love *burns*. We have not fulfilled our destiny when we have sat down at a safe distance from it, purring like overfed cats. "Suffering is the ancient law of love" --& its highest pleasure into the bargain.[5]

One might wince at this view of suffering as love's highest pleasure, until one recalls the tradition of Romantic ideals in literature, familiar to Underhill, which included the exalted place of love's suffering. One might agree, however, that the dynamic process of learning to love God includes purification. The sense of God leads to self-denial and not vice-versa, as Dana Greene has astutely pointed out: "For Underhill, emphasis on mortification is always subordinate to the responses of awe and adoration. This subordination is one of her most important legacies" *(Artist,* 115).

Honoring our Body and our Psyche: Advice in Dryness

A third aspect of Underhill's practical advice concerned our need to honor our body and our psyche, especially when we are fatigued and in dryness. In her wisdom she knew that the thoughts with which we awake are dependent upon those with which we go to sleep. For this reason she pleaded that one not worry in bed. For her, sleep was a time of leisure during which peace and strength were communicated. Taking things bit by bit with trusting adherence to God was for her a way of easing out of spiritual fatigue, rather than anxious mulling over domestic complications:

> It is imitating Martha's most reprehensible habit just at the moment when you have leisure to sit with Mary, and to gain from doing so a strength and peace and rightness of judgement which you can't get in any other way (2/17/1909, *Lt,* 91-92).

Convinced as she was of the value of prayer, she was more convinced of its strength than of its length. When Margaret Robinson was having a hard time, she advised:

> Leave off mental prayer and meditation. Stick to formal prayer... I do not know how long you spend in prayer but very likely now you will *not* be able to spend so long. There is no object in exhausting yourself. You have been poring over the whole thing too much; instead of letting it happen, like a spell of bad weather (2/7/11, *Lt,* 120-121).

At the same time, Underhill was astute enough to recognize the difference between a dark night and nervous exhaustion, as she observed: "I wonder whether you have let your physical health run down and got nervous: because of course that accounts for a lot, and must not be confused with the other" (*Lt,* 121). She preferred to view prayer in the context of one's life of grace, especially when it was difficult or dry, as she indicated to Margaret Robinson:

> Prayer, when one is going through a blank time like this, is really exhausting work and you must be as reasonable in your use of it as in any other form of work. Try to make acts of faith and trust and to cultivate the power of resting in God, even in the darkness. Remember, grace is pouring in on you *all the time* and it is not conditioned by the fact that your eyes are shut (2/6/1912, *Lt,* 132).

She was convinced that dryness was not the time to lengthen quiet time for prayer but to rely on vocal prayer and deeds of service to others, staying quiet inwardly and letting God act.[6] Underhill was aware of our need for rest and relaxation. She urged integration between devotional programs and honoring the limits of our human nature, a balance between what is technically called spiritual reading and reading for pleasure. She advised developing wholesome interests like music or gardening. It was important to her that we get the variety and refreshment needed to avoid stale religious intensity.[7] She gave the following advice in a letter of February 7, 1923: "I know you do feel tremendously stimulated all round; but remember the 'young presumptuous disciples' in the *Cloud*! Hot milk and a thoroughly foolish novel are better things for you to go to bed on just now than St. Teresa" (2/7/23, *Lt,* 313). Notice how she urged her friend to get out of the clouds and to honor the tiredness of her body and her psyche.

Another aspect of this integration was avoiding fatigue and strain in the name of devotions, for example, not getting up for early services when our bodies needed to rest, and taking recreation, sleep, a day off when necessary, and a real holiday.[8] She gave this advice to one who was exhausted:

> Early bed, novels, the flicks and so on are all good and help to minimize the nervous strain. Do not be too ferocious in your exercises in detachment at the moment, and try not to be discouraged, though I know this is hard. Your grief at God's absence is the best of all proofs of your love (10/25/33, *Lt,* 224-25).

She advised taking one day without theology as being a more helpful way to reduce strain than working less on other days (1/18/40, *Lt,* 287). In suffering and in dryness, she urged quiet and confidence, not to struggle but to accept and wait until it passes (11/19/32, *Lt,* 221; *Lt,* 223; 10/29/33, *Lt,* 225).

Still another aspect of this integration was allowing for what she called our unstable psyche in situations of crisis, separation, difficulty of any kind. I believe she showed uncanny insight into human nature when she advised one correspondent who had suffered a profound loss not to blame herself or be afraid of a severe psychological reaction, which she described in as vivid detail as possible: "uprushes of bitter or violent feeling, rebellious thoughts, exasperated nerves, lack of interest or any of the other miseries by which our unstable psyche makes us pay for great strain" (9/12/32, *Lt,* 207). Underhill advised her to offer this suffering humbly to God, and not mull over it during meditation. Underhill was at her best when she counseled a gentle balance that favored active work, short prayers, confiding in a friend, and the avoidance of introspection:

> When it all seems unbearable, talk about it--do not brood or practise suppression. . . When you find in your prayers that you are moving away from thoughts of God to thoughts of your own unhappiness, *Stop!* Get up, read if you can, if not, do not scruple to turn to some active occupation. Short aspirations, constant thoughts of and appeals to God will be better than long prayers just now (9/12/32, *Lt,* 207).

Prayer in dryness meant for Underhill regular weekly worship, vocal prayers, no strain, no attempt at meditation, the development of some nonreligious interest like needlework, no struggle to regain fervor. The avoidance of strain, a quiet, trusting acceptance of the dark and of sacrifice, a focus on secular interests, and no seeking of the Cross were hallmarks of her doctrine on prayer in dryness.[9]

She made a key distinction between the prayerful attitude and the prayerful act; her preference was for the first (9/24/24, *Lt,* 325). At the heart of that prayerful attitude for her was a trustful adherence to God and a willingness to be a channel of grace, much more important in the darkness than our trying to wear ourselves out keeping our times for prayerful acts (8/33, *Lt,* 336). The avoidance of strain and the attempt at tranquillity allows us "like the cats, to see a bit in the dark" (12/36, *Lt,* 338).

She was fundamentally in favor of contemplative prayer, passive prayer in which we do nothing and strain after nothing (3/24/38, *Lt,* 339). This prayerful attitude toward the beginning of our retirement can enable us to hand it over to others in loving trust and greater abandonment to God (4/38, 5/41, *Lt,* 340).

Underhill was fundamentally opposed to self-preoccupation, whether in terms of dwelling on one's unworthiness before God or of preparing for the sacrament of reconciliation.[10] Her advice was always to drop self-scrutiny and to wait quietly for God's self-revelation, sometimes doing something which is not religious and which absorbs our whole attention (4/25/35, *Lt,* 337; 2/36, *Lt,* 338). By this she did not mean that we should avoid the pain of darkness by losing ourselves in activity which brings on exhaustion and depression (12/36, *Lt,* 339).

One contribution which Underhill made to spiritual guidance was her insight into dryness. She herself experienced often the physical fatigue that accompanies intense mental work. Gradually she learned to dispel its effects by turning to some non-religious interest and immersing herself in her gardening, scriptwriting, or bookbinding. For her, dryness is a state of physical and nervous exhaustion. Her letters abound with practical advice about dispelling dryness with a hobby, a hot bath, a movie, or a novel. She was astute enough to perceive, however, the difference between a physical state of dryness and a mystical dark night, between a psychological state of depression and a mystical dark night. In this, I believe she was Ignatian: she urged that one try every human means possible to get back to consolation, that is, proper rest, food, and recreation. Dryness is distinct but not separate from depression which is a psychological state of meaninglessness or of loss of a loved one, a job, or self-esteem. It is also distinct but not separate from the dark night which is a phase of purification marked by the inability to meditate or reflect and an attraction to let go and let God be God. It is possible that someone may think she is in depression or in the dark night when in reality she is suffering dryness. This explains the importance of asking whether the person is sleeping, eating regularly, relaxing, and basically positive relationships, before diagnosing her state and suggesting a path to follow.[11]

Underhill's counsel was not to sustain, much less lengthen, mental prayer at times of dryness, and to garden or read a novel. It may be that the question is not whether we pray in times of dryness, but how. If we are open to variety in our relationship with God, we may not be able to enter into contemplative prayer at this time, but we may find it helpful to journal about our feelings or listen prayerfully to music.

Lent

In her February 17, 1909 letter to Margaret Robinson, Underhill gave three suggestions for Lent revealing her respect for devotional spirituality: weekly Communion, weekly Way of the Cross, and intercessory prayer. For her Communion was not for the purpose of getting help but of offering service. She gave us an insight into her understanding of the redemptive power of the Incarnation when she described the meaning of the Way of the Cross: "To me, the way in which it weaves together and consecrates every misery, injustice, humiliation, difficulty, weariness and squalor incident to human life, raises them to the nth degree of intensity and exhibits them in the full blaze of the Divine, is a sort of inexhaustible marvel" *(Lt,* 92).

Her April 12, 1911 letter to the same urged common sense about avoiding Lenten penances which lead to sleeplessness and slackness. She shared her choice of doing unattractive social duties and giving up all aesthetic pleasures in Lent: music, novels, plays, and poetry (4/12/1911, *Lt,* 124).

In a 1930 letter, Underhill listed notes on mortification from Augustine Baker which sanely advised suffering quietly the difficulties and contradictions of life sent by God, cultivating an habitual quietness of mind, and undertaking only those mortifications which promote humility not strain. Perhaps his prudence informed her own. Underhill's advice for Lent 1936 reflected a growth in her integration of the spiritual and the practical, the inner and the outer. Instead of urging her correspondent to monitor her reading and the theater as she had chosen for herself in Lent 1911, Underhill warned against setting up physical hardships such as lack of sleep, and emphasized turning to God in trust, making the discipline of life of spiritual worth, reading a devotional book each day, accepting failures, being very kind to the animal side of oneself. With this same growing balance, she recognized the tendency to become abstract and impersonal, and advised instead the choice to meet God in the concrete and the personal, in Christ, the sacraments, and prayer experiences. By the Lent of 1938, she had realized that renunciations ought not to be hostile to health and that spiritual mortifications were the real ones. In the Lent of 1939, she affirmed that Lenten spiritual reading is to promote spiritual growth and nourishment, not to get information.[12]

In the summer of 1939, Evelyn Underhill founded a prayer group for twelve women theology students who met monthly to learn about prayer and to pray together. During World War II, they disbanded but Underhill continued to send them at least seven letters for major feasts and liturgical seasons of the year. Her clarion call to adoration, adherence, and intercessory cooperation with God stressed an inward peace based on loving and absolute trust in God. The need to pace oneself with a minimal but regular devotional program was her advice to these women. In one letter, she urged them to beg for the power of the Spirit which changes every situation in which we are placed and which is the only power that can bring in the new Christian society (*Fruits*, 62; *Artist*, 133). In her 1940 Lenten letter to her prayer group, she emphasized abstinence, almsgiving, and prayer. In her 1941 Lenten letter to them, she wrote that chastity is the spirit of poverty applied to the emotional life, purity of heart transforming attachment and possessiveness. What she gave them above all was, in fact, her sense of God. This prayer group was still in existence in 1955 serving the Church of England, with daughter groups in West Africa, New Guinea, Singapore, and India. Most of the members had theological training. Following a simple rule of life, they developed personal friendships and a fellowship in the Holy Spirit.[13]

Aspects of Evelyn Underhill's advice for Lent tended to reflect a former spirituality which concentrated on what I should do when I pray, such as length of prayer time, frequency of Communion, and types of penance. Contemporary Christian spirituality focuses on how I am being led, drawn, by the Spirit, asking such questions as: Where is God in this event, in my life? How can I contemplate the world with Christ's heart, his interests and concerns? Am I seeing Christ in myself and in others, especially the poor and oppressed? How can I live gospel values in today's world?

Identifying with Christ

Underhill believed deeply that our identification with Jesus in his paschal mystery was the Christian life. Christ is to be found in the center of our lives, not in the cozy chair of a chapel isolated from duties and demands. In this belief she was almost severe. She wrote to Margaret Robinson: "I do not think you have ever made the Cross the center of your life *really*. . . And you have *got* to, you know. Nothing else will do. And if you do not accept it deliberately, why then it will be forced on you in some subtle and ingenious way, as it is at the present moment" (*Lt*, 120). She was convinced of the value of surrender and of suffering in faith. She continued in the same letter:

> Humility and *willing* suffering have got to be learned if we want to be Christians, and some people learn them by boredom instead of by torture. But once you really surrender it is extraordinary how the nastiness goes and you perceive that it *was* "shade of His Hand outstretched caressingly" (*Lt*, 121).

Her advice during World War II was to unite one's suffering, darkness, and anxiety to the Cross(10/15/39, *Lt*, 278-79; 10/25/39, *Lt*, 279). While the war increased religious unity, it also destroyed moral integrity with its glorification of bombing (6/22/40, *Lt*, 289). But she granted that it evoked unselfishness and endurance (6/8/40, *Lt*, 290; 1940, *Lt*, 291). For her the Cross implied a realistic acceptance of what is, but her emphasis was on a joyful hope in what is yet to come.

In an August 14, 1925 letter to a theology student, Underhill advised not dwelling much on theological difficulties, granting that our conception of God be wider than our conception of Christ, and affirming that revelation is graded: "It is one and the same living *personal* and loving Spirit whom we feel dimly in nature, more vividly as the inspirer of human goodness and heroism of all sorts, and perfectly (so far as our little souls can bear it) in Christ" (*Lt*, 165). She was convinced that this sense of Christ as God's self-revelation incarnate would grow in us as we humanize and spiritualize our experience of prayer and the service of others.

To one correspondent, she advised that one image of Christ that might be helpful was that of Christ giving himself "for *me*," and an alternate image was Christ as a bridge between the divine and the natural, Catherine of Siena's image (8/4/1929, *Lt*, 183). Dear to her own heart was the Feast of the Sacred Heart in the Roman calendar: the divine in the human (5/30/32, *Lt*, 202). Another experience of Christ for her was praying before the Blessed Sacrament (7/32, *Lt*, 205). Still another image of the Word made flesh in the Gospel portrayal was of something concrete really entering our human world, once again the transcendent in the immanent (9/9/33, *Lt*, 217).

The incarnational principle that underlay her spiritual direction was based on her experience of God incarnate in Christ. Her emphasis on the redemptive power of suffering and of service was rooted in her conviction that Jesus is our personal savior who redeemed us by his self-giving that we might in turn give ourselves with him for others. Her spirituality was never totally Christocentric. In fact, she was more drawn to the life of the Spirit in her later years.

Belonging to the Church

Underhill advised regular participation in church worship as a way of expressing the communal dimension of the Christian life. Much as she valued contemplative prayer, she also promoted intercessory prayer as a way of correcting individualism. She believed in the sacramental principle whereby God is revealed in the everyday, in water, bread, wine, and oil.

Integration was a characteristic of Evelyn Underhill's spirituality and enabled her to enter into a relationship with the communion of saints living and dead. She challenged an overemphasis on one's personal relationship with God by suggesting intercessory prayer as a way of concretizing a personal relationship with other people of faith. To Margaret Robinson who tended to dwell in her mystical relationship with God, Underhill wrote:

> I do so want your life to be properly balanced. To live alone, and be shy, and have a turn for mysticism, makes an individualistic concept of the relation between yourself and God almost inevitable. Such a concept is not untrue: it is half a truth, and when held together with the other half--the concept of yourself as one of the household of faith, related to every other soul in the household, living and dead--it becomes actually true. If this were *quite* true to you, intercessory prayer would become as natural and necessary as passing the salt to your neighbour at table instead of remaining in profound contemplation of your own plate (9/26/1908, *Lt,* 83-84).

Insistent on the social dimension of living the Christian life in the world, she wrote again: "Merge yourself in the great life of the Christian family. Make intercessions, work for it, keep it in your mind. You have tied yourself up so tight in that accursed individualism of yours--the source of *all* your difficulties--that it is a marvel you can breathe at all" (3/17/1909, *Lt,* 96-97). In the same letter, she put it in another way: "Go out as much as you can, and enter into the interests of others, however twaddley. They are all part of life, remember: and life, for you, is *divine.*" In another letter to her, Underhill urged Margaret to seek God not in the intimacy of solitude but in the goodness of other people (1909, *Lt,* 98).

Underhill was convinced that the life of the true contemplative included not only adoration but also mediatorship, a redemptive power at work in others, a cooperation in the work of Christ (8/7/24, *Lt,* 323). Intercession meant to her self-offering in union with Christ and the church's prayer for the world, the individual and corporate aspects of religion (4/16/25, *Lt,* 326; 8/12/40, *Lt,* 293). This share in Christ's action could include stretches of agonizing dark night prayer whereby our suffering avails for others in view of the church's total prayer (3/34, *Lt,* 337).

By March 1924, she wrote to a student that although she did not admire "Churchiness," "a moderate, regular sharing, in the degree suited to each, in institutional practice will always in the end enrich, calm, de-individualize our inner life" (*Lt,* 152). Here, once again, she had found a balance, this time between the mysticism of her interior life and the communal mysticism of worship.

In her August 14, 1925 letter to a student, she warned that "lonely prayers under the sky" will not always mean more to us than corporate sacramental religion which can enrich and steady our private devotional life (*Lt,* 165-166). The student wrote back to ask if she meant "music, beauty and liturgy," and she called them the "chocolate-creams of religion," replying instead: "by sacramentalism I mean the humble acceptance of grace through the medium of *things*--God coming into our souls by means of humblest accidents--the intermingling of spirit and sense. This is the corrective--one of the correctives--needed by your tendency to 'loftiness'"(10/11/1925, *Lt,* 168)!

She viewed intercessory prayer as one form of cooperation with God (1/4/1926, *Lt,* 171). This included offering our prayer and acceptance of dryness to God for the good of others (6/12/30, *Lt,* 190). It also included offering our suffering for the atonement of others' sin (11/6/34, *Lt,* 238).

Underhill revealed one image she had of the church when she was advising a slow and meaningful use of vocal prayer: "You are only a unit in the Chorus of the Church and not responsible for a solo part so that the others will make good the shortcomings you cannot help" (6/12/30, *Lt,* 190).

Another image of the church that she held was that of the redemptive cooperation between Christ and us symbolized in the Eucharist through Christ's self-giving and our self-giving to Christ for the divine work of redeeming the world (11/6/28, *Lt,* 182). This redemptive cooperation and interchange were based on faith not feeling: "Our Lord comes to your soul to *feed* you, not to give you sensations and you will come to offer Him your *whole self,* not just your emotional life" (9/2/30, *Lt,* 191).

A third image of the church that was real to her was how the divine is revealed in creation. This everyday revelation was the basis of her theology of the sacraments as points of supernatural penetration and transformation of the natural world (9/2/30, *Lt*, 191; 8/25/33, *Lt* 215).

She emphasized the value of sacramental religion as being able to feed and steady us by putting the focus back on God(1/25/23, *Lt,* 312; 10/25/26, *Lt,* 172). She was particularly aware of the contribution which our formal prayers could make to the church's prayer and praise in times of dryness (2/7/31, *Lt*, 194). Her experiences and images of the church included its human fallibility and weakness, that which can evoke irritation and impatience as well as that which can evoke admiration and awe. In 1932 she wrote: "The Church is an 'essential service' like the Post Office, but there will always be some narrow, irritating and inadequate officials behind the counter and you will always be tempted to exasperation by them" (*Lt*, 208).

And another image is that the church means "not merely a neat, benevolent and hygienic social order (the Baron used to say 'the Holy Spirit is *not* a Sanitary Inspector') but that transfiguration of the world and of life into something consistent with God's Will, which is the aim of redemption" (12/1/32, *Lt*, 222).

She promoted the value of sacramental religion because she saw Holy Communion as a source of strength. By September 1937, she was convinced that a regular practice of corporate worship could help someone more than the solitary reading of advanced devotional books, by immersing one in the life of the church and putting a check on a tendency to individualism (10/7/23, *Lt*, 317; 9/22/37, *Lt,* 261).

The Life of the Spirit in the World

Underhill's practical advice about living the life of the Spirit was based on her sense of our interconnectedness with the earth and with the universe. For her, the world is a sacrament of God's love, and at the same time, it is in need of redemption. Our cooperation with God's purpose makes us channels of God's love, joy, and peace to others.

Early in her ministry of spiritual direction, Evelyn Underhill underscored the sacramentality of beauty in leading us to God. In her first letter to Margaret Robinson who found the sensuous side of beauty a danger and distraction, Underhill agreed but added that the perception of beauty as the outward sign of the greatest of sacraments prevents one from getting caught in its visible side (11/29/1904, *Lt*, 51).

Underhill's love of beauty and of nature led her to advise others to let their senses be transformed not repressed by detachment. For centuries spiritual traditions had taught mortification through detachment. In this regard, adoration of God in creatures was a higher value for her than mortification. And on this point, she was a bridge to our postmodern sense of being one with all creation. On this point, she invoked Jesus' life of contemplation in action, and, of course, the mystics, as in the following excerpt from a letter to Margaret Robinson: "Remember St. Francis with his love of birds and music, sun and air; St. Teresa's eau-de-Cologne; Ruysbroeck's and St. Bernard's passion for the forest" (7/29/1908, *Lt*, 78). Such real detachment, she observed in the same letter, led Francis of Assisi to glory in God's works and to receive the Stigmata. In a postscript, she quoted from Bernard's testimony that the oaks and the beeches were his real teachers. She discovered that nature can be, like the Judeo-Christian scriptures, a source of God's revelation. In this way she encouraged a sense of our interconnectedness with the earth. She was, however, always talking about detachment for herself, as *Fragments* indicated.[14]

Native North American spirituality and feminist self-awareness are voices affirming our interconnectedness with the earth, with our ancestors, and with the feminine element in creation.[15] Today the new cosmology has challenged spirituality to take account of facts of reality, namely, that matter is not inert, that nature is a medium of God's revelation, that there is a mystical experience of belonging to the universe which is a way of experiencing belonging to God.[16]

The world, for Underhill, was in need of redemption: this was the divine work with which we cooperate (11/6/1928, *Lt*, 182). We do this by agonizing deeply for the world's suffering and loving all things with God's love, without feeling any mystical absorption in life in general, and fulfilling the Second Commandment by concentrating in the First (3/1/33, *Lt*, 209).

Her way of seeing the spiritual in the practical colored her advice about living the daily life of the Spirit:

> Take the present situation as it is and try to deal with what it brings you, in a spirit of generosity and love. God is as much in the difficult home problems as in the times of quiet and prayer. . . Bring your whole situation *en bloc* into your Godward life. Knock down the partition between living-room and oratory, even if it means tobacco smoke and incense get a bit mixed up (9/15/33, *Lt*, 217).

Her advice was always grounded in balance and the Incarnation: being simple and natural with God, avoiding strain, keeping in charity with others. It reflected her specifically feminine concern for the wholeness of human life.[17]

Her advice about not praying to see God but praying to be useful to God sounds more like the counsel of a dutiful daughter who was also a dutiful daughter to God (5/5/30, *Lt*, 188). Is it admirable in North American cultures to be useful to God or, in a way, to be useless to God and still feel loved unconditionally? Wasn't this precisely Underhill's own failure, that she did not allow herself to feel loved unconditionally by God (*Artist*, 150)? On the other hand, she represented a balanced view observing that it is right for us to desire God and to desire to be used by God, arguing that our longing for God must be the kind that longs first for God's will to be done, though that may mean darkness for ourselves (7/20/33, *Lt*, 213). This view certainly counters that of the pseudo-contemplative and confirms the process of the purification of our desires. Underhill warned her directees against individualism, keenly aware of the danger of pseudo-contemplatives to isolate themselves from the responsibilities of daily life, as can be seen in her correspondence with Margaret Robinson and Lucy Menzies.

Underhill's directees were encouraged to free themselves to serve the world not to flee the world. The acid test of their formal prayer was their informal love of neighbor, especially the poor. Deftly, relentlessly, she "set the guidelines for the socially concerned contemplative. She saw the goal of personal and group prayer not only for the salvation of the person, but for the salvation of society."[18]

Conclusion

One of the hallmarks of Underhill's doctrine was her belief in mystical experience and the vision of God in our daily lives. Her way of seeing the spiritual in the practical colored her advice about living the Christian life in the world.

The fact that Underhill wrote as a woman provides us with a point of departure for making an assessment of her ministry of spiritual direction. For one thing, she did not put out her own shingle. She was sought out to preach retreats and give spiritual counsel. For another, although she had high ideals and expectations for herself, her guidance was marked by a gentleness, compassion, and sensitivity that were some of her richest womanly gifts. Perhaps because she herself had to work through a turn from a Neoplatonic idealism to a faith realism grounded in the Incarnation, she was able to help others get out of the clouds and on to the ground. Early on she had learned that the acid test of who we are with God is who we are with ourselves and with others and with everything entrusted to us. For this reason, her gift was a practical mysticism based on doing one's duty with love and delighting in one's cat, listening to someone with love and entering into that person's most trivial interest and concern, breaking down the barrier between the oratory and kitchen, between the oratory and the study, in such a way that one could work prayerfully, that is, in the presence of God.

Her approach was balanced. Even though she herself was not drawn to the spousal metaphor in her relationship with Christ, she was broad-minded enough to focus on its potential for spiritual generativity. Living in comfortable means, she spent time with the poor. Although childless, she reached out to the children in the North Kensington slums.

Evelyn Underhill was a woman of her time and a woman of our time. She was able to indicate lines of a contemporary spirituality that is embodied, ecumenical, interreligious, and open to God's action in the practical duties of daily life. In particular, since women comprised the majority of her retreatants and spiritual directees, she may contribute to a spirituality for women, although she did not set out to do this and did not seem to be conscious of this.

Charles Williams once wrote of Underhill: "The proof of her calling-- or, at least, the value of it--was in her motherhood of souls" (*Lt,* 26). I think Evelyn herself would argue that she preferred a term like "the care of souls" or spiritual mentoring. I am sure she saw herself much more as a midwife than a mother of souls, mediating the birth of new life rather than bringing it to birth.[19] Let us turn now to see how she carried on her care of souls in her retreat addresses and the other works she wrote on the spiritual life.

Suggestions for Prayerful Reflection

Annice Callahan, R.S.C.J.

Evelyn Underhill gave Margaret Robinson practical advice about how to meditate. Try her simple instructions:

1. Put yourself into some position so easy and natural to you that you don't *notice* your body: and shut your eyes.

2. Represent to your mind, some phrase, truth, dogma, event--e.g. a phrase of the Paternoster or *Anima Christi*, the Passion, the Nativity are the sort of things I use. Something that occurs naturally. Now, don't think about it, but keep it before you, turning it over as it were, as you might finger some precious possession.

3. Deliberately, and by an act of will, shut yourself off from your senses. Don't attend to touch or hearing: till the external world seems unreal and far away. Still holding on to your idea, turn your attention *inwards* (this is what Ruysbroeck means by introversion) and allow yourself to sink, as it were, downwards and downwards, into the profound silence and peace which is the essence of the meditative state. More you cannot do for yourself: if you get further, you will do so automatically as a consequence of the above practice. It is the "shutting off of the senses" and what Boehme calls the "stopping the wheel of the imagination and ceasing from self-thinking" that is hard at first. Anyhow, do not try these things when you are tired--it is useless: and do not give up the form of prayer that comes naturally to you: and do not be disheartened if it seems at first a barren and profitless performance. It is quite possible to obtain spiritual nourishment without being consciously aware of it (*Lt*, 73)!

1. Are there areas of your life where you want to trust your experience more? Select one area and choose one action-step for growing in trust.

2. What helps you live the disciplines of regular prayer, service, friendship with the poor, and worship? What is not helpful for you in this regard? Select one discipline and choose one action-step for embodying this discipline in your daily life.

3. How do you feel about Evelyn Underhill's advice for honoring our body and psyche in dryness? Have you experienced her approach to be helpful?

4. Does it help you to shut off your senses or to come to your senses through relaxation exercises? Do you engage your senses in your contemplative prayer?

5. What gives you spiritual nourishment? Is this part of your regular diet for daily, weekly, monthly times of leisure?

Readings

For an edited collection of her letters, see *The Letters of Evelyn Underhill*, ed. Charles Williams (Westminster, Md.: Christian Classics, 1989). For a collection of her writings that can be read meditatively during Lent, see *Lent with Evelyn Underhill*, ed. George Mellick Belshaw (Harrisburg, Pa.: Morehouse, 1993).

Notes

1. See Joy Milos, "Evelyn Underhill: A Companion on Many Journeys," *The Way* 30 (April 1990): 147-159, reprinted in Lavinia Byrne, ed., *Traditions of Spiritual Guidance* (Collegeville, Mn.: Liturgical Press, 1990), 126-41, which uses Underhill's correspondence with Lucy Menzies as a case study of spiritual directon.

2. It has been reinforced by what Gregory Baum called "the Blondelian shift" and by the transcendental Thomism of Karl Rahner and Bernard Lonergan. See Gregory Baum, *Man Becoming* (N.Y.: Herder & Herder, 1970), esp. 1-60; Bernard Lonergan, *Method in Theology*, 2nd. ed. (Toronto: University of Toronto Press, 1990); and Karl Rahner, *The Foundations of Christian Faith: An Introduction to the Idea of Christianity*, tr. William V. Dych (New York: Crossroad, 1978). Cf. George P. Schner, "Appeal to Experience," *Theological Studies* 53 (1992): 40-59.

3. See E. Underhill, *Lt*, 73, 127. On centering prayer, see, for example, Thomas Keating, *Open Mind Open Heart: The Contemplative Dimension of the Gospels* (New York: Amity House, 1986); and *Invitation to Love* (Rockport, Mass.: Element, 1992).

4. For example, see Ada Maria Isasi-Diaz and Yolanda Tarango, *Hispanic Women: Prophetic Voice in the Church. Toward a Hispanic Women's Liberation Theology* (New York: Harper & Row, 1988); Joe Donders, *Non-Bourgeois Theology: An African Experience of Jesus* (Maryknoll, N.Y.: Orbis, 1985; Gustavo Gutierrez, *We Drink from Our Own Wells: The Spiritual Journey of a People*, trans. Matthew J. O'Connell (Maryknoll, N.Y.: Orbis Books, 1984); and Mary John Mananzan and Sun Ai Park, "Emerging Spirituality of Asian Women," in Virginia Fabella and Mercy Amba Oduyoye, eds., *With Passion and Compassion: Third World Women Doing Theology* (Maryknoll, N.Y.: Orbis, 1988), 77-88. Cf. William Callahan, " Spirituality and Justice: An Evolving Vision of the Great Commandment," in Francis A. Eigo, ed., *Contemporary Spirituality: Responding to the Divine Initiative* (Villanova, Pa.: Villanova University Press, 1983), 137-161; Donal Dorr, *Spirituality and Justice* (Maryknoll, N.Y.: Orbis, 1984); Roger Haight, "Liberationist Spirituality," *An Alternative Vision: An Interpretation of Liberation Theology* (New York: Paulist, 1985), 233-256; John C. Haughey, ed., *The Faith That Does Justice* (New York: Paulist, 1977); and Dorothee Sölle, *On Earth as in Heaven: a Liberation Spirituality of Sharing*, trans. Marc Batko (Louisville, Ky.: Westminster/John Knox Press, 1993).

5. "To Margaret Robinson," 13 Oct. 1909, MS. 5128, St. Andrews University Archives, St. Andrews, Scotland, in D. Greene, *Artist*, 45, n. 29.

6. See E. Underhill, 2/21/23, *Lt*, 314; 3/1/23, *Lt*, 314-15; 1/10/34, *Lt*, 231; 5/41, *Lt*, 308.

7. See E. Underhill, 2/7/23, *Lt*, 313; 1/27/1927, *Lt*, 175; 5/14/30, *Lt*, 188; 9/10/30, *Lt*, 192; 2/16/32, *Lt*, 201.

✓ 8. See E. Underhill, 2/21/23, *Lt*, 314; 6/27/23, *Lt*, 316; 1/1928, *Lt*, 178; 6/20/32, *Lt*, 220; 9/29/33, *Lt*, 226; 11/6/34, *Lt*, 239.

9. See E. Underhill, 11/16/23, *Lt*, 318-19; 11/24/23, *Lt*, 319; 2/25/24, *Lt*, 320; 8/7/24, *Lt*, 323; 9/14/24, *Lt*, 324; 10/29/26, *Lt*, 332; 7/29, *Lt*, 335; 12/7/31, *Lt*, 335.

10. See E. Underhill, 11/24/1908, *Lt*, 88; 12/33, *Lt*, 228; 10/19/34, *Lt*, 237; 11/21/39, *Lt*, 282; 9/14/26, *Lt*, 330-31.

11. On the dark night, see John of the Cross, *The Dark Night* in Kieran Kavanaugh, ed., *The Collected Works of St. John of the Cross*, trans. Kieran Kavanaugh and Otilio Rodriguez (Washington, D.C.: Institute of Carmelite Studies, 1979), 295-389. Cf. Constance FitzGerald, "Impasse and Dark Night," in Joann Wolski Conn, ed., *Women's Spirituality: Resources for Christian Development* (New York: Paulist, 1986), 287-311.

On the difference between the dark night and depression, see, for example, Joann Wolski Conn, "Psychological Depression and Spiritual Darkness," *Spirituality and Personal Maturity* (New York: Paulist, 1989), 128-167.

On moving to consolation from desolation, see *The Spiritual Exercises of Ignatius Loyola*, trans. George E. Ganss (St. Louis: Institute of Jesuit Sources, 1992), 122-125, ##317-327. Desolation is understood here as a lack of awareness of God's presence which results in pain, confusion, and turmoil, as well as a movement away from God that is a refusal to love. See also Marian Cowan and John Carroll Futrell, *Companions in Grace: A Handbook for Directors of the Spiritual Exercises of St. Ignatius of Loyola* (Kansas City, Mo.: Sheed & Ward, 1993), esp. 143-179.

✓ 12. See E. Underhill, *Lt*, 124, 193, 252, 265; id., "Men and Books," review of *Amor Dei* by John Burnaby, and *The Knowledge of God and the Service of God* by Karl Barth, *Time and Tide*, 25 February 1939, 242-43, DGC; and id., *Lent with Evelyn Underhill*, ed. George Mellick Belshaw (Harrisburg, Pa.: Morehouse Barlow, 1993). See also E. Underhill, "Keeping Lent," *Church Bulletin* (Christ Church, Hampstead, March 1941), DGC, in which she encouraged prayer, fasting, and almsgiving, suggesting the reduction or temporary cessation of bodily comforts, mental comforts like newspapers and magazines, and personal relationships. This fierce asceticism does not sound like vintage Underhill and may have been written at an earlier period of her life!

13. *Fruits*, 43-72. Cf. Lady Laura Eastaugh, a member of the Prayer Group, "Evelyn Underhill," paper presented on the Friends Festival Day, 1 June 1991, London, DGC; and Agatha Norman, "Evelyn Underhill and her Prayer Group," Folder 57, TS, Evelyn Underhill Collection, King's College Archives, London, 1955, DGC.

14. See E. Underhill, *Fragments*, for example, 34, 36, 50, 52, 62, 86, 88, 101, 115-116.

15. On native North American spirituality, see, for example, Paula Gunn Allen, *The Sacred Hoop: Recovering the Feminine in American Indian Traditions* (Boston: Beacon Press, 1986), 60. Cf. Dhyani Ywahoo, "Renewing the Sacred Hoop," in Judith Plaskow and Carol P. Christ, eds., *Weaving the Visions: New Patterns in Feminist Spirituality* (San Francisco: Harper & Row, 1989), 274-280.
        On feminist self-awareness, see, for example, what Mary Hamilton in analysis with Marion Woodman wrote using active imagination: Mary Hamilton, "Redeeming Eve's Body," in Marion Woodman et al, *Leaving My Father's House: A Journey to Conscious Femininity* (Boston: Shambhala, 1993), 151.

16. See Fritjof Capra and David Steindl-Rast, with Thomas Matus, *Belonging to the Universe: Explorations of the Frontiers of Science and Spirituality* (San Francisco: HarperSanFrancisco, 1991).

17. See E. Underhill, Letter of 12/4/37, *Lt*, 263. Cf. A.M. Allchin, introduction to Delroy Oberg, ed., *Given to God: Daily Readings with Evelyn Underhill* (London: Darton, Longman and Todd, 1992), xi-xv, esp. xii.

18. Susan Anthony, "The Spiral and the Synthesis," *Spiritual Life* 21 (Summer 1975): 145.

19. Underhill referred to the divine motherhood as an aspect of the unitive life (*Mysticism*, 432), to Jesus' "care of souls" (*Abba*, 58), to the church as the "mother of souls" (*Mystery*, 65), and to spiritually educated children becoming "parents of other souls" (*Spirit* 177). Dana Greene found that once Evelyn signed herself "Your affectionate mother" on a letter of March 5, 1940 to Daphne Martin-Hurst, a member of the Prayer Group. See D. Greene, *Artist*, 133, n. 11. Cf. Joy Milos, "Evelyn Underhill, a Companion on Many Journeys," *Traditions of Spiritual Guidance*, ed. Lavinia Byrne (Collegeville, Mn.: Liturgical Press, 1990), 126-41; and "The Role of the Spiritual Guide in the Life and Writings of Evelyn Underhill," (Ph.D. diss., Catholic University of America, 1988).
        On women's views on giving spiritual direction, see, for example,

Kathleen Fischer, *Women at the Well: Feminist Perspectives on Spiritual Direction* (New York: Paulist, 1988); Carolyn Gratton, *The Art of Spiritual Guidance: A Contemporary Approach to Growing in the Spirit* (New York: Crossroad, 1992); Margaret Guenther, *Holy Listening: The Art of Spiritual Direction* (Boston: Cowley, 1992), esp. Chapters on "Good Teachers," "Midwife to the Soul," and "Women and Spiritual Direction;" and Janet Ruffing, *Uncovering Stories of Faith: Spiritual Direction and Narrative* (New York: Paulist, 1989).

Chapter 5

Retreats

Evelyn Underhill gave practical advice for living the Christian life in the world in her retreat addresses and clergy conferences. The first retreat she was asked to give was at the House of Pleshey in 1924 for an interdenominational group called the Time and Talents Settlement. From then on she was asked to give retreats and clergy conferences, mainly to Anglicans. As a laywoman, she must have felt humbled by these requests. In 1927 she was the first woman to preach a retreat at Canterbury Cathedral. Since her books of retreat lectures which she gave form their own genre, they are treated together in this chapter.

The House of the Soul

In her first retreat, "Sanctity: The Perfection of Love," given at Pleshey March 15-18, 1924, for the Time and Talent Settlement, a group of social workers and volunteers, Underhill recommended deepening a sense of God rather than increasing self-knowledge. She favored self-examination that leads us to God in gratitude, and was opposed to self-scrutiny that leads to discouragement (*Ways*, 55-57). This advice might fall on deaf ears to many North American Christians heavily influenced by psychological introspection and self-awareness. I wonder if Underhill was suggesting an emphasis on what is called today receptive prayer.[1]

In her second retreat, "The End for Which We Are Made," Underhill described the seven mansions in Teresa's *Interior Castle* as subjects for meditation, and admitted that self-knowledge, a humbling sense of our littleness, is the first step in the expansion of our soul. But notice that the emphasis is on God not on our egos. She quoted Ignatius' prayer of surrender, the *Suscipe*, which expresses contentment with God's love and grace *(Ways*, 118, 122).

Underhill saw through the resistance which our woundedness can make to simple abandonment to the purposes of God: "The real test of humility is the willingness to risk failure, to take a job with simplicity and let the inferiority complex have a rest" *(Ways*, 216). She also urged dropping all nervous anxiety about our religious needs and preferences. She meant to let grace build on nature not to do violence to our nature. She was aware that what matters is that we respond to God's self-giving where we are, not whether we recite the office or not, use words in prayer, contemplate silently, or practice a particular method of prayer *(Ways*, 219). This conviction reflected her belief in the uniqueness of God's way with each of us.

Underhill recognized the value of psychology to make self-improvement but distrusted psychology's tendency to suggest that we do so by our own resolve *(Ways*, 206-7). She realized that the first step in recovery is the admission of our helplessness and need for a purifying effect beyond our mental health or usefulness *(Ways*, 207). The passive purification provoked by the discovery that we cannot do it ourselves "really kills our self-esteem and leaves nothing, not even self-improvement, in which to take pride. And *then* we begin to be fit to speak to other souls of God" *(Ways*, 211). Here by self-esteem she clearly meant some defence of our ego trying to be independent of God's help. And she perceived clearly that God's patient, purifying action takes place in separations, disappointments, and dealings with difficult people *(Ways*, 211).

One welcomes Underhill's appreciation of the difference between the inexperienced gardener's vigorous campaign of weeding which also does violence to roots and seedlings, and the expert's care to tend patiently the plants that will grow. Second, one agrees with her conviction about the slowness of real growth: "Good gardening is not feverishly sticking in geraniums to get a transient show of bloom" *(Ways*, 172).

Underhill was in favor of the little disciplines and trials which purify self-love and self-will, not dramatic cutbacks or radical sacrifices *(Ways*, 228). While we might quibble about the words she chose, the reality of what she stated is uncontestable: our surrender is the measure of our fruitfulness. She put it another way when she said of heaven: "It does not mean to be clear of jobs, troubles, or sufferings, but merely to be clear of self-regard in every form" *(Ways*, 240). We might prefer to talk about a healthy self-regard as desirable and ego needs as unfavorable, but her message comes through.

A powerful image which Underhill used for the self in her 1927 set of retreat addresses is that of the house of the soul. By this she did not mean a one-room cottage with a mud floor, as some psychologists might assume, or a lake dwelling in the air with no ground floor as extreme transcendentalists might prefer. She meant a house with a ground floor and an upper floor, both of which need our attention. We are not to re-paper the drawing-room, if what is needed is a new sink. The whole house is to become a house of prayer:

> It does not mean keeping a Quiet Room to which we can retreat, with mystical pictures on the walls, and curtains over the windows to temper the disconcerting intensity of the light; a room where we can forget the fact that there are black beetles in the kitchen, and that the range is not working very well (*House*, 8).

Prudence is like a good housekeeper that helps us deal with our situation as it really is not as it ought to be. Another aspect of keeping our house in order is the practice of temperance in seeking God in the ordinary details of our daily lives rather than in moments of ecstasy:

> Some people appear to think that the "spiritual life" is a peculiar condition mainly supported by cream ices and corrected by powders. But the solid norm of the spiritual life should be like that of the natural life: a matter of porridge, bread and butter, and a cut off the joint (*House*, 28).

Fortitude gives us steady endurance to believe that every event mediates God and makes our house a dwelling of the Spirit:

> It is not a week-end cottage. It must be planned and organized for life, the whole of life, not for fine weather alone. Hence strong walls and dry cellars matter more than many balconies or interesting garden design (*House*, 38).

Faith, the soul's watchtower, responds to God by adoration, adherence, and collaboration with God. Hope enables us to recognize the action of God amid the cleaning materials of our daily lives: "The languors and difficulties of ill-health, the friction of uncongenial temperaments, the hard rubs of circumstance, can all leave us cleaner than before" (*House*, 70). Love enables us to unify the upper floor with the basement, mediating divine compassion and generosity to the world.[2]

Notice that Underhill was not a lugubrious, stuffy, or boring retreat director; she kept her sense of humor and light touch, for example, when describing prudence: "She will not serve devotional meringues for breakfast, or try to make beautiful fluffy omelettes full of fervor just when eggs are scarce" (*House*, 16). Underhill acknowledged her indebtedness to Paul, Augustine, and Teresa of Avila for the image of the soul as a house (*House*, 3, 6, 8, 10, 13, 77; *Ways*, 57, 118-19). Her originality, however, was in her amplification and application of this image for English believers, as in her further description of prudence: "The cakes upon her tea-table are suited to the digestion of the guests" (*House*, 18).

This image of our true self is a grounding image inviting us to begin on the ground floor of our lives and work up. Her description of this image demonstrates her wonderful sense of humor, one of the marks of a truly grounded mystic!

The house that she and Hubert shared and made their own became the basis of her image of the self as the house of the soul. Within the metaphor of her English household, she expounded about the levels in the house of our souls, each one of which needs our attention.

The image of the house of the soul conveyed Underhill's conviction that we need to start with the ground floor of our lives, the simple details of our responsibilities and basic body rhythms, in order to discover God at work on both floors. It militates against a Neoplatonic idealism that wants to flee the world and its allurements. It also warns against a quietism which will not get involved in the demands of daily living.

This image, however, may be alien to homeless people who have no sense of what it means to have a house, to have lived in a house. There are homeless women who have all their belongings in a set of garbage bags. What is their fantasy of this image? It may also be inaccessible to latch-key children of divorced couples whose only experience of home is a three-room apartment into which they let themselves in the afternoon while their single parent is working. How can they translate this metaphor in order to let it feed their interior lives?

Some may need to translate this metaphor, but the insight behind Underhill's image of the house of the soul remains valid: grace builds on nature. Her humor was based on her experience as an English barrister's wife used to comfort and convenience except during the war years. Her genius was to adapt truths of the spiritual life to the idiom of her Edwardian culture. Today, however, her thought may need adaptation for our multi-cultural, multi-ethnic global village.

The image of the house of the soul suggests the split-leveled nature of our human condition. We are not only bodies or only spirits: we are embodied spirits in the world. We cannot know in advance how we will pray on a certain day since to live in the present moment we need to acknowledge and accept our body's needs and rhythms, our psyche's material, unconscious dream material, and that day's commitments. Taking care of the house of the soul may mean foregoing some formal time of prayer in order to get much-needed sleep. We may need to allow certain feelings to be, and to be expressed appropriately in order to get in touch with the truth of our being at that time. We may need to engage body and mind in some yoga or deep breathing exercises in order to release stress. We may also need to write out in a journal how we are feeling in the form of a letter to God or Jesus. Some would call all these actions preparation for prayer; others would call them prayer itself.

Some of us cannot forget the beetles in the kitchen or the stove being on the blink, and need to walk upstairs to distance ourselves from practical matters. Others of us can too easily forget and hide ourselves in our quiet room shirking the day's responsibilities; we may need to spend more time in the basement. The image of the house of the soul speaks of our ongoing need for renovation and interior design.[3]

The metaphor of the house of the soul is an apt one for many of us who are looking for an embodied spirituality that engages us where we are and want to be with God where we are, in our gratitude and anger, in our night dreams and daydreams, in our sexuality and creativity, in our work-day as well as in our leisure. This metaphor is also meaningful as an image of the solitude needed for creative work, especially for women trying to find the space and time they need to exercise their gifts.[4]

The biblical theme of the house or household of God has had several interpretations in different times: the line of kings succeeding David, the people of Israel, the Jerusalem temple, and the church. One can trace a shift from Paul's understanding of the house church where the early Christians met to pray, listen to God's word, and share the Eucharist in an open space of equality, to a later understanding of God's household as patriarchal family. Today we take a cosmic view of the universe as the house of God in which human beings and all creatures are called to live as one. Our care for the house of our soul includes our reverence for all creation.[5]

In her 1930 retreat she reflected on the meaning of spirit, the spiritual life, purification, and prayer, as recorded in *The Golden Sequence*. She described the spirit as our consciousness of the eternal (*Golden*, 1-7). The spiritual life begins with the awakening of the ground of our self which is our desire for and taste of God. (*Golden*, 53-62). She called the soul an invisible being that has powers of knowing and loving as well as an emotional drive that needs reorienting. Active purification means the effort of faith, hope, and love to take over the house of the soul, ridding it of destructive powers. Passive purification has to do with the Spirit's creative action in us slowly penetrating and transforming disordered self-love. The ceaseless divine action frees us to be led directly by the Spirit rather than to follow particular guides and methods. Transformation depends on the acceptance of suffering not on its amount. Purification and prayer are two movements of the same process since purification reorients our desire through self-donation and prayer reorients our attention to God (*Golden*, 97-145).

Underhill used her nautical experience to explain the unity of body and soul in the purgative way when she wrote: "There is no watertight bulkhead between the sensitive and spiritual levels of the soul. It is an aspect of our amphibious situation that one part of our being can never be purified apart from the other" (*Golden*, 109). She affirmed the collaboration of psychology with religion since both support the sublimation and redeeming of desire as the way to peace (*Golden*, 111). Her guides for these reflections are the author of *The Cloud of Unknowing* and John of the Cross, particularly *The Ascent to Mount Carmel*.

In her 1931 retreat called *The Mount of Purification* (1960), based on her reflections on Dante's *Purgatorio* in *The Divine Comedy*, Underhill adroitly distinguished between the instinctual I of our surface life that is easily upset and wants to express and develop itself, and the *ME*, our deep soul, our true self. A full-grown spiritual life is one in which God transforms both the *ME* and the *I*. She then proceeded to describe attitudes of heart which feed our spiritual life and counter dispositions which are hostile to the action of God, or what have been known as the seven deadly sins (*Mount*, 1-81).

She saw thanksgiving and humility as correctives to pride. But I would take issue with her denunciation of an anthropocentric religious world as the creation of human pride, and her downplaying of our needs and experiences in the foreground of our spiritual landscape (*Mount*, 22). Both she and I would need to nuance very carefully what we mean by anthropocentric, by pride, and by foreground. I do not use the word "anthropocentric" in a pejorative sense, but rather to signal that human experience is the point of departure for spirituality and theology. I realize that it is too small a term since "cosmocentric" more accurately describes a postmodern spirituality of interconnnectedness. With the emphasis in North American culture on self-assertiveness, it is hard to approach "pride" except as a distorted inflation of our relationship with God and the world. If our needs and experiences are in the "foreground" of our prayer, I trust that God can act through them, with them, and in them through the redemptive power of Christ's risen humanity.

I agree, however, with her insight into our need for spiritual childhood whereby we do not make desperate efforts to grow, but completely accept all that is in our lives. For her an incarnational and sacramental religion finds God in the ordinary circumstances of daily life, not in some mystical heights to which few can attain. Drawing upon the analogy of Zaccheus, Underhill could not resist adding: "There is no use stopping at the top of the theological tree, out of the way of the crowd and dust: a homey welcome is more important than a good view if we have the Spirit of Christ as our guest" (*Mount*, 26). Recalling the story of the pilgrim who had to withdraw from the pilgrimage because his dog was too tired to continue, only to discover a divine presence hidden in the dog, Underhill made a profound statement: "Temptation to desert nature to attain to spirit is one of the most subtle tricks of spiritual pride" (*Mount*, 27). I hear her encouraging us to heed our bodies and our psyches on our spiritual journey, not desert them when they are tired and in need of simple attention for mystical moments.

Another insight that she offered us is: "The texture of the spiritual life is more like a tweed than a tartan" (*Mount*, 27). By that she meant we can let go of what she called pride of intellect, the struggle to fit everything in our lives into a neat pattern; all we are asked to do is to weave all that we are given of God's self-revelation into the fabric of our lives. True humility follows the way of the monkey that clings to its mother rather than the way of the kitten that lets its mother carry it to safety (*Mount*, 29).

Underhill demonstrated her ability as a spiritual psychologist when she went on to describe sacrifice in the sense of self-giving and tranquillity as correctives to anger. Calling impatience a vote of non-confidence in God, she urged us to accept all the ups and downs of our lives as material for disciplining us and making us supple: "God uses a hypodermic syringe quite as often as a surgical knife" (*Mount*, 36).

Continuing to weave together aspects of our eucharistic life with attitudes of heart that counter deadly sins, Underhill proposed communion and love as antidotes to envy, that is, adoring love and compassionate love. She considered commemoration and generosity to be counterpoints to avarice, which she interpreted as our tendency to clutch and grab, our claimfulness. She felt mystery and detachment counteracted greed, and finally zest to be the opposite of sloth (*Mount*, 42-81).

Warning against the destruction of the passion of personal love and desire, she wrote: "The purity of heart which God asks is not the chilly safety of something that is killed in the refrigerator" (*Mount*, 64; *Golden*, 113). She captured our craving for consolation when she said: "Lots of souls enter the spiritual life as a child enters a grocer's shop, simply to ask for a pennyworth of sweets" (*Mount*, 66).

In her 1933 retreat published as *The School of Charity*, Underhill described the inner life as an enduring of a deep process of transformation. She emphasized the fact that we share in the creative process, "beginning where we are, content if our handful of meal can make a cottage loaf, not indulging spiritual vanity with large vague dreams about ovens full of beautiful brioches" (*School*, 22). She recognized the difference between a cook who lets a child watch her make a cake, and a cook who lets the child make her own little cake. This example reveals our collaboration with God.

The life of the Spirit is viewed as an organic process of continuity of the divine action, "not a sudden miracle or a series of jerks" (*School*, 48). Union with God gets demythologized. It is not "a nice feeling which we enjoy in devout moments" but "an entire self-giving to the Divine Charity, such identification with its interests, that the whole of our human nature is transformed in God" (*School*, 49).

One might chafe, however, at her advice to look at God and not to think about our own needs and shortcomings (*School*, 9). We are to love our neighbor as ourselves. Sometimes it is easier for some of us, particularly women, to put others' needs first before our own. Only when we learn how to nourish ourselves can we nourish others out of our fullness rather than out of our deficit need for their attention, affection, and approval.

One might also think that Underhill overlooked the process of human development when she encouraged pious individualists to make a delighted response to God's demand and the needs of others, moving from a consideration of their shortcomings and desires to let go of self-occupation (*School*, 70). We become free enough to be of service when we are in touch with our deep desires.

Some might also challenge some of the terms she seemed to use for what we might call today the ego. For example, she spoke of the pressure of self-will that refuses to focus its being in the peace of the unified and surrendered will (*Mystery*, 23). For women especially who have been trained to put others' needs before their own, a deep and centered willing of one's true self would be altogether appropriate and able to be hallowed. In the same 1935 retreat, Underhill also spoke of the flame of divine love scorching and killing self-esteem (*Mystery*, 45). Self-esteem needs to be strengthened not scorched, encouraged not killed, again especially in women who may have very little self-worth. Ego gets destroyed by encounter with our true self. What she called "the mortification of selfhood" (*Abba*, 45) we might rename today since the affirmation of self and the death of the ego seem more appropriate goals.

Many support Underhill's insistence on the paradox that abandonment to God's will also implies effort in contributing to the divine purpose (*Abba*, 49). Today many of us are convinced that hope implies assertiveness: we must do our part to cooperate with God's self-giving since grace builds on nature. Underhill demonstrated a keenness of psychological insight when she said that peace almost always includes the disclosure of a truth that adjusts us to life, freeing us from fear and anxiety for an authentic obedience to God's will (*Fruits*, 16).

It might be that Underhill's personality was so subjective that focusing on God was indeed more helpful to her than focusing on herself. She knew that her capacity for critical analysis could turn her in on herself. She might have had many bouts with her inner critic that dragged her down to self-doubt and self-pity. In the face of her personal experience, she may have found that her way to God was indeed through adoration from which the incentive to cooperate with God flowed organically. She may have discovered that for her too much psychological introspection immobilized her, whereas spiritual abandonment to God freed her for God's purposes and God's concerns in the world. She certainly had to attend to the delicate balance of her true self, her psyche, and her ego.

A Living Ocean

One of Underhill's favorite impersonal symbols of God was the ocean or the sea. She referred to the ways Catherine of Siena and Mechtild of Magdeburg had used this image. Her own experiences of traveling by sea, yachting, and vacationing by the sea must have made this image very real to her.[6]

In her first preached retreat, Underhill emphasized the value of our elected silence by underlining the gentleness of God's deepest contacts with us. Urging retreatants to follow their own unique way to God, she disclaimed the guru role at once. Insisting on the need to nurture the quiet, she affirmed the Spirit's education in inward stillness. The Christian life was prayer for her. Agreeing that prayer can be called self-suggestion, she called it a method given us by God to suggest to ourselves spiritual ideas. Having been in her own dark night preparing this retreat, she was adamantly opposed to the sunshine school of piety (*Ways*, 51-52, 55, 80, 98).

In her second, fourth, and fifth preached retreats, Underhill quoted Ignatius Loyola's principle and foundation of his Spiritual Exercises that we are created to praise, reverence, and serve God (*Ways*, 111, 115, 141, 144, 150, 198). For her, then, adoration and awe precede service. She went on to attest that all religion is a commentary on the Ignatian saying of our coming from God, belonging to God, and being destined for God (*Ways*, 111, 115-17, 131, 136). She also quoted Janet Erskine Stuart, an English Religious of the Sacred Heart in this century, who urged us to think glorious thoughts about God.[7]

Underhill was convinced that selfless adoration quiets us more than petty or utilitarian thoughts. One of her powerful images of God is that of an ocean of love, the ocean of reality, into whom we throw ourselves in order to touch others (*Ways*, 114). She quoted Ignatius' prayer to give without counting the cost, to fight without heeding the wounds, to toil without seeking rest, and to labor with the sole reward of doing God's will (*Ways*, 128). Prayer is our whole secret and corporate life of communion with God (*Ways*, 135).

In her 1927 retreat, Underhill called prayer the life of encounter with God. The Spirit needs our cooperation unlike a patented cleanser that washes while we are asleep. We are to beg for courage, generosity, and patience. According to Jean-Jacques Olier's approach, we are to live our life of relationship with God in adoration, communion, and cooperation (*Ways*, 147, 160, 154-91). She was in favor of contemplative prayer: "Fussy, anxious, exclusive, practical, this-world prayer does nothing to remodel and enrich Christian character, for it omits the essential first stage" (*Ways*, 176). That is, it does not carry us toward God. This plea for adoration, a kind of centering prayer, a type of receptive prayer, is a healthy counterpoint to all the emphasis today on a kind of "noisy contemplation" which can get so busy that it may not hear the still, small voice of the Spirit.[8]

In her 1928 retreat, having reflected on the stigmata of Francis of Assisi who delighted in birds and animals so much, Underhill concluded that suffering love is at the heart of reality. She called God the soul's country to which real prayer must always bring us (*Ways*, 199-200, 240; *House* 52). That expansive image stretches our hearts to be opened to the breadth of God. It speaks of God's spaciousness and the space God gives each of us to grow, exercise our gifts, and make mistakes.

In her 1930 retreat, Underhill described God as supernatural spirit and father of our souls, self-revealing in cosmic and concrete ways. While the mystics' image of God as ocean captures their experience of communion in depth, the biblical images of God emphasize the divine as distinct and other speaking through the prophets and acting in human history (*Golden*, 8-20). Her experiences and images encompassed both. They were of an impersonal and personal God:

> Sometimes it seems that we are bathed in a living Ocean, that pours into every corner of our being to cleanse, heal and refresh. Sometimes it seems

that a personal energy compels, withstands, enlightens or suddenly changes us; working on our stubborn natures with a stern, unflinching love (*Golden*, 64).

In this passage she was no longer quoting Catherine of Siena or the other mystics who have written about the image of God as the ocean (*Golden*, 14, 151, 172-73). Here she was giving us an inscape of her own spiritual life (*Golden* 94). Another image she used of God is that of artist-creator, just as she had used artist-lover in *The School of Charity*. In so doing, she intimated her awareness of the close connection between creative intuition and contemplative intuition.[9] She also called God the keeper of our soul (*Golden*, 87).

In this retreat, she simplified her approach to the spiritual life, talking about purification and prayer as the two main aspects. Purification has to do with mortification of the senses and of the spirit. An incarnational view requires that we integrate our physical and emotional life with the passion for God. The gentle lead of the Spirit can only be felt in tranquility which is the fruit of a death to all demands of the ego.[10]

She described prayer as adoration which helps us recognize and accept the difference between the creator and the creature. It is a sense of God present as the one real fact and demand pressing on creatures and evoking our self-giving, not as one among other demands and facts (*Golden* 158-67). Underhill's theological insight into God corresponds with Karl Rahner's insight into God as the horizon of all our knowing and loving, not as one object among many of our knowing and loving.[11] She quoted Cardinal de Bérulle's schema of adoration, adherence, and cooperation, translating them as adoration, communion, and intercessory action, and calling them simultaneous not successive responses to the Spirit (*Golden*, 175). Prayer is above all adoration. She showed astuteness in her perception:

We easily become the dupes of our own imaginative and psychological processes (and much of that which passes for 'religious experience' falls under this head); taking that which is less than Spirit for a direct intimation of the spaceless and eternal God (*Golden*, 129).

Our knowledge of God may be only our ideas and feelings about God. The lives of the saints are records of interior conversations, projected images, and daydreams which are the product of memory and imagination accepted uncritically as revelations of the supernatural: "Even so deeply spiritual a work as the *Revelations* of Julian of Norwich shows the influence of religious imagination on every page" (*Golden*, 130). Underhill's point is that we not confuse our remembered images of God with God's presence in prayer. The religious mind can often look like what she called "a mid-Victorian drawing-room" stuffed with draperies, souvenirs, and photographs that reflect our fear of emptiness. The imaginative contemplation of Gospel scenes which Ignatius Loyola fostered is one way to educate and form our Christian consciousness (*Golden*, 130).

Prayer is faithful adherence to God in the sense of willed surrender. It is much like the salmon going down-stream might feel passive in the sea currents but must steer and maintain itself in the face of many movements of adjustment (*Golden*, 11, 24, 55, 61, 152-54, 172). It issues in communion whereby we feel plunged into the ocean of God like a fish in the sea. Playing with the metaphor, Underhill could not resist adding a humorous incentive to the acceptance of our littleness before God: "Far better to be a shrimp within that ocean, than a full-sized theological whale cast upon the shore" (*Golden*, 173-74).

Contemplative prayer is also our cooperation with the divine action, not the abolition of our action: "The 'holy passivity' of the extreme quietist is coma, not contemplation" (*Golden*, 150-51). Our intercessory action, whereby the Spirit acts through us, is part of our intercessory life that is redemptive for others. Its object can be, therefore, particular or general, physical or spiritual. The spiritual life is a cooperation with God's secret action (*Golden*, 67-68, 70-77, 178-96).

In *School*, Underhill called God artist-lover (*School*, 14, 24, 78, 108). She repeated her image of the Spirit as an empowering house guest: "The Spirit is one of those guests for whom space must be made; whose presence makes a difference to the whole house, and not merely to the spare room" (*School*, 85). The process of transformation which is demanded means more than "fresh curtains and a little whitewash" (*School*, 86).

In her retreat meditation on the brooding Spirit of God, Underhill used many different, powerful images for God: poet of the universe, the creative Spirit of God, the great thinker, the eternal artist, eternal love, the ocean of being, creator Spirit, master of the tides (*Mount*, 117-24). It was as if her own creativity was set loose and free to explore new metaphors for the divine as she contemplated the beginnings of creation.

Underhill invited her retreatants to enter into the breadth and depth of the mystery of God, to experience different facets of God, to explore different metaphors for God. Convinced that God is three in one, she herself was drawn to both impersonal and personal symbols for God.

The Light of Christ

The Eucharist is a sacrament of fellowship joining us with the heroes of Christianity and with all heroic lovers of Christ. Love, joy, and peace are the signature of the Spirit of Christ. Love means entering into the petty details of life, not merely putting up with them and not needing to be fed only by consolations which are the chocolate creams of the Christian life. Joy is the self-abandonment of the true child of God. Peace is a tranquil state of will not merely a nice religious feeling that makes us bask in the divine sunshine like comfortable cats (*Ways*, 57-75).

In reflecting on service and election, we are to ask ourselves the threefold question of Ignatius Loyola: "What have I done for Christ? What am I doing for Christ? And what ought I to do for Christ" (*Ways*, 98, 123, 167)? Warning against a demoralizing self-scrutiny, she affirmed and repeated that Christ never makes people feel raw. By contemplation we gaze lovingly at the mysteries of the life of Christ in the Ignatian sense of entering into them with memory, imagination, and will. As Ignatius observed, contemplation of the Passion gives us an inclination to the most perfect things (*Ways*, 56, 108, 149-50, 164).

Underhill understood the meaning of cooperation: "Anyone can love the loveable. For us to love the unloveable into loveableness is the very method and art of redemption" (*Ways*, 234). This is truly the gift of collaborating with Christ in his way of divine love. For her, Christ as the Word is the perfect utterance of God's thought (*Ways*, 239).

In her 1932 retreat called *Light of Christ*, Underhill explained what Ignatius Loyola meant by our contemplating the mysteries of Christ, that is, absorbing rather than analyzing, soaking ourselves in his beauty, seeing the human transfigured by the divine, the way we might look quietly and long at the rose window in the Chartres Cathedral. This long, lingering look at the same mystery from many viewpoints and perspectives is what she meant by contemplative prayer, as she had described it in her letters of spiritual direction (*Lt*, 73, 127). She also invoked Ignatius, repeating his questions about the relevance of a particular scene, the light it sheds on one's life, the call of God (*Light*, 32, 34).

Affirming Christ as the light of the Gentiles, Underhill denounced cosy religious exclusiveness, refusing to identify the light of the world with the sanctuary lamp in one's favorite church. Just as the child Jesus did not go outside the carpenter's workshop, we have no need for peculiar conditions or a separation of life and prayer for our Christian life in the world. What he lived and what we are called to live is an abandonment to God's purpose in and through ordinary life lived in quietness and simplicity. Contemplating the slow and gradual growth of Christ's life can curb our impatience to do before we have learned to accept our slow and gradual growth (*Light*, 36-46; *School*, 39-50).

Underhill warned us to learn the artist's pace, not hurrying or waiting too long, putting on a primary coat and letting it dry instead of rushing ahead while our inspiration lasts only to find a sticky mess (*Light*, 51). Instead of wishing we were different physically or mentally or that we were purely spiritual, we are taught by Christ the teacher within the very circumstances of our unique, everyday life, together with others not apart from them (*Light*, 52-53).

Once again, Underhill lightened up these simple truths with her wonderful sense of humor. Against a Gnostic Christianity, she retorted: "Team games are compulsory in the school of Divine Love; there must be no getting into a corner with a nice spiritual book" (*Light*, 53). And warning against the tendency to reduce the Gospel to the warm humanity of Jesus leaving the mystery of God out, she quipped: "The clue to life He offers is not a bit of soft ribbon but a hard rope that will bear our weight but will also chafe our hands" (*Light*, 55)!

Contemplating Christ as healer, Underhill recognized that even though the man sick with palsy whose friends let him in by the roof might have been an advanced neurotic riddled with fears and obsessions, Jesus did not reprove him but cherished him with a compassionate love that freed him to get up and walk, looking forward not backward. And the man accepted this healing love and got up glorifying God. In the same way, Christ leaves us free to accept or refuse his healing touch. Our cooperation with Christ's healing action lays the Cross upon our hearts, freeing us to pour ourselves out in spendthrift generosity on those who need healing, not those who deserve it (*Light*, 57-67).

Underhill waxed eloquent when she talked about the biochemistry of the soul and our religious duty to arrange our religious meals according to its laws, taking what really nourishes us and giving ourselves time to savor and digest. We are meant to feed on the one word God gives us, not to suffer chronic indigestion reading this and that: "Christ, the soul's healer, gives us or will give us that word which quiets our fever, feeds, steadies and deepens our life, builds up our resistance to the toxins which get into our blood-stream and sap our powers" (*Light*, 64).

Underhill indicated her awareness of and sensitivity to the vagaries of human weakness, such as doubt, disillusionment, grief, and anxiety. By calling Christ the rescuer, she demonstrated her belief in Christ's reassuring presence bringing peace to troubled waters, rather than conveying that Christ removes difficulties or solves problems (*Light*, 68-78).

In her reflection on the Cross, Underhill invited her retreatants and us to integrate inauthenticity, disappointment, loneliness, and the shattering of trust with the sacrifice of love. She also challenged them and us to allow the Eucharist to be the sacrifice of love integrating the divine and the human, incarnating Christ's sacrificial love in our daily lives (*Light*, 79-89).

Contemplation of Christ is important in our life of prayer because we receive more by absorption than by exploration. As the queen bee becomes the parent of new life by being fed on royal jelly, so we are parents of new life by being fed on divine love. Our Christian life in the world is meant to identify with the life of Jesus in the world not only when we feel moved and consoled but also when we need to come to grips with the real problems and pressures of our lives:

> Christ was trained in a carpenter's shop; and we persist in preferring a confectioner's shop. But the energy of rescue, the outpouring of sacrificial love, which the supernatural life demands, is not to be got from a diet of devotional meringues and éclairs (*School*, 40).

Underhill's image of Christ in her 1933 retreat addresses is that of God incarnate, crucified, and glorified, the infinite revealed in the finite. We discover the breadth of divine generosity when we realize that the child who received the magi has "a woman of the streets for His most faithful friend, and two thieves for His comrades at the last" (*School*, 44). It is not Christian for us to separate our life from our prayer or to get out of our job or home situation; the ordinariness of Nazareth sets the tone: "the third-rate little town in the hills, with its limited social contacts and monotonous manual work, reproves us when we begin to fuss about our opportunities and our scope" (*School*, 46). The unity of our Christian life lies in our identification with Christ's paschal mystery: "Those who complain that they make no progress in the life of prayer because they 'cannot meditate' should examine, not their capacity for meditation, but their capacity for suffering and love" (*School*, 54). Humiliation, disillusionment, betrayal, loneliness, disappointment, and the breakdown of trust unite us to the cross (*School*, 59). Karl Rahner, in fact, called them experiences of grace.[12]

In her 1934 retreat, she described Christ's prayer not as action, duty, or experience, but as a vital relationship between us in our wholeness and the being of God, the abiding sense of that tranquil and strong presence (*Abba*, 3-4, 12-13).

In all her retreat addresses, Underhill advocated the principle of the Incarnation: we are committed to the life of the senses and do not seek to be delivered from our creatureliness (*Abba*, 73). So convinced was she of this that she could describe God loving not tolerating "the horrid man at the fishshop, and the tiresome woman in the next flat, and the disappointing Vicar, and the mulish parent, and the contractor who has cut down the row of trees we loved to build a lot of revolting bungalows" (*Fruits*, 15). The tranquillity in which God works is incompatible with speed. We keep our perspective remembering that "it is God that matters, not the elaborate furniture of the sanctuary where you meet" (*Fruits*, 45). God's revelation is always unexpected, as it was at Bethlehem, and so we can only prepare by humble expectancy for the coming of Christ (*Fruits*, 48-52).

Underhill's advice about our relationship with Christ was based, in fact, on his very identity: we are to be incarnational, redemptive, sacramental as he is. That is to say, we are to seek, adore, and reveal God in the details of our daily lives and to collaborate with God in the work of redemption. She accepted the reality and implications of Christ's divinity and humanity. It is Christ who sheds light, heals, teaches, and rescues. It is Christ who was born in a stable, lived in a third-rate town, suffered and died on a cross. Our identification with him is our identification with his paschal mystery.

The Church as an Organism

Underhill used traditional images of the church such as the body of Christ, the bride of Christ, and the communion of saints. Her originality showed, however, when she tried to say what it is by contrasting it with what it is not, describing it as a group of people growing in adoration and active love according to God's will, not a society of specialists (*Ways*, 78). After her long self-imposed exile from institutional religion, she could only advise a regular commitment of communal worship.

In her first retreat addresses, she said that the church is a group of people growing in adoration and active love according to God's will, not a society of specialists. It is the communion of saints, that is, people of heroic love. In her second retreat, she elaborated that saints continue the work of the Incarnation by becoming channels of God's revelation to others. In her 1928 retreat, she spoke of us as members of Christ, children of God, and inheritors of the kingdom of heaven (*Ways*, 78, 82-88, 132, 221-40).

In *Concerning the Inner Life*, a 1926 set of her clergy conferences for Anglican parish priests, Underhill, the first laywoman to address clergy of the Church of England, revealed her sense of the Anglican church in England by calling for a renewal of its priests' life of prayer. She began by insisting that they maintain their own inner life as their first priority:

to be a real person of prayer is the first duty of a parish priest. She assured them that the laity know at once which churches are served with loving devotedness and which are not. A healthy life of prayer maintains us in adoration, nourishes us, educates our faculties, and produces creative work. Discouraging the study of morbid psychology, she urged a deepening of adoration and awe which feed the love of God and our service of others. An inner life based on adoration rather than petition is a remedy for spiritual exhaustion. Loving adherence to God leads to spiritual vitality. It is important for us to discover what nourishes us, be it silent communion or verbal prayer. Distractions can often be alleviated by renewed interest, vocal prayer, the practice of aspirations, appropriate bodily gestures, and muscular movements. Dryness, which is a fatigue state, can best be handled by accepting it, turning to some secular interest, and waiting in faith. A hot bath is better than effort and resistance. Intercession can be viewed as a form of creative work. Three ways for clergy to unite prayer and work are as follows: to pray in their own churches, to make intercession for those entrusted to their care, and to offer spiritual direction to parishioners.[13]

From these addresses, one can detect Underhill's clear belief that the love of neighbor was grounded, for people of faith, in the love of God. She affirmed the dignity of the priestly vocation in the church, and, at the same time, challenged these priests to develop the spiritual dimension of their pastoral care. She did not deliver esoteric thoughts but drove home the value of an ecclesial life of prayer in simple, straightforward terms.

Underhill referred to the church in her 1931 retreat as the bride of Christ and the body of Christ of which we are members (*Mount*, 16-17).

Underhill portrayed an exemplary man of the Anglican Church, Father Wainright, serving fifty years at St. Peter's in the London slum of Dockland, who reached out to the marginalized as Jesus had done, caring for derelicts and drunkards before serving regular church-goers. He would rush to the death-bed of unrepentant people mediating to them God's calming presence. He spent an hour of prayer each morning and the rest of the day in the service of the poor. He was supported by his adherence to and cooperation with God.[14]

In her 1933 retreat lecture on the church, she called it the body, the temple that the Spirit indwells, the mysterious body, the bride of Christ representing the social incarnation of the holy. She went on to give some colorful examples of the point she was making by describing the church as an organism not a mere crowd of souls, a mystery in whom the reality of God abides not a spiritual Rotary Club, an organ of the Spirit not a devotional guild. And the Eucharist is the church's act toward God and others of adoring gratitude and participation in the self-giving life of divine love. For her the Christian life is not an individual quest for solitary perfection but loyal teamwork building communion and freeing us from our selfishness, for membership on which we go into training in Lent. This implies an individual commitment to our process of individuation which may require solitude but which may bear fruit in our transformed capacity for relationship (*School*, 90-104).

Underhill stated that in celebrating the Eucharist, the church celebrates the mystery of its being: God's self-imparting creating the communion of saints, our movement toward union with God, and the coming of God's presence on earth. For her the liturgy reveals the whole mystery of the Incarnation. Binding visible and invisible, the Eucharist makes our gifts holy by offering them with gratitude to God. Christian worship is fundamentally a consecration in that we adore and give ourselves to God (*Mystery*, 1935 Retreat, vii, x, 18, 22, 48).

Once again, Underhill did not lose her sense of humor in describing the costly sacrifice of self that we are called upon to make at the altar by stripping ourselves of our various stances before God. She mentioned the devoted beast of burden, the faithful dog affectionate and obedient, the lamb of purity, and the devotional little mouse. Her conversion from a Neoplatonic mysticism is evident in her conviction that incarnational religion never leaves temporal concerns and duties in order to make a mystical flight to God (*Mystery*, 5, 23-24, 35). She demonstrated her informed ecumenical attitude by quoting prayers at the end of each talk from a variety of liturgies including the Orthodox, the Armenian, and the Roman.

The Life of the Spirit in the World

Underhill advocated a sense of the vastness of the cosmos since it was for her a sense of the vastness of God and a sense of God's presence penetrating the universe. It is remarkable that she verged on a cosmocentric spirituality in her day. The world, our planet earth, was for her a sacrament of God's presence. Her reverence for life was complemented with an acceptance of the principle of destruction and pain in the universe.

In her 1924 retreat, Underhill referred to God as the magnet of the universe exerting a field of force and arranging us in a pattern according to the divine energy. She called the natural world a sacrament of the supernatural in terms of showing us the dynamics of growth (*Ways*, 57, 91).

In her retreat the following year, Underhill again looked at the variety of nature, animals, types of music, languages, and human societies that is involved in creating a tiny planet in an infinite universe. She had an intuition of the vastness of the cosmos. She was convinced of the holy character of daily work as a fruit of authentic prayer (*Ways*, 107, 141). Five years later, Underhill invited her retreatants to reflect on the continuous and steady pressure of God penetrating the universe (*Golden*, 1930 Retreat, 101). She spoke of the Spirit of God filling the entire universe and of our relationship with God as the one thing that matters to us who are "little specks on one small planet" (*Mount*, 1931 Retreat, 21). Her sense of the cosmic vastness of creation gave her a humble perspective from which to view people and God.

Underhill even used analogies from physics to bring home a point. She once referred to Sir James Jeans' thesis in *Mysterious Universe* that one sort of wave turns in on itself and the other set pours out in ceaseless radiation, as a parable of the difference between the avaricious and the generous. Also, just as an electron's possible radiation is only limited by the universe's limitations and therefore it can fill all space by its self-giving, so, too, generous people know no bounds to their sphere of influence. She felt we ought to be content to be inhabitants of an inferior planet without understanding life as long as we are penetrated by God's presence (*Mount*, 58-59, 69-70).

Underhill sketched her cosmic vision of the Church Triumphant stretching its frontiers to embrace the whole universe in its beauty, mystery, and power, and bringing it under the gentle rule of Christ, the radiance of his love. Her mystical breadth and depth stretched beyond the everyday and even beyond the earthly. What she had in mind is that our spiritual life in the world is a commitment to the hallowing of the entire universe in all its dimensions, and religion becomes a demand to face reality not a refuge from reality. And in this way we affirm that Christ glorified is the meaning of the universe (*Light*, 1932 Retreat, 90-98). The world for Underhill, then, is a locus for discovering and revealing God's interests and concerns:

> When we neglect the needs of the sinful and helpless because they conflict with our religious or moral ideas, when we elude the intimate companionship of the Magdalen and the leper, the nerve-ridden clutch of the possessed and all the variety of psychological wrecks which strew the modern scene in their restless loneliness--then we neglect the interest of God (*Light of Christ*, 66).

Underhill cited Julian of Norwich describing through the image of the hazelnut nature's basic holiness: how God's providence brings all into being and sustains all by love despite what we see to be hostility and decay (*School*, 1933 Retreat, 12-14). She observed the cosmic principle of pain, decay, destruction, and death which is balanced by the cosmic principle of joy, growth, development, and life:

> We think of a natural order shot through with suffering, marred at every point by imperfection, maintained by mutual destruction; a natural order which includes large populations of vermin, and the flora and fauna of infectious disease (*School*, 14).

It could be said of her that she kept a cosmocentric spirituality from being totally optimistic and affirmed the paschal mystery within nature itself.[15]

Underhill went on to express how awe of nature can lead us to awe of ourselves: "This loving reverence for life is not to stop short even at the microbe and the worm. It must be extended to ourselves, and the qualities, tendencies and powers which God has implanted or brought forth in us" (*School*, 15). For her, creation is the work of God's love and a symphony wherein each one's melody can find its place: "This truth of the deep unity of creation links us with our lesser relations, and with our greater relations too. It makes us the members of a family, a social order, so rich and various that we can never exhaust its possibilities" (*School*, 16-17). This sense of interconnectedness marks our postmodern paradigm of spirituality.

Underhill had a sense of the cosmic, a sense of the vastness of creation stretching beyond our planet earth. She wrote that the inner life is "as truly there as the cosmic life of infinite space and duration into which we are suddenly caught, when we look for the first time through a great telescope at the awful galaxy of the stars" (*School*, 110). She was very aware of the star that the magi followed.[16]

Underhill was convinced of the incarnational principle that we seek the spiritual in the practical:

> There are still far too many Christians in whose souls a sound-proof partition has been erected between the oratory and the kitchen: sometimes between the oratory and the study too. But the creative action of the Spirit penetrates the whole of life, and is felt by us in all sorts of ways (*School*, 17).

She went on to quote Teresa who found God among the pots and pans and Elizabeth Leseur whose duties were a check on her devotional practices. Underhill commented: "She recognized the totality of God's creative action, penetrating and controlling the whole web of life"(*School*, 18). Later on she used this metaphor of the web again to describe providence: "Now and then it emerges on the surface to startle us by its witness to a subtle and ceaseless will and love working within the web of events" (*School*, 82). Underhill also used the image of weaving when she talked about the transcendent reality of God being shown to us incarnate "so that we may try to weave its pattern into the texture of human life; redeeming that life from ugliness, and making it a garment of God" (*School*, 70).

Underhill was convinced that our life with God in the world has everything to do with our life in the world to come:

> The new, more real life that we expect must penetrate every level of existence, and every relationship--politics, industry, science, art, our attitude to each other, our attitude to living nature--spiritualizing and unselfing all this; subduing it to the transforming action of "the intellectual radiance full of love" (*School*, 105).

The eucharistic transformation about which Underhill wrote has cosmic dimensions which she herself perceived: "Faith looks towards the transfiguration of the whole Universe; that cleansing and perfecting of the natural order which shall make it, on every level, the vehicle of the Glory of God" (*Mystery*, 69). She viewed the Lord's Prayer as our plea for the sanctification of the universe (*Abba*, 23).

Conclusion

Underhill used Jean-Jacques Olier's threefold schema of adoration, communion, and cooperation interchangeably with Cardinal de Bérulle's schema of adoration, adherence, and cooperation. In this she reflected the influence of the French School of Spirituality. For her, adoration meant surrender, communion had everything to do with adherence and self-giving; cooperation meant intercession and collaboration. I would not say, however, that she restricted herself to this schema or to these attitudes of heart in her life or in her reflections on living in the world.[17]

In her retreats, Underhill described mysticism as the heart of all religion, the soul's reaching out to contact with the eternal realities which are the subject of religion. She called mystical theology the loving discernment of reality in and through prayer. In this she distinguished it from a certain kind of scholastic theology which tends to discuss ideas about God rather than describe one's experience of God.[18]

Underhill's spirituality was biblical and liturgical. It was incarnational and holistic. It was practical and provocative of growth. It was individual and communal. It was open to and engaged in ecumenical and interfaith dialogue. It was mainstream Christian, in that it did not latch on to pet phrases or passing trends. Let us turn now to see how her practical advice from her retreat addresses recurred in her other works on the spiritual life.

Suggestions for Prayerful Reflection

Annice Callahan, R.S.C.J.

Get in a relaxed position and ponder what Evelyn Underhill wrote about preparing to make a retreat:

Retreat can be . . . an experience of God's glory, filling the whole universe. But the absolute Light only dazzles us; in its wholeness it is more than we can bear. It needs breaking-up before our small hearts can deal with it. The windows of Christ's Mysteries split it up into many-coloured loveliness, disclose all its hidden richness and colour, make its beauty more accessible to us; convince us of the reality of beauty and holiness and of the messy unreality of most of our own lives. .   There are three things for us to do.

First, looking quietly at the window, bathing in the lovely light that comes through it and which truly gives us God, we shall receive illumination, teaching and healing, a revelation of truth, by absorbing rather than by analysing. ..

Second, we must turn round and apply what we have seen and absorbed to our own inner life which has got to grow up to the fullness of His stature: to put on Christ. He is disclosed both as Saviour and Pattern, especially to those called to the service of Christ. In our daily work and routine, in our religious practice, in our intellectual life . . .; in all these Christ, the Word and Thought of God, is teaching, mending, vivifying us and calling us more and more insistently to love and sacrifice. . .

Third, but that is not enough. A Christian does not stand alone. . . As a member of the Mystical Body of Christ, a unit of the Church, I must in some way show these states and characteristics of Christ in my life, some more, some less, according to my special call. I am part of the organism through which Christ continues to live in the world. I too am required to incarnate something of His all-generous and redeeming spirit, share my knowledge of Him, give myself without stint to heal and save other children of God at my own cost. How does my life stand *that* test?[19]

1. What is it like for you to look and absorb, to soak your soul in beauty? What is it like for you to linger in front of a painting or a piece of sculpture in an art gallery? Are you able to linger over a gospel scene?

2. What is it like for you to put on the mind and heart of another person? What helps you to enter into that person's interests and concerns? Are

you able to enter into a gospel scene and become a character in dialogue with Jesus?

3. What is it like for you to witness to the influence of another person in your life? What helps you to embody that person's kindness, considerateness, compassion? How do you witness to others of the impact of Christ on your daily life?

4. What do you find inspiring in Underhill's retreat addresses?

5. What do you find challenging in her retreat addresses?

Readings

For an excellent introduction to and edited collection of her early retreats, see *The Ways of the Spirit*, ed. Grace Adolphsen Brame (New York: Crossroad, 1990). For contemporary versions of some of her retreats, see *Abba* (Harrisburg, Pa.: Morehouse, 1996); *The Fruits of the Spirit* (Harrisburg, Pa.: Morehouse, 1996); *The House of the Soul and Concerning the Inner Life* (Minneapolis: Seabury Press, 1984); *The Light of Christ* (Harrisburg, Pa.: Morehouse, 1989); and *The School of Charity* (Harrisburg, Pa.: Morehouse, 1991).

Notes

1. See Grace Adolphsen Brame, *Receptive Prayer: A Christian Approach to Meditation* (St. Louis: CBP Press, 1985).

2. See E. Underhill, *House*, 3-87. Cf. Debra Schneider, "Evelyn Underhill as a Spiritual Guide," unpublished paper for my course on Spiritual Guides for Today, Spring 1994, Regis College, Toronto, in which she added to Underhill's list of virtues or attitudes. To prudence, temperance, and fortitude, Schneider added appreciation, patience, and the willingness to suffer in faith. To faith, hope, and love, she added a willingness to enter into the agony and ecstasy of God, and the willingness to abide in the peace of God.

3. One of my students explored this aspect of the house of the soul in a paper in which he wrote the following:

> I need to identify the image of a "house" as my mandala symbol of personal integration and wholeness. Various houses that I review in my dreams and imagination represent a certain progression in my self-understanding. I never go backwards to the house I had built at the beginning of my journey. There is a constant improvement in the quality of a house, its shape, space and attractiveness. The "house" image allowed me to come to the centre of my life, with greater confidence and appreciation of my existence. My pilgrimage, and the conversion experiences lead me through a series of "houses," all indicating the direction of my journey and the attractiveness of "coming home." See Stanley Moszkowicz, "Saint Teresa's Interior Castle as an Image for Conversion," Paper for course on Mystics Then for Now, Regis College, Toronto, Fall 1992, 24.

4. On psychological aspects of prayer, see Ann Belford and Barry Ulanov, *Primary Speech: A Psychology of Prayer* (Atlanta, Ga.: John Knox, 1982).

On the space and time women need for creative work, see, for example, May Sarton, *Journal of a Solitude* (New York: Norton, 1973), esp. 12, 16, 40, 56, 123; and Virginia Woolf, *A Room of One's Own* (London: Hogarth Press, 1929), written during Underhill's lifetime, esp. 6, 79, 158, 166, 171.

5. See Letty M. Russell, *Household of Freedom: Authority in Feminist Theology* (Philadelphia: Westminster Press, 1987); Elizabeth Schüssler-Fiorenza, *In Memory of Her: A Feminist Theological Reconstruction of Christian Origins* (London: SCM Press, Ltd., 1983); and David C. Verner, *The Household of*

God: The Social World of the Pastoral Epistles (Chico, Ca.: Scholars Press, 1983). Cf. Mary Milligan, "You Are God's Household," *LCWR Occasional Papers* 23, no. 1 (Spring 1994): 17-20.

6. On God as the ocean and the sea, see E. Underhill, *Ways*, 114; *Golden*, 64; *Mount*, 68, 73, 119. On her quoting mystics' use of the metaphor of ocean or sea for God, see E. Underhill, *Ways*, 236-38; *Golden*, 14, 151, 172-73; *Light*, 36.

7. See E. Underhill, *Ways*, 108, 113, 115, 178; *House*, 102-3; *Mystics*, 242.
   In "What Is Sanctity?" Underhill referred to Mother Janet Erskine Stuart, R.S.C.J., who urged a fervent novice to beg for common sense. This point struck Underhill so forcibly that she repeated it in a book review. See E. Underhill, *Mixed*, 34; id., "St. Bernard," review of *Studies in St. Bernard of Clairvaux* by Watkin W. Williams, The Spectator, 29 October 1927, 733, DGC.
   In "Education and the Spirit of Worship," Underhill referred to Mother Janet Erskine Stuart, R.S.C.J., who cherished the flowers she brought every day to one of her sick pupils, conveying a sense of the sacredness and beauty of living things (*Papers*, 226-227).

8. This is distinct from a prayerful contemplation that finds God in a busy life. See William Callahan, *Noisy Contemplation* (Washington, D.C.: Quixote Center, 1983); and "Noisy Contemplation: Is Prayer in a Busy Life?" *New Theology Review* 2 (1989): 29-39.

9. See E. Underhill, *Golden*, 65. Cf. Annice Callahan, "Creative Intuition as Analogous to Contemplative Intuition," *RSCJ: A Journal of Reflection* 2 (1980): 77-88; and "Creativity and Prayer," *RSCJ Occasional Papers* 2, no.1 (Winter 1997): 29-43.

10. See E. Underhill, *Golden*, 97-147. On her artful way of urging temperance in mortification, see her letter to the editor, *The Spectator*, 30 January 1932, 147, DGC, in which she noted Bishop Gore's refusal to quit smoking his pipe for a cause, even though he lived a total life of renunciation.

11. See Karl Rahner, *Foundations of Christian Faith: An Introduction to the Idea of Christianity*, trans. William V. Dych (New York: Seabury, 1978), 51-71.

12. See Karl Rahner, "Reflections on the Experience of Grace," *TI* 3: 86-90.

13. See E. Underhill, *House*, 89-151. Cf. Milos, "Chapter Four: The Pastoral Guide," in "The Role of the Spiritual Guide in the Life and Writings of Evelyn Underhill," 134-94.

132 *Evelyn Underhill*

14. See E. Underhill, *Light*, 1932 Retreat, 41, 75; *School*, 1933 Retreat, 33, 44, 97. See also E. Underhill, "Studies in Sanctity: XII. Father Wainright, 1848-1929," *The Spectator*, 9 April 1932, 502-503, DGC, reprinted in *Guide*, 191-96.

15. Brian Swimme, "Canticle to the Cosmos: Destruction and Loss," Study Guide, ed. Bruce Bochte (San Francisco: New Story Project, Tides Foundation, 1990): 21-25.

16. E. Underhill, *School*, 42-44. See also B. Swimme, "Canticle to the Cosmos: The Story of Our Time," 1-5.

17. See E. Underhill, *Ways*, 174-91; *House*, 58, 61, 121; *Golden*, 158-90; *School*, 6, 13, 103; *Abba*, 2, 22-46; *Fruits*, 20, 22. See also D. Greene, "Adhering to God: The Message of Evelyn Underhill for Our Times," *Spirituality Today* 39, no. 1 (Spring 1987):22-38. Cf. *Bérulle and the French School: Selected Writings*, ed. William M. Thompson, trans. Lowell M. Glendon (New York: Paulist, 1989); and Raymond Deville, *The French School of Spirituality: An Introduction and Reader*, trans. Agnes Cunningham (Pittsburgh, Pa.: Duquesne University Press, 1994).

18. See E. Underhill, *House*, 107; *Golden*, 81. Cf. John Barres, "Mysticism, the Heart of Practical Religion: The Spiritual Theology of Evelyn Underhill," *Spiritual Life* 34 (Fall 1988): 139-43.

19. E. Underhill, "Preparation," *Light of Christ*, 29, 32-33. Cf. A. Callahan, "The Light of Christ," *Sisters Today* 69, no. 1 (January 1997): 53-55.

Chapter 6

Other Spiritual Writings

This chapter treats Underhill's works on the spiritual life other than her letters and retreat addresses. In these books, articles, essays, addresses, and book reviews, she emphasized the unity between the practical and the spiritual, between psychology and spirituality, between daily life and worship, and between politics and spirituality. For her the spiritual life simplifies and centers, grounding us in a sense of the divine that gives meaning and worth to concrete details. The peace and strength we experience in prayer is useless unless we also let it touch and shed light on our person, our church and our social life. Her observations and insights offer practical advice on living the life of the Spirit in the world.

A Capacity for God

Underhill called the human person a capacity for God. Two images of the true self before God were, for her, the mystic and the adoring worshiper, both of whom she called creative artists. A third image of the true self before God was that of the saint, a spiritual genius whose life witnesses to the priority of God, a human being who has become "a pure capacity for God," and an instrument of divine action whose personality is transformed not abolished.[1]

In *Man and the Supernatural*, 1927, Underhill elaborated a philosophy of religion by exploring the human impulse to transcendence. Francis of Assisi asked: "What are you? and what am I?" and Ignatius asserted "I come from God, I belong to God, and I am destined for God" (*Man*, 8)! Underhill recognized that this faith claim is practical rather than devotional, intelligent rather than pious. She treated the mystics' declarations regarding God's prevenience, perfection, and eternity. They witness to ultimate reality's concern with human life. They use various kinds of metaphors for God. They assert that the human person can experience God directly. Such experiences are vocational in character, introduce the person to a life of prayer, and transform the personality. They are checked and balanced by the historical, sensible, and intellectual elements of life.[2]

Underhill liked to use the image of the person as a contemplative animal. One could say she meant that the person is a contemplative embodied being. She noted that Aristotle and Aquinas did not write about a contemplative spirit.[3]

Underhill realized that we have an "impulse to transcendence," a craving which nothing in our surroundings can awaken or satisfy, a deep conviction that some larger synthesis of experience is possible to us (*Spirit*, 20-21). She recognized that for those living their relationship with God intensely, spiritual fecundity and not spiritual marriage is the goal of human transcendence (*Spirit*, 44).

Underhill fostered the dialogue between psychology and religion, claiming, for example, that what one calls destructive aspects of the instinctive and emotional life are what the other calls original sin (*Spirit*, 61). The need for conversion is, then, the need for the remaking of the instinctive life, sublimating turmoil and conflicts into new forms of creative energy, and interest into universal objectivity (*Spirit*, 68, 71). This need for conversion rather than for mere beliefs pinpoints religion's invitation to a change of heart not a change of belief. This need for sublimation and transformation which is the first necessity of the spiritual life, she concluded, was founded on solid psychological laws (*Spirit*, 73). Yet, conscious of a childish longing for security, she clarified what she meant when she went on to write that while a sense of dependence on enfolding love is at the heart of religion, "it is of first importance to be sure that its affective side represents a true sublimation of human feelings and desires, and not merely an oblique indulgence of lower cravings" (*Spirit*, 75).

For her, the psyche was a living force within us, "a storehouse of ancient memories and animal tendencies," craving more life and love (*Spirit*, 83). Keenly aware that psychology can criticize contemplative experiences and help discern their authenticity, she maintained that it cannot explain these experiences or reduce God to its own terms (*Spirit*, 85). At the same time, she valued its contribution to our understanding of religious experience. For example, psychology can attest the value of contemplative prayer over vocal prayer because the former engages more of us at both a conscious and an unconscious level (*Spirit*, 93-94).

We need to acknowledge the power of the psychological phenomenon of suggestion in religious experience. For example, Julian of Norwich begged for an illness at thirty years of age and a more personal knowledge of Christ's passion; even though she forgot the prayer, her desire was fulfilled and she became ill when she was thirty. Thérèse of Lisieux was convinced that she was called to be a victim of love, and died of tuberculosis at the age of twenty-four. Without minimizing its transcendental character, Underhill called prayer an exercise of auto-suggestion, in the sense of reinforcing our deep desire for God. Psychology has found that the conditions most conducive to suggestion are quiescence, attention, and emotional interest, which are, as Underhill demonstrated, aspects of contemplative prayer. She went on to show the application of two other laws of psychology to religious experience: the law of unconscious teleology whereby the unconscious will strive to work toward achieving a suggested end, and the law of reversed effort whereby conscious resistances to a suggested end are useless and only tend to intensify it. Underhill's willingness to call prayer auto-suggestion must have revised her view as a teenager that it is not necessary to repeat prayers: she had discovered that it was not God but we ourselves who need such reminders (*Spirit*, 84-114; *Guide*, 87-102; *Essentials*, 196, 205).

In "The Philosophy of Contemplation," 1930, Underhill employed again her image of the house of the soul where Martha and Mary live together: one absorbed in multiplicity, the other gathered into unity, one acting, the other adhering. She also distinguished without separating contemplative knowledge and intuition from artistic knowledge and intuition (*Mixed*, 13-16, 19).

In *Worship*, she reiterated a point she had made in *Mysticism*, namely, that the touch of God is experienced according to our particular education, capacities, and temperament. She referred to the "ground of the soul" several times in several works on the spiritual life.[4]

In an essay on time, Underhill wrote about seeing God's life and work in the present moment as a fresh creation and responding creatively in new ways. In fact, she emphasized seeing the extraordinary within the ordinary.[5]

Our true self, then, has an orientation toward transcendence; it is a capacity for God. While much of prayer is self-suggestion, the divine influence is felt in human life.

God as Spirit

Underhill was convinced that experience is the point of departure for seeking God: "God can and must be sought only within and through our human experience" (*Spirit*, 3). We seek the eternal in the concrete. The life of the Spirit is at all levels of life. In other words, the spiritual life is *one* life. For her God is experienced in three main ways: as a non-personal, cosmic, transcendent reality giving us a sense of security, as a divine companion with whom we are in reciprocal and intimate communion , and as immanent Spirit dwelling within us (*Spirit*, 5-10, 145, 224). Her God desires and demands of us compassion, forgiveness, and gentleness: "The spiritual life is not lived upon the heavenly hearth-rug, within safe distance from the Fire of Love" (*Spirit*, 146). The mark for her of the life of the Spirit is not happiness but vocation: "work demanded and power given, but given only on condition that we spend it and ourselves on others without stint" (*Spirit*, 169).

Underhill offered her views on a spirituality of childhood. Granting the need to foster corporate religious feeling through group prayer at school and at home, she encouraged a sense of the divine in daily life and the development of qualities which express a reverent love for the sacred, a courteous love toward others, and an energetic love which impels to service. The child's attraction for the heroic can be fed by reading the lives of the saints. The child's love of beauty can be nourished by the study of nature and of the arts, including poetry. Since for her the primary goal of education is the molding of the unconscious and instinctive life, the emphasis is not on a particular belief but rather on a spiritual attitude to existence.[6]

In her essay on "The Degrees of Prayer," 1922, Underhill insisted that humble surrender not sustained fervor is the best indication of our cooperation with God. She made five divisions: vocal prayer, meditation, the prayer of immediate acts, the prayer of simplicity, and the prayer of quiet. Psychology supports the articulate recitation of a daily office, litanies, and psalms, since the spoken word has more suggestive power to affect our psychic levels than inarticulate thought. Meditation is thinking in God's presence, which involves our mind, will, and feelings. In the prayer of immediate acts, we make acts of will which establish our attention on God. In the prayer of simplicity we wait on God rather than speak with God, not in the ineffective self-abandonment of quietism. The prayer of quiet is infused, involuntary, intimate union with God. Underhill insisted that when we move to these stages of prayer, we are still to incorporate the other ways of prayer with suppleness and variety. Aware of the findings of psychology, she asserted that in passive stages of prayer, the unconscious presents its material to the intellect and will for transformation (*Papers*, 39-60).

Underhill published an article called "Our Two-Fold Relation to Reality" in 1925, in which she described prayer as attention to and communion with God. The spiritual life is a concrete reality requiring the skillful education of our spiritual faculties for an individual and corporate expression of the spiritual life in adoration and in action. In our balanced approach, everything can become a sacrament of the real (*Guide*, 161-76).

In "Prayer," a 1926 pamphlet, Underhill stressed the life of prayer that needs food, fresh air, and exercise like our bodies. We nourish ourselves through spiritual reading and meditation. We breathe the fresh air of eternity when we open ourselves to God during our day in love, praise, and a sense of the divine presence, letting go of our worries and needs. The exercise of regular private and corporate prayer develops our spiritual muscles. The life of prayer is based on adoration and adherence. It teaches us how to love, work, and suffer. Through it we learn that intercession means not only asking God to do things but also becoming God's fellow-workers (*Guide*, 133-44).

In "Possibilities of Prayer," 1927, Underhill discussed the cultivation of our capacity for God and a redirection of our desires and powers to the single purposes of God. This inner transformation can enhance our physical powers of resistance and give us access to sources of life, light, and love. And it convinces us that intercession is a piece of work not a request which by adoration and self-oblation reaches others, bringing them the redemptive strength of God's forgiving nearness (*Guide*, 145-60).

In *Man and the Supernatural*, 1927, Underhill used the images again of God as country, master, and home. She recalled one of Julian of Norwich's image for God: the ground of our beseeching (*Man*, 194-95). In this book, she reworked her image in *The Golden Sequence* of being bathed in the divine ocean by writing that our observing mind would see our seeking spirits "to be themselves bathed and upheld all the time in and by that very Ocean of Spirit for which they seek and crave" (*Man*, 12). Later on she referred to the supernatural world that "bathes and supports us" (*Man*, 81).

In this same work, Underhill developed her sections on prayer and

sanctification by reflecting on the formula for prayer of the French
School of Spirituality: adoration of the transcendent other, communion
of a person with a divine person, and cooperation with the indwelling
presence. Adoration is a non-utilitarian prayer. Conversion is not only an
initial event but also a life of communion that gives enhancing and
transforming power to those who engage in it. Sanctification
universalizes our will and love. Cooperation has to do with personal
transformation, intercession, and incorporation. Intercession is not only
acts of prayer for the needs of other people but also self-oblivious deeds
that crucify self-interest and magnify beauty, truth, and goodness; it also
implies redemptive suffering as well as the penetration, illumination,
support, and rescue of others. Only integration of the natural and the
supernatural opens us to the divine in human life (*Man*, 204, 207, 220,
233, 235, 237, 251-52, 259).

The threefold approach to God of Jean-Jacques Olier appeared in
"Spiritual Life" where the three forms of prayer are described as worship,
communion, and intercession. Worship or adoration is based on a
realistic sense of God. Self-offering and communion are based on a
realistic personal relationship with God. The life of intercession is based
on a redemptive sense of God's concern for people in the world. Thus it
is not so much begging God to grant particular desires and needs, as
affecting others by mediating God's healing support and light (*Mixed*, 53-
57, 61).

The formula of adoration, adherence, and cooperation held by Cardinal
de Bérulle is recorded in *The Spiritual Life*. We relate to God with
admiring delight, childlike dependence, and disinterested collaboration.
These attitudes nourish a sense of peace and trust in God, which
overstrain and lack of leisure destroy (*Spiritual Life*, 58-103).

Underhill published "God and Spirit" in 1930 in which she explored
the image of God as spirit. The transcendent reality present to us
penetrates and stimulates our embodied spirits to heroic action. That
same year in a book review, Underhill underscored the value of a
personal relationship with God based on faith, hope, and love.[7]

The symbol of God as fire was acknowledged in *Worship*, 1936, as an
attribute of divine self-revelation in Jewish ritual worship and Christian
liturgy, in the Old Testament and the New Testament. Underhill could
not help recalling that both Catherine of Siena and Pascal had
experienced the divine presence as fire. Another imaging of God was the
Holy of Holies, the house of God, the place of the Shekinah, God's
immanent presence, the temple in which ritual sacrifice was offered and
later the synagogue in which Jews meditated on the law, the Torah, God's

covenant (*Worship*, 195, 205-213).

Underhill referred to Ignatius Loyola in several essays. His Principle and Foundation can be embodied in actual life: we are created to praise, reverence, and serve God. Ignatius asserted "I come from God, I belong to God, and I am destined for God." Walter Hilton expressed this singleminded affirmation in Christo-centric terms. The prayer of self-offering, which is called the Offertory in the Christian liturgy, is summed up in Ignatius' "Take, Lord, and receive!" She would like to see this act of consecration recited after our prayers for the alleviation of social and industrial miseries. Christians are called to make Ignatius Loyola's prayer of surrender, *Suscipe*, their own. Ignatius' "contemplation to obtain the love of God" is an example of bridging the temporal and the eternal. We can, in fact, view every form of Christian worship as a contemplation to obtain the love of God. Ignatius used to pause before entering a church to pray, thus revealing his humility and awe in face of the holy. We can know God's will for us by waiting quietly for a pressure or impulse favoring the path we should take, or, in the absence of such a pressure, using the criteria of love and common sense to know what to do, much like the different ways of discerning the spirits that Ignatius proposed.[8]

For Underhill, what counts is not our isolated images of God but our spiritual attitude toward existence. The spiritual life is one life. It implies the molding of our unconscious and instinctive life. We must claim the authority of our personal religious experience.

Jesus the Revealer

In *Man and the Supernatural*, 1927, Underhill portrayed Jesus not as the redeemer but as the revealer of supernatural reality. Christ's divine sonship gives him his identity as God's self-revelation within history. His genius for the ordinary revealed the secret of the supernatural. It presented him not as an interpreter of the mysteries but as a shepherd, comrade, healer, sower of the seed, and master of yokes. Catherine of Siena viewed Jesus as a bridge between the divine and the human. The power of Christ's humanity to mediate grace is captured in the symbol of the Sacred Heart (*Man*, 88, 115-53).

Several of her book reviews indicated her awareness and grasp of issues in Christology at the time. While faulting one author for lacking a metaphysical background, she lauded his book as a revelation of the ultimate in the same breath that she noted the lack of such a revelation in another book which reduced the life of Jesus to insignificant incidents. She urged a balance between objective and subjective atonement as theological notions and as actualities in the spiritual life. She appreciated the historical attempt to establish who moved the stone from the empty tomb. She welcomed Goodier's contribution to our understanding of the historical Jesus, but admitted its avoidance of critical problems and the results of textual research.[9]

Ecclesial Community

Underhill's adult commitment to incarnational, corporate, historical, institutional, and sacramental religion colored her sense of church. She gave fresh meaning to such traditional images of the church as the body of Christ and the communion of saints. Her growing ecumenical and interreligious horizons added depth and breadth to her second classic called *Worship* in which she explored and assessed Jewish worship and various Christian cults.

Having returned to the Anglican communion, Underhill became a firm advocate of the corporate and institutional aspects of religion, that is, of ecclesial community. For her, the church gives its members a religious group-consciousness, an organized cultic ritual, discipline, and the culture of its heritage. She granted religion's employment of instruments of suggestion which reinforce the life of the Spirit (*Spirit*, 121-43).

Underhill described Christians in "Some Implicits of Christian Social Reform," 1922, as conscious members of the mystical fellowship of the living Christ who, like Christ, are committed to the Christianization of society, that is, the interpenetration of God and human life, not the imposition of a new moral code. Christian regeneration sublimates and unifies our instinctual self, bringing us into harmony with God's will. We are called to mediate God's reality to others as workers with Christ. This implies conscious, loving dependence on God as our source of power. A sense of the presence of God can help free us from the grip of materialism. Loving the unlovely into loveableness is a way of freeing us from the spirit of conflict and the defeat of our adversary. Inclusive love can release us from our class and racial antagonisms. The Christian order of society can only be produced by a corporate change of heart. We are to foster the creative aim of divine love. Living in the spirit of prayer, we are to Christianize our every action (*Mixed*, 63-83).

In "Christian Fellowship: Past and Present," 1924, Underhill discussed two aspects of Christian fellowship: its identity of purpose and of a way of life which resembles more that of a family or church rather than that of a hostel or herd. Such community life must serve as a corrective not only to individualism but also to group-arrogance. Communities of

Christian fellowship have their own traditions and customs, the authority of a leader, a common enthusiasm for God, and various types of opposition which have knit the members more closely together. A clear example of Christian fellowship is the experience of community on a retreat which can build unity in silence (*Guide*, 103-116).

In "Life as Prayer," 1928, an address given to a Fellowship of Prayer, Underhill called people of prayer live wires, linking God's grace and the world, agents of God's redeeming power, transmitters of divine love. The possibility of intercessory prayer was, for Underhill, based on the truth of our interconnectedness with one another, our Christian fellowship, which she called the mysterious interpenetration of living souls or spiritual communion. Our intercessory action, including exhaustion, darkness, and suffering, is our share in Christ's saving work. In this sense, intercession is more than a petition; it is work involving communion with the Spirit and sacrifice for the body of Christ.[10]

In "Worship" 1929, Underhill called worship our soul's homage to our origin whereby we praise, reverence, and serve God. It is our humble acknowledgement of God's glory through adoration and sacrifice, not getting information about God, not confessing our sins, and not praying for others. Since we are not pure spirits, we need to acknowledge the sacramental principle of the sacredness of things and deeds. Belonging to an historical religion, we are members of an historical church not pious individualists. A common act of worship releases us from our narrow selfish view of the universe (*Papers*, 73-92).

For Underhill, the church is a society of souls trying to enlarge their own and others' capacity for God. Together they embody the eternal Spirit in a particular time and place as the body of Christ. The church is a small body of Christians sent to save the world by the power of the Cross and of the Spirit of Christ. At the same time, she was aware of the generally unfavorable impression that the church made on its modern critics who sought in vain for outward signs of inward grace. They were repelled by its narrowness, repressive ethical code, resistance to political experiment, entrenched piety, and unwillingness to recognize God in new ways. What opens one's faith vision is to continue to look for the eternal in the accidents of human life. In haphazard and difficult conditions, there is a need for visible homes of the Spirit as centers of light and strength, for churches in the wilderness.[11]

Underhill recognized that modern theology's tendency to emphasize the immanence of God and the prophetic strand in Old Testament spirituality had led Christians to overlook the full religious value of the Eucharist as sacrifice. She saw the need for Christian theology to be reconciled with modern thought, and urged that it be done critically.[12]

In a 1930 review of Dean Inge's book on ethics, she reflected on the relevance of traditional Christian ethics for the social and personal problems of the day. She was opposed as he was to the benevolent materialism of what was called "social Christianity," and convinced that the Gospel is not a message of social reform. She could still not agree with him that a church based on ethical unity and a mystical outlook can continue to uphold Christian values in a secularized civilization without conceding to the evils of institutional religion and dogmatic orthodoxy. In another book review, she reiterated her conviction of the place of a creed in a religion. And in a review of books on the church by T.S. Eliot and Charles Williams, she asserted that Christianity's claim is its offer of transformation, an invasion of reality, and a renewal of life-giving power, not an other-worldly goal or a perfect moral system.[13]

In "What Is Sanctity?" 1932, Underhill called saints spiritual geniuses with a pure capacity for God, possessed by the desire to help, heal, and save. Their joy which endures in darkness and weariness is unlike the happiness of the devotee. They bear the burden of the world's sin and suffering. They believe that contemplation is to make people better shepherds of souls in the church (*Mixed*, 29-43).

An emphasis on cooperation with God as the fruit of communion with God appears in Underhill's essay on "Spiritual Life," 1933. In this work she insisted that due to the interpenetration of spirits, people can become channels of God's life and power secretly transforming an aspect of life. Devotion must issue in costly self-giving or else it may degenerate into self-indulgence. The adoring remembrance of God's reality in our everyday lives evicts pettiness, unrest, and self-occupation. The spiritual life is all that makes us a pure capacity for God through adoration and intercession. It is based on the sheer gift of grace and needs corporate expression. One aspect of cooperation as intercessory prayer and action is what the saints call reparation and without which sanctity is impossible to understand.[14]

Underhill perceived that the spiritual significance of the Oxford Movement was based on its recovery of the historical and institutional elements of religion, its rediscovery of corporate Christianity, its restoration of Catholic tradition, its revival of sacramental and liturgical worship, the disciplined life, and holiness. Its incarnational concern for ceremonial ritual reflected its conviction about the intermingling of sense and spirit in the life of prayer. Its renewed emphasis on the disciplined life of prayer is closely connected with the foundation of retreat houses that flourished. The maturity of holiness within the Oxford Movement exceeds religious individualism in its sweep through the ages of sanctity and in its universal concern for others. One instance was the revival of Anglican religious orders and of the monastic routine which revolves around the corporate worship of God.[15]

In "The Parish Priest and the Life of Prayer," 1936, she called the life of prayer the priest's unique source of pastoral power. Her image of a priest's relationship with God combined adherence to God in prayer with a creative, redeeming love for others. The Curé d'Ars, an obscure peasant priest, became the conscience of France through the depth and strength of his life of prayer. In order to avoid individualism and subjectivity, the prayer of the priest needs to participate in the prayer of the church, that is, the celebration of the Eucharist and the daily Office. This is a prayer of adoration and self-oblation, in Ignatius Loyola's words, a *Suscipe*. Priests can lead their parishes to a life of prayer by developing their own life of prayer, praying in their own churches and thereby making them truly houses of prayer, and forming a weekly prayer group who emphasize adoration and self-offering rather than intercession, and who can include invalids and old people to pray in their homes. The life of prayer is the life of adoration, communion, and cooperation with God. When asked to give instruction about the life of prayer to an individual, a priest ought to balance a critical knowledge of the psychology of religion with a critical openness to anyone developing a passive prayer or claiming visionary experiences (*Papers*, 140-81).

Her 1936 classic work called *Worship* treated various Jewish and Christian liturgies as "chapels of various types in the one Cathedral of the Spirit" (*Worship*, xii). It approached worship as the creature's adoring response to the eternal, an acknowledgement of transcendence (*Worship*, xi, 3, 47, 61, 186).

Using an Ignatian approach, this book described each Christian cult as a contemplation to attain the love of God, leading to adoration, self-offering, and dependence, which override the negative element present. The four chief elements of cult, that is, ritual, symbol, sacrament, and sacrifice, share characteristics of communality and sacramentality, that is, they possess a marked social quality, and they have a visible and an invisible action which combine sense and spirit, habit and attention. The orientation to the unseen and the seen witnesses to God's otherness and nearness in different expressions of Christian worship, such as the monastic reciting the Night Office, the Quaker waiting silently for the Spirit, the old woman boiling her potatoes, the Lutheran singing hymns to the name of Jesus, the Orthodox bowing in adoration of the divine mysteries, the Salvationist marching under the banner of the Cross, and the Catholic praying before the blessed sacrament. Christian worship expresses the paradoxical union of the divine and the human; it aims at the sanctification of life. The Eucharist is a sacrifice and a feast, an act of worship and an act of communion, a historical memorial and the mystery of the divine presence, a source of spiritual energy and a sacrament of fellowship. The Divine Office is based on the sanctification of time. Personal worship consists of adoration and adherence to God, as well as intercession the essence of which is loving cooperation with God, summarized in the Lord's Prayer. Its life is grounded in humility and love. Its goal is self-offering to God embodied through acceptance of the sacrament of the present moment.[16]

> The corporate worship of the Church is not simply that of an assembly of individuals who believe the same things, and therefore unite in doing the same things. It is real in its own right, an action transcending and embracing all the separate souls taking part in it (*Worship*, 86).

This insight into ecclesial communality challenges individualism and supports the Pauline notion of the body of Christ. It recognizes that the church is a concerted group not a collection of prize specimens (*Worship*, 98). Christians do not or should not go to the Eucharist "on an individual errand, even of the most spiritual kind" (*Worship*, 250). We go to participate in the action of the Eucharist which the church offers to God at all times and everywhere.

Christian worship must acknowledge the influence of the Jewish temple ritual and the institutional worship of the synagogue in its liturgical development. They represent the double aspect of our response to God: the ritual demands of the Law and the moral demands of the prophets. Catholic worship is theocentric, incarnational, Christocentric, sacrificial, and social (*Worship*, 208-217, 243-53,).

The church is the communion of saints. Underhill offered some valuable observations in this regard. She described the saints as human beings who have become a pure capacity for God, and therefore tools of the divine action. The cause of their power and holiness is God, who is glorified in their lives and virtue. Christians are called to make their own Ignatius Loyola's prayer of surrender, *Suscipe* (*Worship*, 251-52). Even as an Anglican, Underhill understood the heart of Roman Catholic devotion to Mary:

> The dubious ancestry of some aspects of Marian devotion, its obvious Pagan affinities, the exaggerated position which it has occupied from the Middle Ages onwards, or the many phantasies, superstitions, and sentimentalisms of which it has become the core, must not blind us to the deep spiritual truth which it enshrines (*Worship*, 252).

Granting that Mary was the human agent of the Incarnation, Underhill perceived the theological significance of the phrase "all through Mary."

The Catholic Church is a living organism. It adjusts and expands its worship to meet changing needs and express changing realities. Acknowledging the theological questions regarding the practice of reserving the Blessed Sacrament in church, Underhill was able to see that it can be an incentive to prayer and provide a focus of worship and pledge of the divine presence for the simplest as well as for the deepest believers.[17]

Orthodox worship maintains the characteristics of fourth-century religion in adoring the timeless mystery. The ikon is truly a sacramental mediating communion with the invisible rather than only a focusing devotion or incitement to prayer. Underhill claimed that its veneration in the Eastern Church has a parallel in devotion to the Blessed Sacrament in Western Catholicism. The prayer of the heart is an Orthodox technique of mystical worship; its most familiar form is the Jesus prayer which opens the believer to God's transforming power (*Worship*, 262-75).

Worship in the reformed churches emphasizes a synthesis of the proclamation and preaching of the Word of God, the Christian's response to the Word, and the breaking of the bread of life. Luther's humanistic piety emphasized devotion to the person of Jesus. Calvin's sense of God's otherness and creaturely limitation is a corrective to humanistic piety. Free church worship is characterized by the priesthood of all believers and the universal call to holiness. It is carried to its extreme in the Quaker preference for spontaneous worship and pure inwardness. Underhill called a Quaker meeting an experiment in corporate contemplative prayer which evokes group-suggestion. She viewed Quaker worship as a corrective to ritualism and formalism with its insistence on reverent practice and waiting upon the Spirit. This willingness to pause in awe before worship characterized the saints. Underhill observed that the Society of Friends has produced no great contemplative, and concluded that the great teachers of interior prayer live and worship within institutional, sacramental, and historical religion. She acknowledged that Quaker silence is for them a symbol, although they distrust symbols since they are often used to substitute for the reality of God.[18]

The Anglican tradition combines the Catholic sacramental and corporate ideal of Christian worship with the Protestant biblical and individual ideal. Its authorized missal and breviary is the Book of Common Prayer. The biblical, anti-institutional tone of English religious life is exemplified for Underhill in Richard Rolle who combined an anti-clerical bias and repudiation of formalism with a devotion to the name of Jesus as well as a love of song and music. While the Evangelical revival renewed the prophetic, biblical, ethical aspect of the English religion focused on the ministry of the Word, the Tractarian Movement restored its life of corporate worship centered on the ministry of the sacraments. The spirit of adoration overflows in service to the poor. Underhill claimed that the uniqueness of the Anglican tradition is the equal emphasis it gives to biblical and sacramental worship, that is, to the divine office and the Eucharist. While insisting that the Anglican church should be a thinking church, she considered religious experience, not doctrine, to be the touchstone of Christian belief. Anglican liturgy ensures dignity and historical continuity. Traditional liturgical prayers are to be preferred to beautiful services with modern devotions since these prayers voice the universal church and offer an undiluted spiritual food.[19]

Her insistence on the corporate aspect of Christian life in the world made her fault *The Imitation of Christ* for its excess of other-worldliness and neglect of the horizontal element. At the same time, she was careful to note an unbalanced emphasis on the corporate nature of the Christian life which ignores the place of personal communion with God and can lead to sacerdotalism, an exaggerated reliance on the ordained ministry.[20]

In *The Spiritual Life*, 1937, Underhill described the church as God's tool to save the world, not a comfortable religious club. Every member is to cooperate with the Spirit, most often in secret ways. We transmit as well as receive (*Spiritual Life*, 88-92).

The Universe as God's Self-Expression

Underhill brought to bear the insights and findings of the search for social justice, physics, philosophy, psychology, and politics on her view of the earth and of the universe. Her sense of God's interconnectedness with the world led her to see the interconnectedness of human life with the divine and of non-human life with the human. The realism of her faith led her to describe the universe as God's self-expression.

In her lecture on "The Will of the Voice," delivered at the Copec Conference in 1924, Underhill urged the promotion of justice in the service of faith. She reminded her audience that many people are living in conditions that are not conducive to living the spiritual life while we continue "talking theology, or going to church, or sewing the miserable little patches we call charity and social service into the rotten garment of our corporate life" (*Mixed*, 89). We go on eating the bread of life at others' expense. The Sermon on the Mount is a series of indictments of modern civilization. Following the will of God's voice means living gospel values in a world that does not live by them. The church must become a church of prophecy and vision by living the integrated Christian life of adoration and of action in the world (*Mixed*, 84-94).

Underhill explored "The Christian Basis of Social Action" at the Anglo-Catholic Summer School, Oxford, in 1925. We are called to be God's creative instruments in the world cooperating with the Holy Spirit. This means working to eliminate conditions intolerable for people we love. Christ identifies with our interests; we, in turn, are to identify with others' interests. It also implies that social science ought to be a department of theology (*Mixed*, 95-112).

In *Man and the Supernatural*, 1927, Underhill looked at various philosophies of religion and their attitudes toward the world. First, there is a utilitarian tendency to reject other-worldliness, to subordinate faith to works, to reduce devotional practice to a branch of psychology, and so the emphasis is on a social Christianity. Underhill saw the need for concern with the transcendent order and the performance of non-utilitarian acts of sacrificial love which point to the infinite. Second, a pious naturalism tends to simplify the conception of God in the light of scientific data. The corrective she offered is the mystics' emphasis on awe at the incomprehensible mystery of God. Third, a diffuse immanentism tries to equate the life-force with God's Spirit and views the spiritual life as the outgrowth of creative evolution. The corrective, here, is the balancing of becoming with being, continuity with discontinuity, of belief in the immanent divine presence with belief in the real transcendent Spirit, of self-development with humility and adoration. The mystics insist on the twofold nature of reality as earthly and divine, and of human reality as sense and spirit, nature and grace (*Man*, 53-80).

Underhill insisted on the social and historical context of religious experience. Christ brought to prayer his mind that was inculturated in Jewish tradition, his religious vocabulary colored by the prophets and psalms, and an emotional life influenced by relationships and responsibilities. The mystics' contact with God was and is conditioned by history (*Man*, 100-14).

She was committed to the dialogue between science and religion. She was also aware, however, of some of the ways in which science can stop short of religion. It can seem to make contemplation of reality rather than union the goal of human life, which is given the intuition of being. A pantheistic immanentism that considers the universe God's manifestation can also deny God's distinctness from creatures.[21]

Aware from modern physics that cosmic astronomy and atomic

astronomy explain and complete one another, she observed: "Each atom, with its electrons revolving round the central proton, is as truly a solar system as the most majestic of the stars with its planetary train" (*Man*, 115-16). Likewise, incarnational, historical, sacramental religion reveals within our planetary compass the purpose and nature of the incomprehensible, self-giving mystery we call God. Convinced of the two levels of human experience, Underhill observed: "For the real supernatural life requires a seizing, not a shirking of the most homely: and a using of it as the material of the most heroic" (*Man*, 139). Thus openness to the divine is broadened and deepened by acceptance of the human. Religious symbols and sacraments are so important because "human beings are not able to apprehend spirit unmingled with sense" (*Man*, 167). On this point, Underhill added an interesting insight that a religious symbol can be effective without being beautiful. Crude images can also convey the divine (*Man*, 171).

Evelyn Underhill is to be applauded for recognizing the dialogue that mysticism and science need to have. Her knowledge of science, however, was understandably sketchy and her grasp of the material was uncritical.

Underhill discussed the life of the Spirit in relationship to the social order, bringing out the social dimensions of penitence, surrender, recollection, and work. She urged a corporate repentance for the ills of society, surrender to our spiritual calling, the regular social exercise of recollection, and renewed communal dedication to work. She was convinced of our social suggestibility. For her spirituality was not self-regarding but an education for action according to the incarnational principle. The life of the spirit can be nourished in the social order by periodic retreats (*Spirit*, 200-25).

In "Thoughts on Prayer and the Divine Immanence" (1931), Underhill referred to Sir James Jeans' analogy in *The Mysterious Universe* about the radiation of electrons in the cosmos being bounded only by the limits of that cosmos:

> Thus the outpouring and self-giving energies of one such electron can fill all space; and during our whole lives we are receiving and are conditioned by the radiations and influence of countless worlds and their unimaginable constituents, falling on us, changing us, maintaining us (*Papers*, 93).

For her this was an allegory of the universe of spirit by which she meant the spiritual radiation of the saints. But it breaks down if we understand by it a view of prayer as a purely human activity directed to God rather than as the solidarity of supernatural action generated by the divine energy and directing the corporate activity of those who pray (*Papers*, 94).

In "The Inside of Life" 1931, Underhill observed that the modern dilemma is how to reconcile the truth described in *The Mysterious Universe* with the truth affirmed in "Hark! the herald angels sing." That is, we are meant to be amphibious, at home in both the world of science and the world of spiritual experience. It is amazing that in her day she was aware of the impact which physics could make on spirituality. She admitted that the great fact of our time is the human mind's movement into a new and larger physical world, a sense of the power and vastness of the universe which science has revealed to us. But she reminded us that adoration is still the heart of religion and in the light of which there is no dilemma (*Papers*, 109-121).

Underhill certainly viewed the world as the place in which we cooperate with God to bring about God's purposes. In fact, remarkable for her day, she saw the interdependence of spirituality and politics as a way of expressing the interdependence of God and the world. In other words our convictions about God and the world become moral imperatives for our choices and actions. We learn to judge public issues from the view of eternity rather than from that of national self-interest. Christianity anticipates the redemption of the created order, a restoration of all to conform with the divine purpose. While not allowing itself to collude with new political systems or programs of social reform, it should influence all manifestations of our human life.[22]

The universe is the self-expression of God. Our purpose and destiny are interconnected with it: "The meaning of our life is bound up with the meaning of the universe" (*Spiritual Life*, 19).

Conclusion

According to Underhill, living the life of the Spirit means following God's will in adoration and action. We are to cooperate with the Spirit by identifying with Christ's interests and concerns. An authentic spiritual outlook empowers us to seize not shirk the details and duties of our ordinary lives. The life of the Spirit educates us for action in the world that includes the communal dimensions of individual spiritual attitudes, such as corporate repentance for social evils, surrender to our calling, recollection in our dealings with others, and communal dedication to work. Adoration opens us to the power and vastness of the universe which is God's self-expression. The meaning of our lives is, in fact, bound up with the meaning of the universe (*Spirit*, 200-25; *Papers*, 109-121; *Spiritual Life*, 19).

Connecting our spirituality with our politics is a way of expressing

God's involvement with the world. We are to judge public issues from the view of eternity not from that of national self-interest (*Spiritual Life*, 81, 123-24).

Her distaste for the purely humanitarian and ethical concerns of what was called "social Christianity" blocked the development of her conviction that the gospel is a message of social change. As she became clearer about the need for the socialization of the person and religion, she also began to see the need for the spiritualization of society. In fact, she promoted the development of a personal spiritual life rooted in gospel values as the basis for practical religion, which is always a unity of the love of God and the love of neighbor.

Evelyn Underhill's works on the spiritual life can be considered devotional literature for wealthy English women. On the other hand, Underhill, along with the French Jewess Simone Weil, and the North American Georgia Harkness, has been acclaimed as one of three women who made significant contributions to religious thought, and, in particular, to mysticism and the spiritual life in the early part of this century.[23]

Suggestions for Prayerful Reflection
Annice Callahan, R.S.C.J.

Let us pause for a few moments and consider the following reflection in view of integrating our spiritual life and our practical life, our spirituality and our politics:

We come back to this ordinary mixed life of every day, in which we find ourselves--the life of house and work, tube and aeroplane, newspaper and cinema, wireless and television, with its tangle of problems and suggestions and demands--and consider what we are to do about that; how, within its homely limitations, we can co-operate with the Will. It is far easier, though not very easy, to develop and preserve a spiritual outlook on life, than it is to make our everyday actions harmonise with that spiritual outlook. That means trying to see things, persons and choices from the angle of eternity; and dealing with them as part of the material in which the Spirit works. This will be decisive for the way we behave as to our personal, social and national obligations. It will decide the papers we read, the movements we support, the kinds of administrators we vote for, our attitude to social and international justice. For though we may renounce the world for ourselves, refuse the attempt to get anything out of it, we have to accept it as the sphere in which we are to cooperate with the Spirit, and try to do the Will. Therefore the prevalent notion that spirituality and politics have nothing to do with one another is the exact opposite of the truth. Once it is accepted in a realistic sense, the spiritual life has everything to do with politics. It means that certain convictions about God and the world become the moral and spiritual imperatives of our life; and this must be decisive for the way we choose to behave about that bit of the world over which we have been given a limited control (*Spiritual Life*, pp. 79-81).

1. What helps us harmonize our everyday actions with our spiritual outlook?

2. What hinders us from doing so?

3. Do we view the world as the sphere in which we are to cooperate with the Spirit and try to do God's will?

4. How can we let our spiritual life influence our politics?

5. How can we let our spiritual life influence our attitude and behavior toward our planet earth and toward the universe?

Readings

For an updated version of her 1921 Oxford University lectures, see Evelyn Underhill, *The Life of the Spirit and the Life of Today* (Harrisburg, Pa.: Morehouse, 1995). For a reliable first edition of her 1936 classic, see Evelyn Underhill, *Worship* (New York: Crossroad, 1985). For a second abridged edition, see Evelyn Underhill, *Worship* (Guildford, Surrey: Eagle, 1991; Wheaton, Ill.: Harold Shaw, 1992). For an excellent introduction to an edited collection of her essays, see *Evelyn Underhill: Modern Guide to the Ancient Quest for the Holy*, ed. Dana Greene (Albany, N.Y.: State University of New York Press, 1988).

Notes

1. See E. Underhill, *Mount*, 111; id., *Worship*, 251; id., "Studies in Sanctity: I. The Meaning of Sanctity," *The Spectator*, 23 January 1932, 102-103, DGC, reprinted in *Mixed*. Cf. D. Greene, *Artist*, 122-23.

2. See E. Underhill, *Man*, 1-51; and "Man and the Supernatural," letter to the editor, *The Spectator*, 15 October 1927, 606, DGC.

3. See E. Underhill, *Man*, 113; *Mixed Pasture*, 2.
    Her use of Aristotle's and Aquinas's description of the human person as a contemplative animal has much in common with Bernard Lonergan's description of the human being as a symbolic animal. Self-transcendence is the dynamism of human reality integrating love of family, love of country, and love of God. It integrates the world of immediacy, which includes the data of sense and of consciousness, with the world of meaning, which asks questions and arrives at and implements correct answers. It integrates cognitional and moral authenticity with religious authenticity. Even in preconscious activity such as dreams one can detect an orientation toward self-transcendence. See B.J.F. Lonergan, "Religious Experience," and "Religious Knowledge," in *A Third Collection: Papers by Bernard J.F. Lonergan, S.J.*, ed. Frederick E. Crowe (N.Y.: Paulist, 1985), 113-45, esp. 119, 123-24, 131-34, 141. For this reference, I am indebted to Michael Vertin, philosophy professor at the University of St. Michael's College.

4. On the uniqueness of God's way with each of us, see E.Underhill, *Worship*, 170-71. On the ground of the soul, see idem, *Worship*, 171, 178, 190, 309, 311; *Man*, 197-98, 247; *Mixed*, 27, 59.

5. See E. Underhill, "The Mastery of Time," in Grace Adolphsen Brame, "Evelyn Underhill and the Mastery of Time," *Spirituality Today* 42, no. 4 (Winter 1990): 344-349. See also Grace Adolphsen Brame,"Continuing Incarnation: Evelyn Underhill's Double Thread of Spirituality," *The Christian Century* (October 31, 1990): 997-999; "Evelyn Underhill and the Mastery of Time," *Spirituality Today* 42, no. 4 (Winter 1990): 341-351; and "The Extraordinary within the Ordinary: The Life and Message of Evelyn Underhill," *Feminist Voices in Spirituality*, ed. Pierre Hegy, Studies in Women and Religion, Vol. 38 (Lewiston, New York: Edwin Mellen, 1996), 101-124.

6. See E. Underhill, *Spirit*, 172-99.
    Robert Coles, a noted North American child psychologist, author, and Harvard professor, would agree with Underhill's fostering of the spiritual life of children in *The Life of the Spirit and the Life of Today*. Like her, he is keenly

interested in promoting the dialogue between psychology and religion. In examining his interviews with children, Coles discovered that in focusing on their moral life and their political life, he had failed to hear the clues they had given about their spiritual and religious life through a remark, a picture, a dream, or a nightmare. Out of 293 pictures of God that children drew, all but thirty-eight of them are of God's face. Many of his interviews are about children's experiences of nature and art. Like Underhill, Coles was more interested in these children's spiritual attitudes to existence than in their religious beliefs. In talking with Christian, Jewish, and Islamic children, as well as children with no apparent religious affiliation, Coles concluded that children engage in secular soul-searching as pilgrims trying to make sense of the universe, its meaning and purpose, as well as the meaning and purpose of their daily lives. See Robert Coles, *The Spiritual Life of Children* (Boston: Houghton Mifflin, 1990), esp. 277-335. For this reference, I am indebted to Patrick Henry, Director, Institute for Ecumenical and Cultural Research, Collegeville, Minnesota, February 18, 1993.

7. See E. Underhill, *Guide*, 177-90; and "God and Man," review of *God in Christian Thought and Experience* by W.R. Matthews, and *Psychology and God* by L.W. Grensted, *The Spectator*, 1 November 1930, 636-37, DGC.

8. See E. Underhill, *Man*, 8; *Papers*, 73-92, 157; *Worship*, xii, 251-52, 311; *Mixed*, 22, 43, 56, 102, 202; *Spiritual Life*, 113-14. See also Ignatius Loyola, "Rules for the Discernment of Spirits, Weeks 1 and 2," in *The Spiritual Exercises of St. Ignatius*, trans. George E. Ganss (St. Louis: Institute of Jesuit Sources, 1992), 121-128, ##313-336. Cf. Michael J. Buckley, "The Structure of the Rules for Discernment of Spirits," *The Way Supplement* 20 (August 1973): 19-37.

9. See E. Underhill, "Cujus Filius Est," review of *The Life of Jesus* by J. Middleton Murry and *The Historical Life of Christ* by J. Warschauer, *The Spectator*, 29 January 1927, 155, DGC; id., "A Guide-Book to the Gospels," review of *Jesus of Nazareth* by Charles Gore, *The Spectator*, 2 March 1929, 339, DGC; id., "Recent Theology," review of *The Atonement in History and in Life* by L.W. Grensted, *Essays in Christian Theology* by Leonard Hodgson, and *The Principles of Theology: an Introduction to the Thirty-nine Articles* by W.H. Griffith Thomas, *The Spectator*, 29 March 1930, 533, DGC; id., "Easter Morning," review of *Who Moved the Stone?* by Frank Morison, *The Spectator*, 19 April 1930, 670, DGC; and id., "A New Life of Christ," review of *The Public Life of Our Lord Jesus Christ: an Interpretation* by A. Goodier, *The Spectator*, 24 May 1930, 868, DGC.

10. See E. Underhill, *Papers*, 63, 65, 67, 71. See also "The Hill of the Lord," *The Spectator*, 19 November 1927, 870, DGC, in which she called human religion a live wire along which the energy love is transmitted to us from God and returns

again to its source.

11. See E. Underhill, *Guide*, 189, 215; id., "Pax Domini," *The Spectator*, 27 December 1930: 1003-1004, DGC; and id., "Churches in the Wilderness," *The Spectator*, 1 August 1931, 146-47, DGC.

12. See E. Underhill, "Recent Theology," review of *The Fullness of Sacrifice* by F.C.N. Hicks, *The Christian Faith in the Modern World: a Study in Scientific Theology* by E.O. James, *Studies in the Philosophy of Religion* by A. Seth Pringle-Pattison, and *The Grace of God* by N.P. Williams, *The Spectator*, 27 September 1930, 418, DGC.

13. See E. Underhill, "The Christian Standard," review of *Christian Ethics and Modern Problems* by W.R. Inge, 20 September 1930, 386, DGC; and "The Skeleton of Faith," review of *Doctrines of the Creed* by Oliver P. Quick, *Time and Tide*, 13 August 1938, 1150-51, DGC; "Poet-Prophets," review of *The Idea of a Christian Society* by T.S. Eliot and *The Descent of the Dove* by Charles Williams, *Time and Tide*, 4 November 1939, 1416-1417, DGC.

14. See E. Underhill, *Mixed*, 51, 55, 61; "Trench Warfare," review of *In Defence of the Faith* by Charles Gardner, *The Spectator*, 22 January 1927, 119, DGC; and review of *The Elements of the Spiritual Life: a Study in Ascetical Theology* by F.P. Harton, *The Criterion* 12, no. 47 (January 1933): 282-84, DGC.

15. See E. Underhill, *Mixed*, 123-46; and "The Oxford Group Movement," letter to the editor, *The Spectator*, 27 August 1932, 260, DGC.

16. See E. Underhill, *Worship*, xii, 22-32, 68, 70, 77-81, 117, 137-38, 165-69, 186, 189, 224-29, 242.

17. See E. Underhill, *Worship*, 256-57. On devotion to the Blessed Sacrament and its formative influence on the saints, Underhill quoted von Hügel in an unpublished letter he had written her. See *Worship*, 257, n. 2.

18. See E. Underhill, "Some Books on Religion," review of *History and Thought* by W.R. Matthews, *Holiness of Religion* by A. Barratt Brown, *Physical Justification of Religion* by R.S. Hansen, *The Spectator*, 10 August 1929, 193, DGC; and *Worship*, 276- 313. On the view that her book on worship showed her brilliant understanding of the liturgical form of worship but a weak grasp of the genius of free Protestant worship, see Douglas V. Steere, "Underhill, Evelyn (Mrs. Stuart Moore)," in *The Twentieth Century Encyclopedia of Religious Knowledge*, 1955 ed.

19. See E. Underhill, *Worship*, 314-38; "The Art of Worship," review of *Liturgy and Worship: a Companion to the Prayer Books of the Anglican Communion*, ed. W.K. Lowthar Clarke and C. Harris, *The Spectator*, 16 December 1932, 870-71, DGC; id., "Churches Full and Empty," letter to the editor, *The Spectator*, 22 May 1936, 934, DGC; and id., "A Thinking Church," review of *Doctrine in the Church of England*, *Time and Tide* (January 22, 1938): 100-101, DGC. Cf. Robert Gail Woods, "Evelyn Underhill's Concept of Worship," (Ph.D. diss., Southern Baptist Theological Seminary, 1971), esp. 93-123, 153-234.

20. See E. Underhill, "Signposts," review of *The God-Man* by E.L. Mascall, *The Re-Creation of Man* by T.M. Parker, *The Church of God* by D.M. MacKinnon, and *The Necessity of Worship* by P. McLaughlin, *Time and Tide* (September 21, 1940): 948, DGC; and "Men and Books: Thomas à Kempis," *Time and Tide* (1 March 1, 1941): 173, DGC.

21. See E. Underhill, "Aspects of Reality," review of *Religion in the Making* by A.N. Whitehead and *Reality: a New Correlation of Science and Religion* by B.H. Streeter, *The Spectator*, 18 December 1926, 1118, DGC; "Spirit and Life," review of *The Sciences and Philosophy* by J.S. Haldane, *The Spectator*, 22 June 1929, 975, DGC; and "A Three-fold Universe," review of *Matter, Life, and Value* by C.E.M. Joad, *The Spectator*, 19 October 1929, 547-48, DGC.

22. See E. Underhill, *Spiritual Life*, 81, 123-24; and "Men and Books," *Time and Tide* (March 26, 1938): 424-25, DGC.

23. See John Macquarrie, *Twentieth Century Religious Thought* (Philadelphia: Trinity Press International, 1989), 4th ed., 148-53, esp. 151-52.

Part Three

Legacy for the Third Millennium

Introduction

This section offers three ways of approaching Evelyn Underhill's legacy for the third millenium. The first chapter presents and assesses Underhill's approach to mysticism. It also evaluates her study of visions from the perspective of Karl Rahner's study of visions. The second chapter discusses her contribution to the ministry of spiritual guidance. The third chapter indicates ways in which her spirituality for daily living can speak to future generations of Christians.

Chapter 7

Study of Mysticism

Underhill was one of three major English exponents of mysticism in her day. Dean William Inge, author of *Christian Mysticism*, 1899, was the pioneer. Baron Friedrich von Hügel, author of *The Mystical Element of Religion*, 1909 and 1923, insisted on the institutional and intellectual elements in religion undergirding authentic mystical experience. Underhill was the distinguished popularizer and educator of a religious public, many of whom regarded religion as ethical idealism or as a set of orthodox opinions. She helped them understand the importance of mysticism and worship by presenting mysticism as the adventure of holiness, and liturgy as a reliable bridge between the divine and the human.[1]

The originality of Underhill's book on *Mysticism* "lay in the fact that it redefined what it is to be human and what it is to be religious" (*Artist*, 54). Being human is for her being in union with God. Being religious has more to do with an attitude of adoration and service than an attention to doctrinal correctness and theological precision. Being a mystic included for Underhill being sane and practical. Mysticism was for her a source for the study of life: "Her genius lies in the fact that she discovered this subject, recognized its power and influence, and wrote about it with such elegance, power, and immediacy."[2]

Descriptions and Distinctions

One of Evelyn Underhill's original contributions to the study of mysticism was her understanding of its four characteristics. She was familiar with the four marks of the mystic state noted by William James: ineffability, noetic quality, transiency, and passivity. By these James meant that mystical states must be experienced because they defy expression, they are states of inarticulate knowledge, they do not last long, and in them the subject feels held by a superior power. But Underhill wanted to capture the holistic and integrating aspects of James' four marks. For her, mysticism is a life process that is practical and active, not theoretical and passive. Second, it is a spiritual activity done for its own sake not for any other purpose. Third, its method is love which includes surrender as well as perception, whose object is living and personal. Fourth, it involves a development of the whole self under the impetus of its search for the transcendent.[3]

Another original contribution of Underhill to the study of mysticism is her schema of five stages in the mystical process. Christian tradition had spoken of three: purgation (*via purgativa*), illumination (*via illuminativa*), and union (*via unitiva*). She included awakening as an initial stage, and observed that the dark night of the soul precedes union (*Mysticism*, 165-451; *Ruysbroeck*, 119).

All of us are attracted by something transcendent. We step back and are afraid of sacred experiences like intimacy. The phases of the mystic way are in our daily lives when we feel called to go beyond our experience. Spiritual awakening means moving from the unconscious to a conscious search for God, and is often felt as a hunger for God. Purgation is the process of becoming free of all the things God wants us to be free from in order to grow in our following of Jesus. Illumination can be insight for some, and an affective, loving sense of God's closeness for others. The dark night might include a mid-life crisis, a communal impasse, a loss of meaning, of a significant relationship, or of a familiar way of being with others. Union with God can be felt to be as passionate as a lover's embrace or as silent as an elderly couple sitting on a bench comfortable in each other's presence.

Her book on *Practical Mysticism* is an attempt to simplify a description of the reality and stages of mysticism. It gives the five stages of the mystic way an experiential base. I personally disagree, however, with Underhill's description of these as stages that appear in a sequential order. For example she calls purgation "the second stage in the training of the human consciousness for participation in Reality" (*Practical*, 59). I prefer to view these stages as phases of which we go in and out at different times in our lives. I also resist her classification of the three levels of reality which she called the natural world of becoming, the metaphysical world of being, and divine reality. I believe that each of us is in a state of all three all the time (*Practical*, 45, 90).

In her biography of Jacopone da Todi, we find these five stages of his growth: a new consciousness, cleansing, illumination, suffering, and union with God. Jacopone experienced an impasse signaling his transition from purgation to illumination which involves total abandonment to God and detachment from personal desire. His initiation into the illuminative way included alternating states of rapture and anguish. Like other mystics, his times of enlightenment were followed by instability (*Jacopone*, 58, 96-97, 119, 150, 197, 226). It is interesting to observe that Underhill later simplified her five-fold schema, discussing, for example, only purification and prayer in her retreat addresses called *The Golden Sequence*.

Underhill made a significant contribution to the study of mysticism. Refusing to reduce mysticism to unconnected moments of illumination, she insisted that it is a way of life, marked by active deeds of love and leading to the development of the whole person. Her recognition that purgation, illumination, and union also include an initial stage of awakening and a transitional dark night before union, prompted her to expand the traditional schema. She perceived that the dark night of the soul is more than a state of exhaustion: it is God's invitation to transformation through a mystical death to self.

In her work *Mysticism*, Evelyn Underhill was aware of the importance of an authentic philosophy of mysticism. Beginning with one's quest for the real, she discussed the limitations of various theories of reality such as naturalism, idealism and philosophical skepticism, and concluded that mysticism is the science of the real since it claims communion with the absolute. In contrast with empiricism and rationalism, her thought reflected her affinity with the romanticism of her day. Basing her approach on Henri Bergson's notion of vitalism as a dynamic philosophy of becoming generated by a vital impulse, the *élan vital*, she called mysticism a spiritual vitalism. Underhill later recognized the corrective that mysticism can be to vitalism by its insistence on a dual vision of reality as being and becoming, life and fruition, rest and change. She admitted the benefits of critical realism and the defects of vitalism, and acknowledged the impact which philosophy makes on mysticism.[4]

Underhill also recognized the impact of psychology on mysticism, and adverted to such issues as hysteria, automatic states, and the function of contemplation in altering the field of consciousness. Today, she would have written very differently because of advances in the field of psychology. I am in awe, however, of her willingness to tackle this area, to cite multi-cultural references, and to acknowledge problems about secondary parapsychological phenomena without feeling she had to solve them.[5]

She demonstrated her outstanding grasp of difficult material regarding the psychology of mysticism. For example, aware that some psychologists were skeptical of the mystics' sense of the presence of God, attributing it to projection or wish-fulfillments, she referred her readers to Delacroix's studies which approach mysticism as projection. She then noted that a balanced view can be found in Maréchal's studies in the psychology of the mystics where mysticism is treated as God's gift to one who is open to the gift. For Underhill, the criterion of authenticity for ecstatic states such as visions and voices, as to whether they are of divine origin or due to imagination, intense reverie, or psychic illness, is their life-enhancing quality. Her knowledge of material is evident in the Bibliography (*Mysticism*, 242, n.3; 266-68, n.1; 270; 475-507).

Conversant with mystical theology, Underhill could see the value of the different ways the mystics experience the mystery we call God. Some emphasize divine transcendence, others divine immanence, and still others reflect both approaches in their writings. She urged that mystical theology accept both ways of interpreting our experience of God according to our temperament and situation, rather than hold that positing one theory implies the rejection of its opposite. Christianity provided a sound approach for Underhill since it combines the metaphysical and personal aspects of the divine in the Trinity and the Incarnation.[6] Union with the divine can be experienced as union with transcendent mystery, union with the personal aspect of God, or union with the divine life indwelling in the world and in one's self. She presented three classes of mystics' symbols for God and three ways of seeking God, which reflect different cravings of the self and different temperaments. Various mystics express their way to God as the marriage of the soul, or the mystic quest including the search for the hidden treasure and the quest of the Holy Grail, or the spiritual journey as reflected in Dante's *Divine Comedy* and Bunyan's *Pilgrim's Progress*. Underhill's balanced perception understood that this journey contains the gamut of symbolic expression about God as transcendent, incarnate, or indwelling.[7]

Reflecting on the marriage of the soul motif, Underhill recounted the traditional view that medieval mystics had used bridal imagery because the Song of Songs was a popular allegory of the spiritual life. But she then took an alternative view, that mystics love the Song of Songs because they see in it a mirror of their own experiences. Descriptions of spiritual marriage are free, for the most part, of physical imagery, as with

Teresa of Avila and Richard of St. Victor, and the spouse of God develops a maternal generativity mediating divine life and grace to others.

The great work of new birth, of divinization, is expressed by such mystics as Jacob Boehme and William Law who used alchemical symbols such as fire, gold, and the white stone. In assessing magic in relation to mysticism, Underhill revealed her own dabbling with it and her disenchantment with its dangerous involvement with the occult and separation of knowledge and love.[8]

Technically, mystics are those whose experience of God includes mystical phenomena. In a more general sense, they are also those who consciously and freely experience God in their lives. In other words, everyone can have a mystical experience that differs not in kind but in intensity from that of those we technically call mystics.

Evelyn Underhill was at her best debating a difficult topic like visions and voices. She was able to distinguish the mystic's authentic visions from psychopathic visions reflecting a temporary loss of balance: Julian of Norwich seeing the fiend clutching at her throat or Teresa dismissing Satan from the top of her breviary by the use of holy water. Underhill agreed that these pathological phenomena are a type of hallucination and was willing to grant that visions and voices can be regarded as mystical automatisms translating the suggestions of the subconscious to the conscious personality and slowly transforming it. Relying on Teresa and John of the Cross, Underhill established criteria of certitude, peace, and joy to substantiate visions.[9]

As with visions, Underhill distinguished between healthy and psychopathic kinds of ecstasy. Her openness to and grasp of the psychology of mysticism caused her to call ecstasy a complete mono-ideism, that is, a conscious attention to one thing and inattention to everything else. She called the divine voice which Catherine of Siena claims spoke to her soul the intuitive perceptions of the deeper self. Ecstasy for Underhill was a mystical act of perception extending the spiritual consciousness in the direction of the transcendent. She was aware that ecstasy is the development of infused contemplation, and considered its distinguishing note to be entrancement. Whereas ecstasy is a gradual involuntary process, rapture is an abrupt and irresistible absorption in the divine vision (*Mysticism*, 358-79).

Underhill presented herself as an astute psychologist of mysticism in her description of the dark night of the soul as a fatigue state that follows a time of sustained mystical activity. But she was quick to add that it can contribute to transformation in God. This means that it is a state of transition between two worlds, a shift from a center marked by pleasure-affirmation to a center characterized by pain-negation. It is, therefore, a growth to a new state of consciousness that is accompanied by many different kinds of growing pains. She proved herself to be a careful scholar when she refused to generalize reducing the dark night to one kind of experience. Granting that it is a negative and painful state normally intervening between illumination and union with God, she insisted on the diversity of types of darkness as she had affirmed the diversity of types of illumination, which often depends on the diversity of temperaments: the anguish of the lover who has just lost the beloved, intellectual confusion, the passive purification described by John of the Cross as a state of misery, a total self-abandonment lived in strenuous activity as described by Suso. It can include a sense of sin, the absence of God, dryness, psychic turmoil, feelings of helplessness and distress, desolation, a dark rapture which concentrates painfully upon the divine absence. This stage purifies the will to abandon its individualistic standpoint. It is a mystic death (*Mysticism*, 380-412).

Underhill began her study of the unitive life claiming that the goal of the mystic way is union with God. From the viewpoint of a psychologist of mysticism, she also claimed that it represents the final form of consciousness: a union of the *anima* and the *animus*. She described the unitive life in metaphors suitable to different kinds of mystics: deification for the transcendent-metaphysical mystic and spiritual marriage for the intimate-personal type. One symbol of deification is that of fire filling the universe and setting deified people ablaze, as described by Mechtild of Magdeburg, Catherine of Siena, Boehme, and Dante, among others. Another symbol of deification is being in the ocean of God's love, as described by Ruysbroeck and Suso. The spiritual marriage is a metaphor for union that issues in divine fecundity, a heroic and apostolic life. Underhill did not hide her partiality for Ruysbroeck and quoted from him to accentuate the unitive life's double movement of activity and rest. Nor did she fail to report that Catherine of Genoa in her unitive state sang nursery rhymes to God, becoming like a little child, discovering the transcendent in the homey (*Mysticism*, 413-43).

She developed a healthy skepticism regarding visions and ecstasies and applied her principle that their value lies not only in the fact that they are transient moments of ineffable knowledge of God, but also in their ability to enhance life. She was willing to grant that visions are the suggestions of the unconscious, while not denying the divine influence. She asserted that mysticism is an organic process, refusing to equate mysticism with ecstasies and raptures. She urged defenders of the faith to study carefully the psychological states and abnormal faculties that recur in the history of religion.[10]

Although she called mysticism the science of the real, Underhill knew that mystics' descriptions of their experiences are impressionistic rather than scientific. These descriptions are for her practical, that is, they help us get closer to God not to some philosophical schema. Underhill was very careful not to give a definition of mysticism but to offer a working hypothesis that had changing metaphors. In one place she wrote of mysticism as the science of the real, in another place, as the art of union with the real, later on, as the experience of union with God.[11]

Underhill's originally a-historical approach and her psychological method allowed her to posit the basic unity of all mystical experience, pagan or Christian, Eastern or Western, and to ignore the socio-historical context in which mystics live and write. One of her descriptions of mysticism as an innate feeling about the mystery at the heart of our lives enabled her to disregard what name is given the end of mystic union. She has been criticized for using such idioms as the God of Christianity, the world-soul of pantheism, and the absolute of philosophy as indifferent alternatives. She has been faulted for an anti-intellectual bias in her interpretation of mysticism but I believe she was trying to say that in the true mystic what she called the transcendental consciousness dominates the normal consciousness. Mysticism for her was not only a theory of the intellect or a hunger of the heart but a transformation of the whole self in the interests of the transcendental life. Today we talk more clearly about the human person's orientation to transcendence and to the unifying process of conversion.[12]

Underhill called the mystic a spiritual genius with a power to reveal to others an apprehension of and craving for God, just as the artistic or scientific genius conveys the structure and significance of the physical world. A religious genius grows in understanding and creative power through devoted attention to a reality distinct from self. Religious experience, as opposed to vague spiritual feelings, is marked by a profound sense of something done to it and to be done by it. It contains a surplus of meaning which defies the resources of language. The use of images and symbols conveys contemplative intuition as well as creative intuition. Detachment and recollection are part of poetic and mystical purgation. According to Henri Bremond, the poet can fall short of the mystic's full experience of the real due to the artistic urge toward self-expression. Gerard Manley Hopkins is to be regarded as an authentic man of the Spirit who occasionally wrote poems rather than a mystical poet.[13]

The critical acceptance of mystics' reports must be based on scientific criteria, namely, unity of witness, absence of contradictions, and the power of uniting in one system many facts:

> In their own words, the mystics may transcend reason but they must not contradict it. Neither must they contradict, though they may improve the general religious and moral sense of the group in which they arise. Moreover, the reality disclosed by these experimental theists must in some measure be valid for all (*Man*, 50).

In this way the objectivity of mystics' truth claims can be assessed and judged. Their spiritual peaks must be seen in the context of everyday life. In other words, there is a communal and historical dimension of mysticism, that is, a corporate history, practice, and tradition (*Man*, 82).

Underhill viewed mysticism as a way of life of the whole person, not a series of intellectual advances culminating in an illuminating intuition. There was for her a continuity between the self and God; mysticism is the essence of religion. Her focus was on mysticism as a practice not as a world view.[14]

A Rahnerian Perspective

Since Underhill's works on mysticism were written, countless others have appeared. A scholarly treatment of these books is beyond the scope of this work. Since I am fascinated by the common ground covered by Underhill and Karl Rahner, a German Jesuit mystic and theologian of the twentieth century, I plan here to concentrate on this one approach and then explore their common emphasis on a mysticism of daily life. Evelyn Underhill's study of visions sheds light on the psychology, philosophy, and theology of mysticism. Her contribution can be assessed from the perspective of the mystical theology of Rahner, who also made a study of visions.

For both Underhill and Rahner, mystical experiences are always experiences of faith, hope, and love. The mystics' extraordinary experiences deepen and purify the ordinary life of faith. A key point of Rahner's mystical theology is precisely this connection: "mystical experience is not specifically different from the ordinary life of grace (as such)."[15] For him, mystics in the strict sense differ from mystics in the broad sense in that their experiences are a particular mode of our religious experience according to their psychology and abilities, that is, according to unusual psychological manifestations. In other words, many people have peak experiences but not all are explicitly aware of them. The experience of transcendence involves a forgetting of self for the sake of the other, the surrender to mystery and its acceptance by mystery that is mysticism's goal made historically visible in Jesus' death.[16]

The two agreed on the incarnational structure of Christian mysticism, the fact that God's self-communication is conveyed through a sign like a word, picture, or Christ's humanity, evoking the response of a human act of some sort. Underhill noted that Teresa of Avila saw the humanity of Christ and Ignatius Loyola saw the Trinity in the image of three spinet keys (*Mysticism*, 271-72). Rahner affirmed the possibility of private revelations of God in historical apparitions (*Visions*, 13-17).

In describing the characteristics of mysticism, Underhill was clear that mysticism is active, not theoretical and passive, evoking a response of love (*Mysticism*, 82-90). Rahner added that even in an imageless mystic, there is a participation in Christ's mystical emptying: "this emptying of self will not be accomplished by practising pure inwardness, but by the real activity which is called humility, service, love of our neighbour, the cross and death" (*Visions*, 14, n. 12).

Underhill mentioned that mystics refuse to consider their visionary experiences important and prefer to be timid and self-critical about them (*Mysticism*, 280). Rahner affirmed that we can apprehend God in the sign, but cautioned that we are to focus on the ultimate reality not to cling to the sign: "The sign must be welcomed and passed by, grasped and relinquished" (*Visions*, 14, n. 12).

Both agreed on the classification of visions into three main groups: intellectual, imaginary, and corporeal. Intellectual visions have to do with a definite but indescribable consciousness of God's presence, a pure apprehension of God's presence as in Teresa's vision of Christ at her side. Imaginary visions are interior and distinct. They can take a symbolic or personal form. In the symbolic form, one is shown truth under an image, for example, Mechtild of Hackeborn seeing a virgin with a ring in her hand in the heart of God. In the personal form one does not learn new facts but is convinced of a living presence, for example, Margaret Mary Alacoque's vision of the Sacred Heart. Regarding both forms to be types of passive imaginary visions, Underhill introduced another category which she called active imaginary visions which expressed a change in the self usually after some psychological crisis. Her examples are the visions of Francis of Assisi receiving the stigmata, Catherine of Siena's mystic marriage, and the transverberation of Teresa. The corporeal vision externalizes intuitions, memories, or thoughts, for example, the ring which Catherine of Siena always saw upon her finger though no one else saw it and which was the way the cross appeared to her.[17]

Rahner also classified visions as intellectual, imaginative, and corporeal. While Underhill connected an intellectual vision with an apprehension of either a personality or knowledge, Rahner considered it to be without images. He was convinced that the imaginative vision is the normal case. He would not distinguish symbolic and personal imaginative visions since the visions of the Sacred Heart, for example, are symbolic as well as personal. He developed his theology of devotion to the Sacred Heart in an essay on the theology of the symbol.[18]

Underhill wrote about mystical visions which individuals receive that are to be concealed, and prophetic visions that are to be declared (*Mysticism*, 279). Rahner made the same distinction between mystical visions that concern the person's life with God and spiritual growth and prophetic visions which convey a message to the church of instruction, warning, mandate, or prediction about the future. A prophetic vision contains an imperative for the church in a concrete historical situation. From this perspective, he viewed the visions which Margaret Mary Alacoque claimed to have received to be prophetic because they contained a message for the church recommending devotion to the Sacred Heart (*Visions*, 17, 26-27).

Underhill considered visions and voices to be "the normal if rare methods by which a certain type of intuitive genius actualizes its perceptions of the spiritual world" (*Mysticism*, 267). They accompany the mystic life without being its content. They are automatisms, suggestions already in the mind, that characterize all creative genius. Mystic automatisms are helps to transcendence. She combined her study of the psychology and theology of mysticism when she made the following plea:

> If we would cease, once for all, to regard visions and voices as objective, and be content to see in them forms of symbolic expression, ways in which the subconscious activity of the spiritual self reaches the surface-mind, many of the disharmonies noticeable in visionary experience, which have teased the devout, and delighted the agnostic, would fade away. Visionary experience is--or at least may be--the outward sign of a real experience (*Mysticism*, 271).

Just as artists express themselves in paintings, poems, and musical compositions, visions and voices are the artistic expressions and results of thought, intuition, and direct perception. Just as artistic automatisms affect the artist's work, mystical automatisms transform that mystic's personality (*Mysticism*, 272). The imaginary visions of Blessed Angela of Foligno were vivid artistic reconstructions including symbols of things she had felt and known, such as her conversation with the Holy Spirit on the way to Assisi in which she imagined the Holy Spirit telling her she was loved more than any other in the valley of Spoleto. Her intellectual visions were imageless intuitions of truth, immediate apprehensions of absolute reality. The imaginary visions of Julian of Norwich can be considered the result of unconscious memory whereby she constructed graphic pictures from the artistic and religious conceptions of her youth (*Essentials*, 160-98).

Instead of viewing visions as a form of artistic expression, Rahner approached visions as the overflow of God's self-expression. Visions are the secondary parapsychological phenomena of a spiritual process: "The imaginative vision, which presupposes such infused contemplation, is only the radiation and reflex of contemplation in the sphere of the senses, the incarnation of the mystical process of the spirit."[19] In other words, the imaginative vision expresses infused contemplation but does not substitute for it. From this perspective, one can understand why classic mysticism is indifferent to and critical of imaginative visions, even authentic ones, because God is always greater than any image. It is suspicious of imaginative visions that occur outside the context of the mystical process, which, for Teresa and John of the Cross, meant the stage of mystical betrothal (*Visions*, 61).

Underhill probed the authenticity of visions by asking whether they represent merely the visionary's objectified dreams and fantasies, or whether they represent some force, personality, fact, spiritual power: "Is the vision only a pictured thought, an activity of the dream imagination: or, is it the violent effort of the self to translate something impressed upon its deeper being, some message received from without, which projects this sharp image and places it before the consciousness" (*Mysticism*, 269)? She granted that all visions borrow their shape, not their content, from suggestions already present in the visionary's mind. She was astute to realize that given the active subliminal consciousness and unstable nervous organization of mystics, their visionary experiences are often a mix of authentic and pathological visions (*Mysticism*, 267-71).

In her essay on "The Essentials of Mysticism," 1920, Underhill admitted that she wanted to probe mystical states and revelation in light of current movements and stripped of their monastic dress to ask:

> What elements are due to the suggestions of tradition, to conscious or unconscious symbolism, to the misinterpretation of emotion, to the invasion of cravings from the lower centres, or the disguised fulfilment of an unconscious wish? And when all these channels of illusion have been blocked, what is left (*Essentials*, 2)?

Having established that the essential of mysticism is the consciousness of a living God not our symbols of God, Underhill concluded that very few secondary phenomena are mystical in a technical sense:

> Just as our normal consciousness is more or less at the mercy of invasions
> from the unconscious region, of impulses which we fail to trace to their true
> origin; so too the mystical consciousness is perpetually open to invasion
> from the lower centres (*Essentials*, 19-20).

She included in her examples Catherine of Siena's mystical marriage and
Teresa of Avila's wound of love as lapses to lower levels, incidents
which add nothing to our knowledge of the work of the Spirit, divine
favors which are really disguised satisfactions that fall short of union
with God which is the essence of mysticism (*Essentials*, 19-20).

Rahner distinguished the divine influence in an authentic vision from
the subjectivity of the visionary whereby the content may be prone to
historical inaccuracy, theological error and distortion, or aesthetic bad
taste. Due to these variable factors, he concluded that authentic
imaginative visions are generally only indirectly caused by God. The core
of such visions is infused contemplation. Human subjectivity expresses
itself. For this reason he further concluded that while we may accept the
divine origin of a particular vision, we may not be able to accept its
entire content. Since he did not believe there could be pure, infused,
unmediated contemplation, it seemed to him inevitable that given human
bodiliness, the mystics bring their own interpretation to the experience
of God.[20] It is clear that both had studied carefully and critically the
psychology and theology of mysticism.

Underhill argued that the life-enhancing quality of visions
distinguishes those of real transcendental activity from those due to
imagination, reverie, or mental illness. In "The Authority of Personal
Religious Experience," 1925, she proposed criteria which can be used
in assessing authenticity: consensus of witness which means a
comparison of a message with the church's religious sense, and life-
giving power affecting the whole life into which the message came.
Religious experience cannot be authoritative if it tends to isolate us from
our historical or social background. It must generally emerge from and
be supported by our corporate experience. The religion of the spirit must
correspond with the religion of authority (*Guide*, 119-123).

Second, authentic religious experience has a transforming effect which
may be fed by tradition and environment. Augustine was transformed.
His conversion was mediated through traditional suggestion and an
authentic experience traditionally expressed. His reading of books by
Plato could lead him to an ecstatic gaze but could not sustain that gaze.
His experience of God and selfless life were not based on books.

Conversion leads us to a sense of mission, impelling us to service, quickening love for others. The voice that told Augustine "Take and read" compelled the sacrifice of his career of rhetorician and its transformation into a ministry of proclaiming the Word of God (*Guide*, 123-126).

The authority of personal religious experience is the authority of mystics and saints, an authority of personality not of information, an authority of certitude not of logic in argument. Our experience of God is never received on a *tabula rasa* and so is not discredited by traditional terms of expression. It is distinct but not separate from symbolic formula. Genuine religious experience evokes a response that is life-giving for others (*Mysticism*, 270; *Guide*, 126-31). While Underhill guarded against individualism in underlining the value of the authority of corporate experience, she may have overlooked the witness of prophetic counter-cultural vision.

Rahner proposed some criteria for authentic visions. He considered the following inadequate: piety, personal honesty, bodily and mental health. Infused contemplation and an external miracle authenticate a vision. Criteria of authenticity cannot be established from observing the process of the sensory effects of a vision since similar visionary phenomena can occur in people who are not necessarily under the divine influence. A sounder criterion is an attitude of humility signaling "a decisive transformation, a religious deepening of the person that comes with the experience and endures" (*Visions*, 61). More would need to be said by both to make a just assessment of their reflections on criteria for establishing the authenticity of religious experience.[21]

In *The Mystics of the Church*, 1925, Underhill described mysticism as the direct intuitive experience of God, a life based on conscious communion with God, a life which aims at union with God. It is for her another name for what we call the spiritual life. She claimed that everyone has a capacity for God. She maintained that the mystics have a social meaning for others, supplying the prophetic element of religion. She underscored the importance of the mystics' socio-historical background. She distinguished theocentric mystics who focus on God, from Christocentric mystics who focus on their personal relationship with Christ. Contrary to her former agnostic individualism, she spoke of the communion of saints as the interdependence of all Christians. For her the mystics' personal sense of communion with God differs in degree rather than in kind from the spiritual life of others (*Mystics*, 9-28, 54).

Rahner offered a nuanced view of the term mysticism by stating that each of us is given an unthematic basic experience of being oriented to

God that is so constitutive of who we are as human beings that while it can be repressed it cannot be destroyed. This mystical experience has its climax in what mystical theology calls infused contemplation, that is, the felt presence of God that is sheer gift. From this perspective, he could describe everyone as an anonymous mystic since each of us experiences ourselves in relation to mystery. The ones we call mystics in a technical sense are given this experience with a special depth and intensity. In other words, their experiences differ in degree not in kind from the core experience given to every human person. This difference has to do with the person's sensitivity to God's presence; the mystic is one who is very aware of this.[22]

Both Underhill and Rahner would agree that the experience of grace is possible in non-Christian mysticism. Underhill quoted pagan philosopher mystics and Sufi mystics. Rahner's theory of the anonymous graced one supports this view.[23]

Underhill took for granted that mystical experiences are one all over the world. When she wrote *Mysticism*, Underhill assumed the unity and universality of mystical experience. She held to what is called today the undifferentiated unity of mystical experiences.[24] Karl Rahner, on the other hand, believed in union with a difference, in irreducibly plural forms of mystical experience.[25]

In addition to the common ground that both Evelyn Underhill and Karl Rahner covered regarding visions, there are also similarities in their approach to a mysticism of daily life. Her practical mysticism has much in common with his mysticism of everyday life. Both were convinced that we are called to discover and reveal God in our daily lives. Underhill wrote often of finding the transcendent in the homey details. Rahner wrote often of experiences of grace, of God's self-communication in daily successes and failures. Underhill quoted mystics who had experienced visions and voices, but she quoted their images of God and the world that helped them in their everyday faith. Rahner threw into relief the mysticism we can nourish in our simple, uneventful lives of faith, hope, and love. Underhill described activities in which we can meet God as when baking a cake, tea-time, gardening, and housekeeping. Rahner also touched on aspects of our lives which are themselves graced, such as drinking, eating, seeing, sitting, sleep, and standing.[26]

Underhill experienced many bouts with nervous and physical exhaustion. It is understandable, then, that she wrote often and convincingly about dryness and desolation, advising the cultivation of nonreligious interests, accepting our limits, and trusting that this fatigued state could open us to God. Even though she entered into the aging process of her parents over lunch everyday with them, she did not write about aging or death as such, apart from a letter about her own aging process and the need to let go and let others take over (*Lt*, 340). Rahner, on the other hand, advised old people to start or keep up their social life and hobbies. Being reduced to incapacity may lead us to hand ourselves over to God. He regarded loneliness, disappointment, and the ingratitude of others as experiences of grace. For him the Ignatian mysticism of joy in the world was counterbalanced by a mysticism of selfless service based on surrender to the darkness and to death. Their background in the mystics gave both Underhill and Rahner a deep understanding of the mystical death to self which lets go in order to let God be God. For both the mystics of daily life are those who live the courage of their convictions in fidelity to their conscience, accepting the whole of their lives even in diminishment.[27]

It is interesting to note that just as Underhill stressed personal prayer as an essential aspect of priestly life, Rahner emphasized other points, namely, theology as an indispensable element of pastoral work, the spirituality of a parish and its pastor as the spirituality of a basic community, the loneliness of one's decisions of faith and of one's religious experience, and the common experience of the Spirit as fellowship in faith. For Rahner, a priest of today must be someone who can pray in a personal way, someone who gives poverty a positive emphasis in daily life, and a servant of the faith of others, someone whose love of neighbor and of God has a political dimension.[28]

Underhill's understanding of the Roman Catholic devotion to the Sacred Heart as mediating God incarnate under the symbol of a heart burning with love points to the mystery of God's self-giving. In describing early medieval mystics of the church, Underhill wrote that pictorial visions of Christ and the saints or allegorical revelations were the chief media of spiritual apprehension: "Thus St. Gertrude's vivid sense of the self-giving love of God found expression in the beautiful symbol of the Sacred Heart" (*Mystics*, 79). Karl Rahner's theological reflection on this devotion has gone further and shed light on the human heart as the center of freedom and the place of our surrender to the mystery of God. In the same manner, the heart of Christ is the center of his freedom, the place of his surrender to the mystery of God. As we surrender ourselves in adoration of God and compassion for others, we become women and men of the pierced heart. While Rahner also treated the medieval mystics' understanding of the Sacred Heart, he considered the piercing of the side of Jesus the origin of this devotion.[29]

Underhill's insistence on the incarnational principle of finding the divine in the human marked her as a Christian spiritual guide. Her insistence that we not separate our life and our prayer helped her correspondents to see that their practical life was also spiritual. Hers was not a mysticism of visions but a practical mysticism of sacrificial love. Karl Rahner coined a phrase which captures Underhill's life and prayer: "a mysticism of everyday faith."[30] Her mysticism and theology were based, like his, on the unity of the love of God and the love of neighbor, as we can see in her advice about relating to friends, enemies, and the poor.[31] Her conviction about our mystical awareness of God's presence in our daily life is a way of finding God in all things, an Ignatian theme in Rahner's mysticism. She would have readily agreed with Karl Rahner's prophecy: "The devout Christian of the future will either be a 'mystic,' one who has 'experienced' something, or will cease to be anything at all."[32]

Conclusion

Underhill perceived in her own way that visions remain isolated unless they are integrated into the fabric of one's daily attitudes and choices. In other words, the experience of God touches not only our minds but also our hearts and our wills. Conversion effects not only a change of mind but also a change of heart and a change of will. Andrew Tallon has written about heart-knowledge as affective connaturality:

> The mystical can fail to make an ethical difference if there is no change of heart; this could not be true were the ethical and mystical but operations of head and heart as separate faculties rather than degrees of actualization of one continuum. Affective connaturality applies to both the ethical and mystical because of their deeper unity.[33]

For Underhill, mystics are models of genuine human life. The mystics retain their own uniqueness in their union with God. She was intent on underlining the universality of mystical experience. Some would say she overemphasized the Christian tradition to the exclusion of non-Christian mysticisms. But perhaps that is to assess her work in an anachronistic way, disregarding her pioneering efforts to make mysticism accessible to an English-speaking public.[34]

Underhill encouraged a unitive knowledge of mysticism that was based on a knowledge of the mystic's own experience as well as on a knowledge of its interpretation. She helped to foster a contemporary philosophical understanding of mysticism and laid foundations for further studies in the comparative study of religion.[35]

Underhill observed that prior to purgation, there is a phase of growth that opens us to mystical experience. She called this a new consciousness or awakening. Today, given advances in cognitional theory and epistemology, we can expand her vocabulary to describe our knowledge of the mystery of the human person as a conscious subject with an unrestricted openness to knowing and loving, as conscious intentionality that mediates the world through meaning and feeling, as an embodied spirit that is open to transcendence, and as an existential participant who must act responsibly in the world.[36] Karl Rahner claimed that we are given a pre-mystical consciousness of the original experience which is the mystery of God. In other words, our knowledge and conscious activity is grounded in a pre-apprehension of reality as incomprehensible.[37]

When she wrote *The Mystics of the Church*, Underhill was keenly aware of the context in which a mystic lives and writes. She granted the pluralism of types of religious experience: "It is obvious that since the Reality of God transcends all human conceptions, there is room for many differing types of mystical experience, and all will be incomplete" (*Mystics*, 13). Since the history of mysticism is the history of how many different temperaments react to one reality, it does not put before us "one particular kind of experience or one uniform type of perfection" (*Mystics*, 15). The historical setting of the mystic includes that person's environment as well as religious background and ancestry, "and cannot be understood in isolation from it" (*Mystics*, 17). She distinguished carefully between the message coming from the outside world and the perceptions and memories of the mystic receiving and transmitting the message (*Mystics*, 19). It would seem, then, that at the time she wrote the first edition of *Mysticism*, she believed that all mystical experiences are the same and their descriptions transcend differences. At the time she wrote *The Mystics of the Church*, she may still have believed that all mystical experiences are the same, but she granted that the mystics' descriptions of their experiences reflect cultural and religious diversity.

Underhill recognized the given character of the mystical experience as well as the gradual efforts of living the Christian life in the world. She was more interested in the fruits of mystical experience than in, for example, visions in and of themselves. She distinguished between mystics in a technical sense who are spiritual geniuses touching depths unknown to most and pointing the way, and mystics in a general sense in which we can say that each of us is a mystic because each of us is given a core experience, a desire for God, a taste of God, a touch of God, a word of God.

Suggestions for Prayerful Reflection

Annice Callahan, R.S.C.J.

Consider the diagram below. What would you add, alter, or dispute?
Innermost Circle: Our Core Religious Experience

Each of us is given a core religious experience. We may not know how
to put it into words. We may not even be conscious of it. But all of us are
given a taste of God. We can say that all of us are mystics; that is, each
of us has personally experienced God.

Second Circle: Secondary Parapsychological Phenomena

Some of us are given secondary phenomena that give images to our
experience of God such as visions, locutions, ecstasies, raptures. Notice
that not all of us are given these. Notice also that they are not our core
experience. In the past, we have tended to reserve the term "mystic" for
one who has been given a vision, locution, or ecstasy, like Catherine of
Siena or Teresa of Avila. We put mystics on a pedestal. Today we have
toppled that pedestal by acknowledging the core experience that makes
each of us a mystic.

Third Circle: Our Psycho-socio-cultural-historical Context

Our experience of God is always conditioned both by our psycho-
social history and our particular culture. Mysticism is always in a
context, a particular language. Julian of Norwich lived at the time of the
Black Death with the threat of possible extinction. It rings true that her
message to the people of her day and of our day was: "All shall be well,
and all shall be well, and all manner of thing shall be well." What they
needed most was hope.

Fourth Circle: Expressions of our Religious Experience

Our religious experience also includes our attempts to articulate our
experience of God--when we try to share it with a friend or spiritual
director, when we try to draw it or express it in some other artistic
medium, or when we write it down in a journal or in a book. Julian of
Norwich recorded her visions in what we now call *Showings* or
Revelations of Divine Love. But notice how the third circle and the

second circle and the first circle intersect somehow with this fourth circle. Julian wrote in Middle English. Not many of us can read that. What we read is a translation, in fact, an edition of a translation of *Showings*. Notice how many steps removed we are from Julian's core experience! We need to keep this in mind. Why? Because it means that we need not accept all her visions but we can affirm her core experience. One can read many books about Julian's showings and these are yet another expression of religious experience.

Notice that these circles interface with other circles in a spiral fashion. The themes, content, and imagery of secondary phenomena spring from a person's lived praxis. In their devotional life, medieval Christians focused heavily on the crucifixion. It is not unlikely, then, that Catherine of Siena and Francis of Assisi were given the stigmata, the five wounds of Jesus, hidden from all but themselves. Our core experience is received by us in the context of our socio-historical situation and psychological conditioning. A North American native living in the woodlands experiences God as the great Spirit and the earth as mother. A North American business executive living in Rio de Janeiro may turn to God and yet continue to use technology to exploit the earth.

1. In *Mysticism*, Underhill described mysticism as the science of the real that claims communion with the absolute. How would you put that in your own words?

2. For William James, the characteristics of mysticism are ineffability, noetic quality, transiency, and passivity. For Evelyn Underhill, mysticism is a practical and active life process, a spiritual activity the object of which is love, and the benefit of which is the development of the whole person. Can you think of other characteristics of mysticism?

3. Tradition has described the stages of growth in our relationship with God as purgation, illumination, union. Evelyn Underhill discovered five stages of the mystic way: awakening, discipline, enlightenment, self-surrender, and union. Can you think of others? Are they stages or phases for you?

4. Underhill described the mystics' personal and impersonal symbols of God such as the lover, the ocean of being, the bridegroom and the abyss. What is your symbol for God at this time in your life?

5 Underhill discussed three symbols of our search for and union with God--the mystic quest, the spiritual marriage, and the new birth. What is the metaphor of your religious experience?

6. How would you distinguish the dark night, depression, and dryness?

Readings

For her 1920 study of various mystics, see Evelyn Underhill, *The Essentials of Mysticism and Other Essays* (New York: E.P. Dutton & Co., 1960). For her 1925 study of the mystics, see Evelyn Underhill, *The Mystics of the Church* (Harrisburg, Pa.: Morehouse, 1997).

Notes

1. See Horton Davies, *Worship and Theology in England 1900-1965*, Vol. 5 (Princeton: Princeton University Press, 1965), 134-50. For the influence of her books on mysticism on Alan Watts, see John W. Donohue, "Two in Search of the Spirit," *America* 135 (August 7, 1976): 52-53.

2. D. Greene, "Evelyn Underhill," Paper presented at King's College, London, June 15, 1991, 8. On Underhill's insistence on the practical value of mysticism, see review of *Mysticism*, *The New York Times Review of Books* 16 (July 30, 1911), DGC; and R.O.P. Taylor, review of 12th edition of *Mysticism*, *Theology* (February 1931), DGC.

3. E. Underhill, *Mysticism*, 81-94, 331. Cf. William James, *Varieties of Religious Experience* (New York: Collier, 1968), 292-94; and Harvey D. Egan, *Christian Mysticism: The Future of a Tradition* (New York: Pueblo, 1984), 7-11.

4. E. Underhill, *Mysticism*, 3-43; and "Bergson and the Mystics," in *Guide to the Holy*, 49-60, published a year after *Mysticism*. Bergson believed that the whole of *reality* is a becoming animated by a vital impulse of life, the *élan vital*. See Henri Bergson, *Essai sur les données immédiates de la conscience* (Paris: Alcan, 1889), and *Les Deux Sources de la morale et de la religion* (Geneva: Editions Albert Skira, 1945). Cf. I.M. Bocheński, "Philosophy of Life: Henri Bergson," in *Contemporary European Philosophy* (Berkeley: University of California Press, 1964), 102-113.

On her use of the term "critical realism," see *Fragments*, 28, for its correspondence with von Hügel's intellectual approach to the twofold reality of sense and spirit according to which the finite is sacramental of the infinite. For a contemporary understanding of the term in cognitional theory, see Appendix: A Note on Critical Realism.

5. See E. Underhill, *Mysticism*, 44-69. On the difference between psycho-analysis and moral theology, see E. Underhill, "The Physician of Souls," review of *Absolution* by E. Boyd Barrett, *The Spectator*, 1 October 1932, 412, DGC.

6. E. Underhill, *Mysticism*, 95-124. Underhill wrote that Ruysbroeck and Tauler emphasized divine immanence, John of the Cross divine transcendence. Catherine of Siena and Julian of Norwich, Dionysius the Areopagite, and Meister Eckhart acknowledged both God's transcendence and immanence. See *Mysticism*, 97-102.

7. See also E. Underhill, "Two Books on Dante," critical review of *New Light on the Youth of Dante* by Gertrude Leigh, and *Symbolism in Mediaeval Thought and its Consummation in the divine Comedy* by Helen Flanders Dunbar, *The Spectator*, 1 February 1930, 167-68, DGC; and "Men and Books," review of English translation of *Dante's Purgatorio* by Laurence Binyon, *Time and Tide* (October 29, 1938): 1494, DGC.

8. E. Underhill, *Mysticism*, 125-64; and "A Defence of Magic, " *Fortnightly Review* (Nov. 1907): 754-76, and *Putnam's*, 3 (November 1907): 177-85, reprinted in *Guide to the Holy*, 33-46.

9. See E. Underhill, *Mysticism*, 270-71, nn. 2,3,4; 272-73, n. 2; 274-75; idem, "Spanish Mysticism," review of *Studies of the Spanish Mystics* by E. Allison Peers, *The Spectator*, 5 February 1927, 194, DGC.

10. See E. Underhill, " Men and Books," review of *Prophecy and Divination: a Study of Man's Intercourse with the Unseen World* by Alfred Guillaume, in *Time and Tide* (November 26, 1938): 1664, 1666, DGC.

11. On the symbolic nature of mysticism, see E. Underhill, "Men and Books," review of *Symbolism and Belief: Gifford Lectures* by Edwyn Bevan, *Time and Tide* (August 27, 1938): 1202-3, DGC.

12. See E. Herman, Introduction, *The Meaning and Value of Mysticism* (London: James Clark, 1915), esp. 6-29, 98-99, 248-91.
    On her ignoring the historical settings of the mystics, see Herman, 7.
    On his criticism of Underhill's hypothesis about a special mystical faculty and her seeming identification of it with emotion, intellect, and will raised to their highest potency, see Herman, 23-29. Cf. *Mysticism*, 58-69, 75, 87.
    On his misunderstanding of her choice not to differentiate various ways of describing the end of mystic union, that is, the God of Christianity, the world-soul of pantheism, and the absolute of philosophy, see Herman 98. Cf. *Mysticism*, x.
    On his critique of Underhill's seemingly anti-intellectual interpretation of mysticism, see Herman 244-251, 278-279, 288-291. On Underhill's insistence that mysticism is not only knowledge but a life transformation of the whole self, see *Way*, 8, 64, 85 ff.

13. See E. Underhill, *Man*, 22, 24-25, 30, 32; "Poet and Mystic," review of *Prayer and Poetry* by Henri Bremond, *The Spectator*, 21 January 1928, 86-87, DGC; "Men and Books," review of *Further Letters of Gerard Manley Hopkins* edited by C.C. Abbott, *Time and Tide* (May 21, 1938): 721-22, DGC. On Bremond, see also E. Underhill, "A Historian of the Soul," review of an English translation of Vol. 1 of *A Literary History of Religious Thought to France from*

the Wars of Religion down to our own Times by Henri Bremond, *The Spectator*, 22 December 1928, 963, DGC; and "Types of Holiness," including a review of *L'Abbé Tempète: Armande de Rance* by Henri Bremond, *The Spectator*, 1 June 1929, 865, DGC. Cf. Annice Callahan, "Creative Intuition and Contemplative Intuition," *RSCJ: A Journal of Reflection* 2, no. 2 (1980): 77-88.

14. See Margaret Lewis Furse, "Mysticism: Classic Modern Interpreters and Their Premise of Continuity," *Anglican Theological Review* 60, no. 2 (April 1978): 180-93; and *Mysticism: Window on a World View* (Nashville, Tenn.: Abingdon Press, 1977), 157 ff.

15. K. Rahner, "Mysticism," *Encyclopedia of Theology* (New York: Seabury, 1975), 1010-1011.

16. See K. Rahner, "The Logic of Concrete Individual Knowledge in Ignatius Loyola," *The Dynamic Element in the Church*, trans. W. J. O'Hara (New York: Herder and Herder, 1964), 126-147. Cf. Abraham H. Maslow, *Religions, Values, and Peak-Experiences* (New York: Viking Press, 1970), 22, 86, 88-90.

17. E. Underhill, *Mysticism*, 281-93. On the difficulty of distinguishing the psychological mechanism of imaginative visions from that of pseudo-hallucinations, see Joseph Maréchal, *Studies in the Psychology of the Mystics*, trans. Algar Thorold (London: Burns Oates & Washbourne, Ltd., 1927), 168-70.

18. See K. Rahner, *Visions*, 31-47. See also earlier versions of this book in K. Rahner, "Ueber Visionen und verwandte Erscheinungen," *ZAM* 21 (1948): 179-213, and "Les Révélations Privées: Quelques Remarques Théologiques," *RAM* 25 (1949): 506-514. Cf. H.D. Egan, *Christian Mysticism: The Future of a Tradition* (New York: Pueblo, 1984), 307-9.

　　　See also K. Rahner, "The Theology of the Symbol," *TI* 4:221-52. Cf. Annice Callahan, *Karl Rahner's Spirituality of the Pierced Heart* (Lanham, Md.: University Press of America, 1985); and "Karl Rahner (1904-1984): Theologian of Everyday Christian Life," *Spiritual Guides for Today* (New York: Crossroad, 1992), 61-78.

19. K. Rahner, *Visions*, 57. In *Visions*, 101, he defined parapsychological as "natural, though extraordinary, mental phenomena."

20. K. Rahner, *Visions*, 55-75. By infused contemplation as opposed to acquired contemplation, Rahner meant what the Spanish mystics described as infused contemplation, that is, the full mystical union, from the "spiritual betrothal" to "the spiritual marriage," which is the sheer gift of God's self-communication that cannot be demanded or earned. See *Visions*, 57.

21. On criteria for establishing the authenticity of religious experience, see, for example, Richard Bergeron, "Towards a Theological Interpretation of the New Religions," *Concilium: New Religious Movements,* eds. John Coleman and Gregory Baum, Vol. 161 (New York: Seabury, 1983): 74-80; Michael J. Buckley, "The Structure of the Rules for Discernment of Spirits," *The Way Supplement* 20 (August 1973): 19-37; Michael Downey, "Understanding Christian Spirituality: Dress Rehearsal for a Method," *Spirituality Today* 43 (1991): 271-280; Edward Kinerk, "Toward a Method for the Study of Spirituality," *Review for Religious* 40 (1981): 3-19; Christopher O'Donnell, "Neo-Pentecostalism in North America and Europe," *Concilium: New Religious Movements,* 35-41; Walter Principe, "Pluralism in Christian Spirituality," *The Way* 32, no. 1 (January 1992): 54-61.

22. See K. Rahner, *Opportunities for Faith,* trans. Edward Quinn (New York: Seabury, 1970), 125; and "Reflections on the Problem of the Gradual Ascent to Christian Perfection," *TI* 3: 3-23; "The Ignatian Mysticism of Joy in the World," *TI,* 3, 280-81; and "Mystical Experience and Mystical Theology," *TI* 17, 90-99. Cf. Harvey D. Egan, " 'The Devout Christian of the Future Will . . . Be a "Mystic." ' Mysticism and Karl Rahner's Theology," *Theology and Discovery: Essays in Honor of Karl Rahner, S.J.,* ed. William J. Kelly (Milwaukee: Marquette University Press, 1980), 139-58,esp. 148-49. On the universal vocation to mysticism, see William Johnston, *Christian Mysticism Today* (San Francisco: Harper & Row, 1984), 40-41.

23. See K. Rahner, "Mystical Experience and Mystical Theology," *TI* 17: 95. I first heard Professor Rahner use the phrase "anonymous graced one" instead of "anonymous Christian" in a private interview in Innsbruck, Austria, on February 25, 1982. On tape.

24. On the argument in favor of the unity and universality of mystical experience, see Aldous Huxley, *The Perennial Philosophy* (New York: Harper & Bros., 1945); Huston Smith, "Is There a Perennial Philosophy?" *Journal of the American Academy of Religion* 55 (1987): 553-565; Walter T. Stace, *The Teachings of the Mystics* (New York: New American Library, 1960) and *Mysticism and Philosophy* (New York: Macmillan, 1960). Cf. H.D. Egan, *What Are They Saying about Mysticism?,* 14-18, 32.

25. On plural types of mystical experience, see R.C. Zaehner, *Mysticism Sacred and Profane* (Oxford: Clarendon Press, 1957), and *Concordant Discord: The Interdependence of the Faiths* (Oxford: Clarendon Press, 1970); and Ninian Smart, "Interpretation and Mystical Experience," *Religious Studies* 1, no. 1 (1965): 75-87; and "Understanding Religious Experience," *Mysticism and Philosophical Analysis,* ed. Steven T. Katz (New York: Oxford University Press, 1978), 10-21. Cf. William Lloyd Newell, *Struggle and Submission: R.C. Zaehner on Mysticisms* (Washington, D.C.: University Press of America, 1981);

Frits Staal, *Exploring Mysticism: A Methodological Essay* (Berkeley: University of California Press, 1975); and H.D. Egan, *What Are They Saying about Mysticism?*, 32-39. Cf. H.D. Egan, *What Are They Saying about Mysticism?*, 6-18, 32-50.

On the influence of texts, ontologies, and models, see Steven T. Katz, "Language, Epistemology, and Mysticism," in *Mysticism and Philosophical Analysis*, ed. Steven T. Katz (New York: Oxford University Press, 1978), 22-74; "The Conservative Character of Mystical Experience," *Mysticism and Religious Traditions*, ed. S.T. Katz (New York: Oxford University Press, 1983), 3-60; and "Mystical Speech and Mystical Meaning," *Mysticism and Language*, ed. Steven T. Katz (New York: Oxford University Press, 1992), 3-41.

For a critique of Katz's cognitional theory and approach, see James R. Price, "The Objectivity of Mystical Truth Claims," *Thought* 49 (January 1985): 81-98; "Lonergan and the Foundation of a Contemporary Mystical Theology," *Lonergan Workshop*, Vol. 5, ed. Fred Lawrence (Chico, Calif.: Scholars Press, 1985), 163-195; and "Typologies and Cross-Cultural Analysis of Mysticism: A Critique," in *Religion and Culture: Essays in Honor of Bernard Lonergan*, ed. T. Fallon and B. Riley (Albany: State University of New York Press, 1987), 181-90, esp. 182-83. Cf. Cf. D. Granfield, *Heightened Consciousness*, 41-55; and Bernard McGinn, *The Foundations of Mysticism*, Vol. 1 of The Presence of God: A History of Western Christian Mysticism (New York: Crossroad, 1991), 275. For other criticisms of Katz' approach, see Anthony N. Perovich, "Mysticism and the Philosophy of Science," *Journal of Religion* 65 (1985): 63-82, esp. 71; and Wayne Proudfoot, *Religious Experience* (Berkeley: University of California Press, 1985), 124-36.

Underhill would have welcomed today's plethora of books on mysticism which promote ecumenical and interreligious dialogue, such as *Mystical Union and Monotheistic Faith: An Ecumenical Dialogue*, ed. Moshe Idel and Bernard McGinn (New York: Macmillan, 1989).

26. See K. Rahner, *Belief Today*, trans. Ray and Rosaleen Ockenden (New York: Sheed, 1967), 13-43;"The Ignatian Mysticism of Joy in the World," *TI* 3: 277-93; "On the Theology of Worship" *TI*, 19: 147; and "Eternity from Time," *TI* 19: 169-77. Cf. Harvey D. Egan, "The Mysticism of Everyday Life," *Studies in Formative Spirituality* 10/1 (February 1989): 7-26; and "Karl Rahner: Theologian of the *Spiritual Exercises*," *Thought* 67 (September 1992): 257-69.

27. See *Karl Rahner--I Remember: An Interview with Meinold Krauss*, tr. Harvey D. Egan (New York: Crossroad, 1985), 101-6; and *Karl Rahner in Dialogue: Conversations and Interviews, 1965-1982*, ed. Paul Imhof and Hubert Biallowons, tr. ed. Harvey D. Egan (New York: Crossroad, 1986), 90, 241-47; K. Rahner, *Biblical Homilies*, trans. Desmond Forristal and Richard Strachan (New York: Herder, 1966), 77. Cf. H.D. Egan, "Rahner: Theologian of the *Exercises*," *Thought* 67, no. 266 (Sept. 1992): 262-64.

28. See K. Rahner, "Priestly Existence," *TI* 3: 239-62; "Part Two: Priesthood," *TI* 19: 55-138.

29. See K. Rahner, "The Eternal Significance of the Humanity of Jesus for our Relationship with God," *TI* 3: 35-46; "'Behold This Heart!': Preliminaries to a Theology of Devotion to the Sacred Heart," *TI* 3:321-30; "Some Theses for a Theology of Devotion to the Sacred Heart," *TI* 3:331-52; and "The Man with the Pierced Heart," *Servants of the Lord*, trans. Richard Strachan (New York: Herder & Herder, 1968), 107-19.

Cf. A. Callahan, *Karl Rahner's Spirituality of the Pierced Heart: A Reinterpretation of Devotion to the Sacred Heart* (Lanham, Md.: University Press of America, 1985), esp. Chapter One, 37, 46-48, 75-77, 90-100; *Spiritual Guides for Today* (New York: Crossroad, 1992), 66; and "The Visions of Margaret Mary Alacoque from a Rahnerian Perspective," *Modern Christian Spirituality: Methodological and Historical Essays*, ed. Bradley Hanson (Atlanta, Ga.: Scholars Press, 1990), 183-200; and Donald Gelpi, "Karl Rahner's Theology of Devotion to the Sacred Heart," *Woodstock Letters* 95 (1966): 405-17.

30. See Karl Rahner, *Everyday Faith*, trans. W.J. O'Hara (New York: Herder and Herder, 1968). Cf. Harvey D. Egan, "The Mysticism of Everyday Life," *Studies in Formative Spirituality* 10/1 (February 1989): 7-26; and Edward Carter, *The Mysticism of Everyday* (Kansas City: Sheed & Ward, 1991).

31. See K. Rahner, "Reflections on the Unity of the Love of Neighbor and the Love of God," *TI* 6: 231-49; and *The Love of Jesus and the Love of Neighbor*, trans. Robert Barr (New York: Crossroad, 1983).

32. K. Rahner, "Christian Living Formerly and Today," TI 7, 15. See K. Rahner, "Spirituality of the Secular Priest," *TI* 19, 115; and "The Spirituality of the Church of the Future," *TI* 20, 149. Cf. Harvey D. Egan, " 'The Devout Christian of the Future Will . . . Be a "Mystic." ' Mysticism and Karl Rahner's Theology," *Theology and Discovery: Essays in Honor of Karl Rahner, S.J.*, ed. William J. Kelly (Milwaukee: Marquette University Press, 1980), 139-58.1

33. Andrew Tallon, "The Heart in Rahner's Philosophy of Mysticism," *Theological Studies* 53 (1992): 708.

34. See Harvey D. Egan, "Chapter Four: Mysticism as a Way of Life I. Evelyn Underhill," *What Are They Saying about Mysticism?*, 40-50. Cf. Jean M. Bartunek and Michael K. Moch, "Third-Order Organizational Change and the Western Mystical Tradition," *Journal of Organizational Change Management* 7/1 (1994): 24-41, which describes mystical experience as a model for developing third-order change capacity in organizations, using Teresa of Avil . as

the model of a mystic as change agent.

35. See, for example, E. Underhill, "The Alpine Spirit," review of *The Zermatt Dialogues: constituting the outlines of a Philosophy of Mysticism* by Douglas Fawcett, *The Spectator*, 16 January 1932, 87-88, DGC. Cf. Richard Woods, ed., *Understanding Mysticism* (Garden City, N.Y.: Doubleday, Image, 1980), 1-15, esp. 2, 3, 11, and 13.

 In emphasizing that mysticism and mystical theology are distinct and not separate, Bernard McGinn quoted Underhill who distinguished between mystics who taste religious experience and mystical philosophers who analyze the data of religious experience, granting that mystics are mystical philosophers but not all mystical philosophers are mystics. He viewed her familiarity with the mystics and freedom from Inge's prejudices as advantages. According to him, the drawbacks of *Mysticism* are her florid prose, a looseness in her mode of argument, an identification of mysticism with the core of religion, her position about a transcultural and transreligious unity to the stages of the mystic path, and her lack of sympathy with certain more speculative forms of mysticism. See E. Underhill, *Mysticism*, 83, 95; and Bernard McGinn, *The Foundations of Mysticism: Origins to the Fifth Century*, Vol. 1 of The Presence of God: A History of Western Christian Mysticism (New York: Crossroad, 1991), xiii, 273-75.

36. See Bernard J.F. Lonergan, *Method in Theology*, 2nd ed. (Toronto: University of Toronto Press, 1990), 8; and "The Subject," *A Second Collection*, ed. William F.J. Ryan and Bernard J. Tyrrell (Philadelphia: Weminster, 1974), 69-86. Cf. David Granfield, *Heightened Consciousness: The Mystical Difference* (New York: Paulist, 1991), 5-28.

37. See K. Rahner, *Foundations of Christian Faith*, trans. William V. Dych (New York: Seabury, 1978), 33.

 Bernard Lonergan asserted that our conscious intentionality is fulfilled by being in love with God; mystical experience is an intensified and differentiated experience of that state of being in love with God. B. Lonergan, *Method*, 106. Cf. Granfield, *Heightened Consciousness*, 29-41; and Harvey D. Egan, *What Are They Saying about Mysticism?*, 98-116.

Chapter 8

Spiritual Guidance

This chapter describes Evelyn Underhill's ministry of spiritual guidance. The examples of her spiritual mentoring are drawn from her letters, the retreats she conducted, and her other works on the spiritual life, such as her reflections on education, as indicated below. The discussion of her retreats as a form of spiritual mentoring indicates the influence of Ignatian spirituality on her own.

Evelyn Underhill was an excellent listener and did accompany those with whom she walked in their spiritual journey. She did more than that. She helped them sort out a viable devotional program, encouraged them to balance their spiritual lives with other interests, brought her study of mysticism to bear on their problems and difficulties in helpful and sometimes humorous ways, and proclaimed the good news of God's presence in an idiom with which they could readily identify in their own practical lives.

A Spiritual Mentor

One can claim that Underhill's spiritual mentoring reflected the dynamics of conversion. In *The Life of the Spirit and the Life of Today*, she wrote about our need for conversion as the need for the remaking of the instinctive life, a need for sublimation and transformation. Her second classic, *Worship*, underlined the formative and transformative power of worship. In *The Spiritual Life*, Underhill wrote explicitly about conversion as a change of heart. In "The Authority of Personal Religious Experience," she affirmed that conversion leads to a sense of mission, impelling us to service, and quickening love for others. She was convinced that conversions are gradually accomplished. Her conviction was that Augustine did not experience a miraculous conversion but the struggles of a genius thirsting for reality to harmonize belief with appropriate action, the platonic worldview with a Judeo-Christian way of life.[1]

Underhill's call to affective conversion marked her as an outstanding spiritual director. She was very conscious that conversion is a human experience, that God acts with, not in spite of our selfishness, and that conversion is a lifelong process including the integration and acceptance of our gifts and limits, strengths and weaknesses, desires and disordered affections.[2]

Another of her strengths as a spiritual guide was her knowledge of the mystical tradition. She was interested in the mystics' lives and writings not for information but only for formation, formation of the heart. At one point, they were her first spiritual guides. She continued to mediate their wisdom to others in appealing ways.

Letters

As a figure of authority within the Church of England, she helped to shape English spirituality. One must bear in mind that authority in religious circles of her day was predominantly male, clerical, and institutional. As Terry Tastard has observed:

> The authority associated with Underhill is very different. As a woman and layperson, she had to find another way of being recognized. Feeling her way forward, she had to rely on a combination of scholarship, integrity, and a responsiveness to where God might be leading her. It was who she was rather than the office she held which compelled recognition and acceptance. It enabled her to outflank the formidable prohibitions against women teaching in the Church.[3]

One of the ways she taught as a churchwoman was through her letters of spiritual direction. Here she synthesized not only all that the mystics had taught her, but also all that her own religious experience had taught her. Her own ability to trust her experience and capacity for discerning God within the individual freed her to empower others to do likewise"

> Her belief in each person's spiritual capacity gave her that fundamental prerequisite for spiritual directors, an attentive respect for each person's experience of God within the circumstances of their life. Applied to herself, it gave her confidence in God's work in her own

life, calling her forward into prominence in roles which the churches
had regarded as male preserves.[4]
Her capacity for discernment led her to move from the individual level
to the social level in her pacifist position from which she challenged the
church to counter violence with peace.

In her letters we can also see Evelyn Underhill as an adept spiritual
mentor.[5] Her advice revealed her capacity for compassion and
encouragement, her ability to adapt principles to particular situations,
and her sense of the uniqueness of the individual. She did not lay down
rules and regulations. Instead, she took a person where she was and
helped her settle on a few key aspects of a devotional program
appropriate to her way of life. She did not try to be an overbearing
spiritual guru and abhorred that idea greatly (*Lt*, 61). Instead she was
open to becoming a soul-friend who shared another's spiritual journey as
one who walked beside her not ahead of her. Perhaps it was her own
proneness to being in a muddle now and then that gave her the humility
to accept her ministry of spiritual mentoring as a sheer gift rather than an
achievement. She acknowledged the needs of the whole person for
nourishment, advising rest when the body and psyche were
overstimulated, quiet when the mind could let go of thinking and the will
could let go in surrender, spiritual reading of the mystics not so much as
food for prayer as guidance in Christian living, friendship with the poor
as a way of engaging the emotions in an appropriate focus. As a spiritual
mentor, Underhill's focus was on integration between the human and the
divine, between the limitations of our psychophysical condition and our
spiritual aspirations, between an individual's unique way to God and
tradition's witness to the mystic way. She put surrendered self-giving at
the heart of the spiritual life whether it be in the form of surrender to God
in prayer, surrender to our bodily and psychic limits, surrender to others
in service, surrender to the dark, or surrender to dryness. For her peace
had more to do with willed abandonment than any feeling of contentment
(*Lt*, 64, 90, 204, 247, 304).

Her style in spiritual direction was an unobtrusive and unpretentious
sharing of what had been helpful to her, inviting the directee to trust her
own experience and take what advice is pertinent. She was neither
overbearing nor "preachy." Being a shy person herself, Underhill waited
patiently for a person to open up to her. She did not push, she did not pry
(*Lt*, 71, 164).

Her support of a minimal but regular devotional program including
the disciplines of prayer, communal worship, service, and friendship with

the poor, showed her balance as a director. For her, meditation was not thinking about a pious subject but letting God become the center of life and thought. Intercessory prayer and action flow from and feed contemplative prayer in her view. Her study of the mystics had convinced her that the mystic way includes a purgation not only in one's life of formal prayer but also in one's daily life of service to others. Her fear of pseudocontemplatives helped ground her in the rugged routine of responding to people's needs, in particular, those of the poor. She believed that faith is active in sacrificial love. Her study of mysticism and her own years without church attendance had convinced her of the balance that institutional, sacramental religion can provide by providing a life of communal worship and an atmosphere of shared faith. Adoration, in fact, was more important to her than mortification: the focus was on God (*Lt*, 70-72, 81, 149, 244-45).

On the subject of dryness and desolation, Underhill waxed eloquent as a spiritual mentor, probably from her own frequent experiences of nervous exhaustion. She had learned to value the strength of formal prayer rather than the length thereof. When fatigue set in, she recommended a change of diet from the living waters of the prayer of quiet and a spiritual classic to hot milk and a foolish novel. She had also learned the wholesome balance which our broader interests can give to our life of prayer. She knew personally how self-analysis can block prayer. At such times she urged that a person stop praying, talk to someone, and get involved in an activity that will hold the attention. The avoidance of strain was a hallmark of her plea for peacemaking with oneself and with God (*Lt*, 201, 207, 313-14, 318).

Underhill was a woman of God and a woman of the church. Her spiritual mentoring reinforced a person's commitment to church attendance and participation. As well, it recognized the intercessory value of the communion of saints, that is, ourselves as active members of the household of the faith. She had come to see that sacramental religion can have an enriching and steadying effect on our devotional lives, and passed on her insight. As an antidote to individualism, she invited her directees to take an interest in the tiny details of others' lives, no matter how mundane. As another dimension of intercession, she perceived that our surrendered self-giving, especially in the dark night and in dryness, are part of Christ's self-giving, a share in his redemptive work, a participation in the church's prayer for the world (*Lt*, 83-84, 96-97, 165-66, 293, 326).

Underhill's love of beauty and of nature led her to advise others to let their senses be transformed not repressed by detachment. For centuries spiritual traditions had taught mortification through detachment. In this regard, adoration of God in creatures was a higher value for her than mortification. And on this point, she was a bridge to our postmodern sense of being one with all creation *(Lt,* 78).

She urged her directees to see the creative and redemptive aspects not only of our spiritual life but also of our work in the world. For her communion with God was of a piece with the unspiritual aspects of practical life. She believed that surrender is the principle of unity: our abandonment to providence is not only a pious feeling that makes us feel safe and secure in prayer; it is a courageous risk to trust God in all the pleasant and painful things that happen to us. The peace we taste in prayer is an atmosphere in which we are to perform our duties of the day. In this perspective, ordinary life is the medium of God's self-revelation. She urged her directees to integrate life and prayer. For her, life is one: our spiritual life and our practical life are one. For her, our practical life is spiritual. Her advice for living the spiritual life in the world was to live the whole of our life with God *(Lt,* 152-55, 179, 217).

Her advice as a spiritual mentor about avoiding self-preoccupation by focusing on God does not seem to honor the psychological growth steps of the spiritual journey. She wrote to one directee that in all we do, think, or pray about, we are to throw the whole emphasis on God, God's work, God's call, God's creating us moment by moment, and our whole purpose in life as being to praise, reverence, and serve God (9/23/1929, *Lt,* 187). This is not entirely possible or even desirable before one has grown enough in a sense of self and self-esteem and self-worth. It can short-circuit some valuable inner work of self-affirmation.

It is remarkable how much Underhill was able to convey through the written word. Many of her letters of correspondence are letters of spiritual direction. She was able to read between the lines and respond to the person's heart, not only to what was written.

Retreats

Underhill showed herself to be a gifted retreat leader as well as a guide, capable of helping people in their spiritual journey. She was persuaded that real prayer depends on our response to God's action and invitation in our daily lives, not upon all our fussing about our times of prayer, its content, or method *(Ways,* 224-25). In this I believe she spoke with real wisdom.

In her letters Underhill wrote often about dryness and gave practical advice for accepting it. She capsulized her doctrine on dryness in *Concerning the Inner Life* where she counseled prudent awareness of our bodies and our psyches to the Anglican priests attending a clergy conference. She called it, in fact, a psychological condition, a fatigue state, an intensity of desolation, a state of spiritual exhaustion which normally follows upon a time of spiritual progress. Rather than focusing on it or trying to fight it, we are to use every human means possible to rest and relax, diverting our attention to some nondevotional interest. Her balance, sensitivity, and common sense marked her as an apt spiritual director who would help people live peacefully rather than on the heights or in the depths of their own musings (*House*, 130). A contemporary Anglican priest who directs a retreat center in North America keeps rediscovering the gift of balance which reflective, recreative rest can give us. She has written: "God graces us with rest; and, as we respond with our gratitude, receiving the gift, we begin to enter into that balanced life which is our destiny as the people of a loving Creator."[6]

Evelyn Underhill developed her own original and womanly style of preaching a retreat. Although she demonstrated her familiarity with the Spiritual Exercises of Ignatius Loyola, she felt no need to imitate him. The closest she came to integrating her insights with his was in *Light of Christ*. The impetus of his apostolic spirituality was an inspiration for her own. For example, she resisted a quietistic, passive idealism in favor of a collaborative realism:

> To rest in the Lord does not mean sinking into the devotional cushion
> and putting the tail over the nose: it means the restful harmony of a
> ship that has found herself, in which all parts work together in perfect,
> selfless collaboration under the Captain's will (*Mount*, 74).

This is a reflection of Ignatius' view of the contemplative in action, not avoiding God's purpose but cooperating with the divine initiative. Another instance where an apostolic spirituality helped her focus was when she suggested that the question for committed Christians is not "What is best for my soul?" but "Where has Christ put me and what does he want me to do?" (*Mount*, 76)? Once again we are invited to be centered and sent by Christ to serve others wholeheartedly. A sense that our ministry is no longer right for us, however, may prompt us to search elsewhere. A third way in which Underhill reflects the influence of Ignatius is her description of what it means to find God in all things: "I can and should find all things in God and God in all things. *Things*--the gas-stove and the typewriter, the tube and the bus, streets and shops and all they contain" (*Mount*, 76).

A fourth example of the Ignatian influence on her spirituality is her emphasis on a service mysticism rather than a bridal mysticism: "Practical life is for most of us our school of divine service" (*Mount*, 78). Drawing on the analogy of working in God's kitchen as fellow-workers who have zest, she added tongue-in-cheek: "We must not play with the flour, help ourselves to the sultanas and leave the job half-finished if we get tired" (*Mount*, 79). A fifth indication of Ignatian spirituality in her writings is her description of meditation as a way of contemplating a mystery in the life of Jesus, entering into the scene by watching and listening, and letting it enter into our lives by talking about it with God (*Mount*, 85-86).

A sixth way she incorporated the Ignatian tradition into her own spirituality was her appreciation for and reliance on de Caussade's simple but soul-searching doctrine of abandonment to divine providence in our outer and inner experience which seeks and finds God in the sacrament of the present moment. Like him, she was convinced that the divine action penetrates the entire universe. Like him, she brought her common sense to bear on the problems of the interior life.[7]

Her method of taking a theme and developing it from several points of view was in reality her method of what she called meditation, turning a phrase, truth, or event over and over like fingering a precious possession, seeing it from many points of view as she had described it (*Lt*, 73, 127). It is a method of contemplative prayer which enabled her to contemplate in faith the reality of life as she experienced it. It can also be used as a way of contemplating a Scripture passage.[8]

Underhill ran a house. Her use of the metaphor of the house of the soul was appropriate since it rang true to her experience of her own life. It rang true when she said: "We are not washed and ironed in order to be put in the spiritual linen-cupboard but in order to live a new life" (*Mount*, 75).

Another way she approached a topic for one of her retreats was to take a theme she had been researching and praying over in another context. At the time she wrote her second classic called *Worship*, 1937, she preached a 1935 retreat later published as *The Mystery of Sacrifice*, 1938. In this way, she stayed with what was real and uppermost in her mind and integrated it with her heart.

Underhill revealed herself as a seasoned spiritual director when she insisted that the indwelling Spirit can act through image and form, whether adequate or inadequate. A hymn annoying to an intellectual can lead another person to adoration. Hearts can be softened watching crude

religious art. The sick person looking long and hard at a badly built
crucifix can experience the Spirit in a way that is not possible for those
whose taste forbids them to gaze. Holy people often foster outdated
devotions (*Golden*, 42-43). Today when we live in an era marked by
biblical and liturgical spirituality, we may raise our eyebrows to see a
pious person or family enter a church and say together some devotional
prayer. Are we denying that the Spirit can act in many, many ways, not
only the most relevant or even the most reliable?

Another way Underhill offered spiritual direction to us was in her
insistence on the interpenetration of the Spirit of God and the whole
human person. She claimed that a full spiritual life is obedient to the
Spirit in reality, even though it may not be filled with either devotion or
good works. Its goal is cooperation with God rather than some beatitude
or special awareness (*Golden*, 61-62). This approach encourages a
humble abandonment to divine providence in one's life circumstances,
at the same time that it warns against a religiosity or piosity. It is
interested in one's acceptance in faith and hope of life just as it is, not
only in taking a spiritual thermometer of one's progress by re-reading the
journals of one's spiritual journey to trace themes and turning points.

She assured us of her gift for spiritual direction when she also said
that the form and kind of prayer, that is, the use of words, the practice of
meditation, the amount of imageless prayer, is of as little importance as
distinctions of dress and custom. What matters about any "degree" of
prayer is that it be our unstrained response to our light and vocation, to
the truth of our being, if you will (*Golden*, 153). To illustrate her respect
for the wide diversity of how people pray, she took her metaphor from
the symphony:

> We are not to criticize our neighbor's monotonous performance on the
> triangle, censure the first violin's deliberate silence, or look dubiously
> at the little bit of score we have received. All contribute to one only
> music; and this alone gives meaning to their prayer (*Golden*, 154).

Later on, she demonstrated again her skill in the care of souls by
asserting that communion can be experienced through personal or
impersonal symbols: a peaceful abiding in Christ's presence, an inflow
of quiet love in sacramental communion, a tranquil mulling over of a
word, a phrase, or a mystery, or an imageless action (*Golden*, 174). She
acknowledged the diversity of ways in which God acts in us.

Still another way in which she pierced the truth of a mystery that
comes up in spiritual direction is in her reflection on the power of
intercessory action which flows from our surrender to God and union
with the Spirit:

> For this action depends primarily, not on the intensity of our
> sympathetic interest, our psychic sensitiveness, the sustained energy
> and confidence of our demands, or our telepathic power--though all
> these may contribute to its effectiveness--but on a profound and
> selfless devotion to the purposes of the Divine Charity (*Golden*, 186).

Convinced of the mingling of the human and the divine, she was also
convinced of the primacy of God in mediating love and grace.
Furthermore, she was convinced of the redemptive interconnectedness
of all people whereby we can suffer for another and cannot save
ourselves. Effective intercession meant for her our adoring openness to
God, our compassionate openness to the needs of the world, and our
humble openness to accept suffering and darkness in faith as the price of
our redemptive power (*Golden*, 187-90).

A last way in which she exercised her gift for spiritual direction
ministry in her retreats and clergy conferences was to empower others to
exercise their gift for spiritual direction. In *Concerning the Inner Life*,
she specifically urged priests to undertake the spiritual guidance of others
following the law of discipleship that God comes to us through others.
For her spiritual values are caught not taught. She saw this ministry of
spiritual mentoring as much needed in the Church of England as a
contribution to the renewal of its life of prayer (*House*, 96, 141, 147-48).

Other Spiritual Writings

Underhill continued her mission as a spiritual teacher outside of her
formal spiritual direction and conducting of retreats. In describing the
psychology of religious experience in an essay called "The Place of Will,
Intellect and Feeling in Prayer," 1913, Underhill also revealed valuable
insights for spiritual direction. Christianity stands out for its acceptance
of humanity in its wholeness and of life in its wholeness. The balanced
exercise of our human faculties in prayer avoids excesses like an
isolation of philosophical or theological acumen, sentimentality, or an
arrogant reliance on our own powers. Simplicity does not imply a neglect
of reason, vagueness, or a want of logic. An active and disciplined
intelligence can inform our humility and love. By turning our will and
desire to God, we open ourselves to self-donation. Feeling inflames the
will with desire to act. Feeling based on a sense of the beautiful can also
express itself in adoration (*Essentials*, 99-115).

In this essay, Underhill showed her ability to reinterpret traditional
faculty psychology which tended to dichotomize intellect, emotions, and

will. She began to work out her practical advice for spiritual dryness: when we are feeling mentally dull or emotionally flat, it is useless for us to push ourselves. Drawing on a nautical metaphor she wrote: "The most spiritual of emotions is only a fair-weather breeze. Let the ship take advantage of it by all means, but not rely on it. She must be prepared to beat to windward if she would reach her goal" (*Essentials*, 108). She showed herself as adept at helping intellectuals get in touch with an affective dimension of prayer, as helping romantics get their feet on the ground and put their poetic words into deeds.

Reflecting on the education of the spirit in 1916, Underhill revealed herself as an astute spiritual mentor. She asserted that the teaching of doctrine divorced from practical experience is not enough. What is needed is moral training which should include reflection on the gifts of the Spirit and a reinforcement of the essential connection between work and prayer. What is also needed is a linking up of the devotional life with the instinct for beauty. Contemplation is attention to the things of the spirit.[9] She was aware that disciplining the attention and will can lead us to practice the presence of God, for example, when we see or listen to works of art. This secular approach to contemplation is welcomed today by those who strive to find God in all things, in the works of nature and in the works of human beings.

In an address to religion teachers called "The Teacher's Vocation," 1927, Underhill gave practical advice which can also apply to the ministry of spiritual direction. Her image was that of the sheep-dog that helps most by sitting very still, looking at the shepherd, delighting in its relationship with the shepherd which was the center of its life, not by barking or fussing. So, too, our best resources for spiritual direction are those which feed our personal relationship with God: our faith, hope, and love, that is to say, our vision of God's glory, our quiet certainty that God's purposes will prevail, and our generosity which adapts itself to an individual's pace and requirements. But the sheep-dog also keeps its eye on the sheep. In the same way, we need to look on each person as unique and infinitely dear to God, to put all our confidence in God, and to love each one entrusted to us with compassion. While we need to honor the physical and psychological aspects of those we are feeding, we also need to keep in mind that the service which psychology renders us is never meant to dominate. A careful discernment of spirits enables us to respect differences and meet people where they are. This entails sitting beside the shepherd to get the shepherd's outlook on the sheep as well as sitting beside the sheep to understand each one's outlook and aptitude. It also means teaching people how to be nourished by finding God in their daily lives, for example, in the office, the factory, and the home. Through intercessory prayer and action, we can cooperate with God in helping the people entrusted to us to discover and reveal divine love. The work we do for them in the hiddenness of our own interior life may be the most real and enduring, releasing God's creative power (*Papers*, 182-99).

Her analogy of the sheep-dog captures the double focus we are to keep on God and others. Ministry is not some exalted state in a rarefied realm of ideas; it is a homey embodying of faith, hope, and love in the real world of each day's duties and demands. Our ability to experience God's nearness in all that happens to us is our ability to empower others to do the same.

In "The Spiritual Life of the Teacher," 1934, Underhill added other principles of developing an interior life which may be of help to spiritual directors today. Our Christian life in the world must be marked by adoration, communion, and cooperation with God. It is founded on a deep and steady devotional life which keeps us teachable and subordinate to God. It is the symphony of the prayer life of the church, not a series of duets. It implies a self-oblivious generosity whereby we share even those resources we thought would barely meet our own needs, trusting them to God's purpose. It also implies a fidelity to the contemplation of the mysteries of the life of Jesus, looking humbly and steadily at the pattern of gospel values (*Papers*, 200-217).

Teachers need to be teachable; spiritual directors need to be able to be led by the Spirit. Our prayer life is part of the corporate life of the church not the cultivation of a Jesus-and-me exclusiveness. Perhaps self-oblivious generosity needs to be tempered today by a respect for our own needs and the limits of our resources. Gospel values are caught not taught by those who find a mirror experience with people trying to live them. We are invited to enter into life, learning to look at it with the eyes of the artist creator as it really is, and then giving ourselves to it. Many of us, perhaps, can identify with Underhill's prayer for wisdom:

> That we may stand by you, the divine wisdom, and know and love and help your creation--or whatever bit of your creation is given us to care for and love and work at--with that selfless knowledge, and that disinterested love, free from all claimfulness, which does not conflict with your holy knowledge and love (*Papers*, 206).

In "Education and the Spirit of Worship," 1937, Underhill developed points which can also be used as practical advice for spiritual directors. Her emphasis was on developing a spirit of worship in oneself rather than in those one serves. This means a deep reverence for life which enables us to interpret life. It also means an acknowledgement of the glory of God. This unpossessive delight will convey the sacramental nature of the world to those who are interested in a religionless Christianity. And it colors our outlook on those in our care when we look on them with reverence and delight. Faith, hope, and love are the key elements of the spirit of worship, that is, a selfless devotion to the great purposes of creation (*Papers*, 218-40).

The spirit of worship goes beyond kneeling in a pew or preaching in a pulpit. It extends to our attitude toward nature as well as our attitude toward other people. There is, as it were, a secular spirit of worship that reverences life in all its forms and manifestations, respecting each one's unique way of imaging the creator. In our Western culture that is so satiated with the pressures of competition and commercialism, the promises of psychological analysis for healing and freedom, and the prestige of wealth and fame, it is refreshing to be invited to a spirit of worship that is more interested in promoting God's glory than one's own status, more open to adoration than analysis, more drawn to learn from the indwelling Spirit than driven to earn money.

Conclusion

Underhill was called a "mediator of God's reality" (Cropper, 102). She had a "special power of making the things of the Spirit seem both tremendous and homely, and curiously attractive" (Cropper, 138). Underhill's insistence on the centrality of the incarnational principle of reality enabled her to be a spiritual guide for those living the life of the Spirit today.[10]

Underhill's lack of social and political consciousness and her spirituality as fostering a private manner of speech and cosy, mystical chatter over the tea-cups, have been criticized.[11] That view sees the curse; the blessing was Underhill's unusual ability to bring home a point in a way that spoke to women of her day who were thirsty for a personal relationship with God. Underhill's emphasis on work with the poor and her own final commitment to pacifism gave her the courage to be in the vanguard of those whose spirituality includes social justice.[12] She needed, however, to grow in the conviction that social change is what the Gospel is about.

Underhill was criticized indirectly by the Anglican, Martin Thornton, who stated that his era had given rise to an enthusiasm for esoteric forms of mysticism and that some viewed any Christians who said their prayers affectively as mystics.[13] Did he understand with any empathy Evelyn's own personal search for meaning in her enthusiastic study of the mystics? And did he sense the service she rendered Anglican and in a broader sense Christian spirituality by broadening our notions of the mystics to include those of us who cherish our core experience of God in our daily lives without having experienced secondary phenomena?

One can argue that there were two Evelyns, the joyous discoverer of the eternal and the older religious leader who taught many the meaning of Christian living.[14] On the other hand, one can observe that Christianity helped her to integrate these facets of her personality, freeing her to develop a personal relationship with Christ and to reverence the wisdom of other world religions.

Her "care of souls" was a feminine way of nurturing others. One wonders if she nurtured herself as carefully. Her development of other interests ended up being an affirmation of her femininity and a way to balance her research and writing. They are creative outlets for not measuring up to patriarchal standards and for feeling good enough without proving oneself.[15]

It is remarkable that Underhill advocated an embodied spirituality in her day, one that urged rest for the body and relaxation of the mind. She and her directees would have benefited greatly from techniques of relaxation that can slow the mind, reduce blood pressure, and eliminate stress, techniques with which we are familiar today.[16]

In her spiritual direction correspondence, Underhill mentioned types of formal prayer as helps to the spiritual life, such as communal worship, mental prayer, and vocal prayer. Many of us today also find dreamwork, active imagination, and guided imagery ways of getting in touch with the unconscious and honoring the unconscious as a medium of God's revelation. Journaling in other forms can be very helpful.[17]

Underhill's creativity was a rich resource for her own Christian life and for her ministry to other Christians. Her ability to re-interpret the Gospels in the metaphors of her day gave the scriptures a freshness and immediacy that could be disarming. Her ability to integrate her own experience creatively with the material she studied freed others to engage their experience with their faith convictions. She experienced in herself the interaction of the creative process, relaxation, meditation, and the resources of the Judeo-Christian tradition. She offered this synthesis to others in her letters, retreats, and other writings. Her early dabbling in various art forms such as poetry and novel-writing was her foundation as a word artist, a creator of words. In the end, perhaps her own art form was the essay which formed the basis of her retreat conferences and spiritual books. Her recurring need to relax the strenuous pace at which she lived and worked opened her to recognize that same need in many who sought her out. The fruit she discovered in a form of meditation that was quiet, nonverbal, contemplative, was perhaps the richest gift she held out for others to taste. Her approach to scripture was pastoral rather than academic. Her creative adaptation of scriptural passages had more to do with touching the heart than teaching the mind. Her scholarly grasp of mysticism moved beyond reportage into her own constructive analysis of aspects of mysticism. Here again one perceives her originality at work. No wonder she called God artist creator. She herself was an artist co-creator. Today many are discovering their own creativity as a medium of God's self-revelation and their way of revealing the creator.[18]

Evelyn Underhill made a significant contribution to Anglican spirituality.[19] She had a scholarly knowledge of the mystics, an ability to adapt the principles and process of mysticism to the idiom of English Edwardian life; she moved from an agnostic, anti-institutional stance to commitment to the Anglican communion. The freshness of her metaphors was drawn from her own life as a married laywoman, her ability to help others live gospel values in troubled times, her love of beauty, art, and worship, her freedom to translate the classics of the mystical tradition into down-to-earth sayings for Christians living in the world of the early twentieth century. She felt at ease in not attaching herself to any one school of spirituality but taking the best of each of them, perhaps above all living her own life of prayer and service humbly and wholeheartedly.

Suggestions for Prayerful Reflection
                                  Annice Callahan, R.S.C.J.

I invite you to relax, sit back in a comfortable chair, breathe deeply, and close your eyes. Let go of all you may be thinking and feeling. Let yourself become quiet inside.

Evelyn Underhill's knowledge of mysticism was based on both her own personal experience and her interpretation of others' religious experience. She gave us an insight into the depth of her own mystical experience when she wrote: "Sometimes it seems that we are bathed in a living Ocean that pours into every corner of our being to cleanse, heal and refresh. Sometimes it seems that a personal energy compels, withstands, enlightens or suddenly changes us"(*Golden*, 64).

Let us take this passage as an invitation to contemplation and pause for a few moments to enter into this image of being bathed in a living ocean. Enter into the peace within.

Taped Music: "Seascapes" or other music of sounds of the sea

Imagine yourself by the ocean, by the sea.

Listen to the sounds of the ocean--the tide rolling in, the waves crashing over rocks, sea gulls overhead, the foghorn blowing.

Watch the sights of the ocean--the movement of the water, sea creatures, boats, the shoreline.

Imagine yourself going into the ocean to float or swim, being bathed in a living ocean, being in the sea, plunging or being plunged into a deep and peaceful sea.

What is that like for you? How do you feel underwater, out of control?

Imagine God as a living ocean, the deep and peaceful sea drawing you, holding you, pouring into every corner of your being to cleanse, heal, and refresh.

Imagine your self as a living ocean, pouring into every corner of your being to cleanse, heal, and refresh.

Imagine your self as a living ocean pouring life, energy, and peace into every corner of our planet earth, every corner of our universe, to cleanse, heal, and refresh. Slowly, in your own time, open your eyes.

1. Adoration, adherence or communion, and cooperation were important attitudes of heart for Underhill. I find gratitude, trust, and compassion more meaningful in my own spirituality. How would you describe the key attitudes of your own spirituality?

2. What do you find helpful in Evelyn Underhill's mode of spiritual mentoring, from the point of view of the spiritual directee and the retreatant?

3. What do you find helpful in Evelyn Underhill's mode of spiritual mentoring from the point of view of the spiritual mentor and the retreat conductor?

4. Based on your own experience, what aspects of spiritual mentoring, spiritual direction, and spiritual companionship, would you add to those which Underhill experienced, discussed, and embodied?

5. Underhill experienced God as a living ocean and a personal energy. What image speaks to you of your experience of God at this time in your life? What images of God have spoken to you in the past?

Readings

For a recent publication of her 1938 meditation on the liturgy, see Evelyn Underhill, *The Mystery of Sacrifice* (Harrisburg, Pa.: Morehouse, 1991).

On Evelyn Underhill as a spiritual director, see Joy Milos, "The Role of the Spiritual Guide in the Life and Writings of Evelyn Underhill," Ph.D. diss., Catholic University of America, 1988; and "Evelyn Underhill, a Companion on Many Journeys," *Traditions of Spiritual Guidance*, ed. Lavinia Byrne (Collegeville, Mn.: Liturgical Press, 1990), 126-41. See also Annice Callahan, "Evelyn Underhill (1875-1941): Pathfinder for Our Way to God," *Spiritual Guides for Today* (New York: Crossroad, 1992), 25-42, 141-147.

Notes

1. See E. Underhill, *Spirit*, 68-75; *Worship*, 3-19; *Spiritual Life*, 99, 114; *Guide*, 117-31; idem, "St. Augustine," review of *A Monument to St. Augustine, St. Augustine's Conversion* by W.J. Sparrow Simpson, and *St. Augustine* by Eleanor McDougall, *The Spectator*, 30 August 1930, 285, DGC; idem, "The Human Mind," review of *Study of Conversion* by L. Wyatt Lang, *The Spectator* 15 August 1931: 221, DGC. Cf. Milos, "Chapter Five. Guidance in Worship," "The Role of the Spiritual Guide," 195-217; Delroy Oberg, "Evelyn Underhill and Worship," *Australian Journal of Theology* 3, No. 1 (May 1991):31-41, DGC.

2. On the development of his point about affective conversion, see Paul Robb, "Conversion as a Human Experience," *Studies in the Spirituality of Jesuits* 14, No. 3 (May 1982): 1-50; and Donald Gelpi, "The Converting Jesuit," *Studies in the Spirituality of Jesuits* 18 (January 1986):1-38. On affective conversion, see also Walter Conn, *Christian Conversion: A Developmental Interpretation of Autonomy and Surrender* (New York: Paulist, 1986), 316-17, n. 59.

3. Terry Tastard, "Divine Presence and Human Freedom: The Spirituality of Evelyn Underhill Reconsidered," *Theology* 104, No. 762 (November/December 1991): 428; see also 426-32. On restrictions on women in the Church of England, see Brian Heeney, *The Women's Movement in the Church of England 1850-1930* (London: OUP, 1988), esp. 43-44, 121-25.

4. Tastard, "Divine Presence and Human Freedom," 431.

5. See Henry Bodgener, "Evelyn Underhill: A Spiritual Director to Her Generation," *London Quarterly and Holborn Review* (January 1958): 45-50; Joy Milos, "The Role of the Spiritual Guide in the Life and Writings of Evelyn Underhill," (Ph.D. diss., The Catholic University of America, 1988), esp. 218-47, and "Evelyn Underhill, a Companion on Many Journeys," *Traditions of Spiritual Guidance*, ed. Lavinia Byrne (Collegeville, Mn.: Liturgical Press, 1990), 126-41.

6. Elizabeth J. Canham, "A Rest Remaining," *Weavings: A Journal of the Christian Spiritual Life* 8, no. 2 (March/April 1993): 26-32.

7. See E. Underhill, "Père de Caussade," review of *Prayer: Spiritual Instructions on the Various States of Prayer* by J.P.de Caussade, *The Spectator*, 25 July 1931, 133, DGC; id., "The Ignatian Tradition," review of *Abandonment to Divine Providence* by J.P. de Caussade, *The Spectator*, 28 November 1931, 737-38, DGC.

8. For a description of *lectio divina*, a form of contemplative prayer used in the monastic tradition, such as Benedictine spirituality, see Matthias Newman, "Contemporary Spirituality of the Monastic *Lectio*," *Review for Religious* 36 (1977): 97-110. For a description of gospel or imaginative contemplation used in apostolic spirituality, such as Ignatian spirituality, see Philip Sheldrake, "Imagination and Prayer, " *The Way* 24 (April 1984): 92-102.

9. See E. Underhill, *Essentials,* 86-98. Cf. J. Milos, "Chapter III: The Educator as Spiritual Guide," in "The Role of the Spiritual Guide in the Life and Writings of Evelyn Underhill," 102-33.

10. See Annice Callahan, "Evelyn Underhill (1875-1941): Pathfinder for Our Way to God," *Spiritual Guides for Today* (New York: Crossroad, 1992), 25-42, 141-147.

11. Valerie Pitt, "Clouds of Unknowing," *Prism* 3 (June 1959): 7-12.

12. On the growing place of social justice in her spirituality, see Terry Tastard, "Evelyn Underhill and God in the Present," *The Spark in the Soul: Four Mystics on Justice* (New York: Paulist, 1989), 68-94.

13. See Martin Thornton, *English Spirituality: An Outline of Asceticial Theology according to the English Pastoral Tradition* (London: S.P.C.K., 1963), 13.

14. See Anne Bancroft, "Evelyn Underhill," *Weavers of Wisdom: Women Mystics of the Twentieth Century* (London: Penguin Books, 1989), 82-93.

15. M. Murdock, 68-69.

16. See, for example, Lucy Lidell with Narayani and Giris Rabinovitch, *The Sivananda Companion to Yoga* (New York: Simon & Schuster, a Fireside Book,1983; J.M. Déchanet, *Christian Yoga* (New York: Harper & Row, Perennial Library, 1960); Jack Forem, ed., *Transcendental Meditation: Maharishi Mahesh Yogi and the Science of Creative Intelligence* (New York: Bantam Books, 1978); Norvell, *The Miracle Power of Transcendental Meditation* (New York: Harper & Row, 1972); Herbert Benson, M.D., *The Relaxation Response* (New York: William Morrow and Co., 1975), and with William Proctor *Beyond the Relaxation Response* (New York: Times Books, 1985); Charles F. Stroebel, M.D. *QR: The Quieting Reflex* (New York: Putnam's, 1982); Barbara Brown, M.D., *New Mind: New Body* (New York: Harper & Row Bantam Paperback, 1979), and *Stress and the Art of Biofeedback* (New York: Harper & Row, 1977); Edward A. Charlesworth and Ronald G.

Nathan, *Stress Management: A Comprehensive Guide to Wellness* (New York: Ballantine Books, 1984). Cf. D. Granfield, *The Heightened Consciousness*, 119-47.

17. On active imagination, see Robert A. Johnson, *Inner Work: Using Dreams & Active Imagination for Personal Growth* (San Francisco: Harper, 1986). On journaling, see Jan Johnson, "Journaling: Breathing Space in the Spiritual Journey," *Weavings: A Journal of the Christian Spiritual Life* 8, no. 2 (March/April 1993): 34-41.

18. See E. Underhill, *Golden*, 65; *Mount*, 117-18, 122; *School*, 14, 24, 78, 108. Cf. Julia Cameron, *The Artist's Way: A Spiritual Path to Higher Creativity* (New York: Jeremy P. Tarcher/Perigee Books, 1992); and Brenda Ueland, *If You Want to Write: A Book about Art, Independence and Spirit* (St. Paul: Graywolf Press, 1987), 2nd ed.

19. See, for example, A.M. Allchin, "Evelyn Underhill and Anglican Spirituality," and Michael Ramsey, "The Mysticism of Evelyn Underhill," in A.M. Ramsey and A.M. Allchin, *Evelyn Underhill Anglican Mystic* (Oxford: SLG Press, 1996), 5-34, esp. 13, where Ramsey lauds Underhill's ability to show the theological foundations of the life of prayer, witness to the interpenetration of prayer and theology, and express an Anglican spirituality.

On Anglican spirituality, see, for example, John Macquarrie, *Paths in Spirituality*, 2nd. ed. (Harrisburg, Pa.: Morehouse, 1992); John R. H. Moorman, *The Anglican Spiritual Tradition* (London: Darton, Longman, & Todd, 1983); Michael Ramsey, *The Anglican Spirit* (Cambridge, Mass.: Cowley, 1991); Frank C. Senn, ed., *Protestant Spiritual Traditions* (New York: Paulist, 1986); and William J. Wolf, *Anglican Spirituality* (Wilton, Ct.: Morehouse Barlow, 1982).

Chapter 9

Spirituality for Daily Living

The legacy of Evelyn Underhill for the future is not only her study of mysticism and her spiritual guidance, but also her spirituality for daily living. One can see this in her life and in her writings.

In Her Life

Her tours of the Continent were a source of her practical mysticism. Her love of beauty led her to visit not only museums and natural sites of loveliness, but churches and shrines as well. In her book on *Shrines and Cities of France and Italy,* she discussed architecture as a history of the mystic life. Commenting upon a Madonna and Child statue in a church in Arezzo, Italy, she observed that Mary seems to hold the Eucharist in her raised left hand as if to say, " 'But here He is! Here and now! With you and in you, even unto the end of the world!' I thought this a fine and original conception: the symbols of the historic and implicit Incarnations side by side in the arms of the Church."[1] Underhill wanted to make the Incarnation real for us by describing her interpretation of the statue.

Evelyn Underhill, a lapsed Anglican and then theist, became a spiritual guide whose practical mysticism was a call to conversion. She herself experienced a slow process of conversion in her own life and one can trace aspects of this conversion. The shift from Neoplatonic idealism toward what eventually came to be labeled "critical realism" was a step in her intellectual conversion whereby she eliminated the myth of

Plotinus' world of ideas as the real world and affirmed a duality of nature and grace. Her choice to lead a life of prayer and penance signaled a moral conversion to change the criterion of her decisions from satisfactions to values. Her appreciation of Christian art and architecture led her to the artist-creator and became a context for her being grasped by ultimate concern. Two other occasions in her religious conversion were a retreat at a Roman Catholic convent, when she was convinced that Roman Catholicism was true but she could not accept its hierarchical condemnation of Modernism, and her first retreat at the Anglican House of Retreat at Pleshey. After quietly rejoining the Anglican communion, her life of prayer was simplified and deepened, steadying her in tranquil surrender. Her growing acceptance of her own call to holiness led her to invite others to accept their universal call to holiness. Her process of what certain later thinkers would call "psychic conversion" is more difficult to trace; her journal reveals her lifelong obsessive preoccupation with her faults and weaknesses, making it difficult for her to experience God's love and forgiveness.[2]

Her gradual process of conversion was more than one development; it was an interconnected series of developments which transformed all levels of her life. Her conversion was personal, communal, and historical, and led her to find a communal expression of worship and service, and to ally herself with an historical religious tradition, namely, Anglicanism.[3]

Her choice to rejoin the church of her youth was based on her personal mystical experience and her study of mysticism which led her to value corporate, institutional religion. She re-discovered this value as a check to our Western tendency to individualism. It also embodied the sacramental principle whereby the divine is mediated through the human. At the same time, her renewed commitment to church life was also a form of redemptive cooperation with Christ. Her renewed participation in the Anglican communion was ecumenical and interreligious.

In Her Writings

Study of the Mystics

Underhill never studied theology formally and she was not a systematic theologian. Underhill was not a mystical theologian in the strict sense. But one can argue that her study of the mystics was a source for her theological reflection on her religious experience as well as on that of others.

The mystics were for Underhill a rich source of images for self, God, Christ, the church, and the world. Her pastoral concern for people's spiritual life caused the shift from her keen interest in mysticism to a zealous desire to make mysticism accessible to all in their daily lives.

Her advice to trust one's own experience must have been based, in part, on her knowledge that the mystics trusted their experience of God, even in the face of misunderstanding or opposition. She referred to Francis of Assisi who became God's troubadour, Catherine of Siena, an illiterate laywoman who dominated Italian politics after a mystic marriage, Ignatius Loyola who became our Lady's knight, and Teresa of Avila who started the Carmelite Reform obedient to the inner voice (*Mysticism*, 430).

Underhill's advice about living the disciplines of prayer, regular communal worship, service, and friendship with the poor sprang from her own life as well as the lives of the mystics. In fact, are not these disciplines a way of concretizing her thesis that mysticism is a way of life and not transient experiences of illumination? She saw that her own life needed the balance of communal worship and work with the poor. She also saw that contemplative prayer and active service are part of the daily diet of the mystics.

Underhill observed that the absolute is revealed in the everyday. Only our surface-consciousness keeps us from seeing. Mystics stand out because of their heroic and self-oblivious love, not because they remove themselves from human interests and reactions.[4] "In some least expected moment, the common activities of life in progress that reality in whom the mystics dwell slips through our closed doors, and suddenly we see it at our side" (*Mysticism*, 449). This conviction about the divine self-revelation in daily life is the hallmark of her spirituality.

Underhill made her study of mysticism a call to conversion. When she described mysticism as "a way of life" and "an organic life process," I believe she was describing conversion as a slow and gradual transformation not only of consciousness but of lifestyle. She was more interested in the mystics' lives than in their visions because life for her is prayer, not only rare moments of enlightenment and union. She concentrated on the mystic way rather than the mystic state because for her mysticism is about integrating our spiritual outlook with the circumstances of our daily lives. It is by their fruits that we shall know the true mystics. Intimacy with God widens the circle of our love and strengthens our capacity for selfless sacrifice for others. Underhill realized that mystics do not wait for visions but beg to see Christ in others; they do not sit around in rapture but bear the anguish of the world's suffering in their bodies as well as in their hearts. In her mid-life, she perceived that mystics not only are often members of the church, but also contribute to the church by their prayer, penance, and lives of witness to the reality of God. Before and after their visions, those we call mystics in the technical sense were still in need of conversion just as we are.

Letters

In her letters we see Evelyn Underhill's practical mysticism in the way she made her study of the mystics accessible to her correspondents. Her advice about handling dryness and desolation came from her experiences of trying to pray when tired or discouraged, and from her scholarly treatment of the dark night. She became, in fact, adept at distinguishing physical or nervous exhaustion from an authentic dark night as a call from God (*Mysticism*, 380-412; *Lt*, 121).

Underhill used her background in mysticism to emphasize the value of surrender especially in dryness and in the dark. Her own call to surrender in the void was reinforced by mystics of the dark. She had a special penchant for John of the Cross (*Lt*, 235).

As in her books on mysticism, she continued to quote the mystics in her letters and refer to their lives and writings. They were so real to her that they were her friends. On her trips to the Continent, she would make a point of seeing where they had lived, prayed, and served. She wrote her fiancé about her trip to Siena on Catherine of Siena's feast in 1907, when she was able to see not only Catherine's house but also the hospital cell where Catherine had gone to rest when nursing the sick. After living for a time in a hotel with a group of noisy Italians, Underhill wrote her secretary that she understood why Catherine had secluded herself in one room for three years! To one directee who was drawn to find everything in God, Underhill suggested Catherine's image of Christ as a bridge between the human and the divine. Explaining to another directee about our being members of Christ to atone for sin, Underhill cited Catherine as an example of having said to criminals: "I will bear the burden of your sin" (*Lt*, 61-62, 158, 183, 238). Catherine was in a real relationship with God and with the world. Underhill invited us to be in our real relationship with God and with the world.

Underhill sprinkled her letters with references to the mystics she had studied. In one letter in which she was encouraging her directee to avail herself of the communion of saints by asking them to help her, Underhill quoted Teresa about knowing God by frequenting the company of God's friends. Underhill appreciated in special ways her trip to Avila in 1928, regaling Lucy Menzies with the details of visiting Teresa's birthplace, the Convent of the Incarnation, and the Convent of St. Joseph. She saw the grill where John of the Cross sat to hear Teresa's confession and the choir where Teresa had her vision of the spiritual betrothal. Writing to E.I. Watkin about ecstatic phenomena as the by-product and not the essence of mystical experience, Underhill proved their connection with the physiological rhythm by observing that the mature Teresa who wrote the *Foundations* was more united to God than in her ecstatic period described in the *Life*. Here again, Underhill demonstrated her awareness of the psychology of mysticism as well as its theology. And it was her keen understanding of the psychology of mysticism which led her to advise balance and leisure, especially to those in an exhausted state.[5] Underhill demonstrated her familiarity with the mystics in recommending that her directees read books by them.[6]

In a March 1924 letter to a student, her insight into the unity of work and prayer was revealed:

It is only when we grasp the redemptive and creative side of spiritual life and *our* obligation, in respect of it, that we escape the evil of setting up an opposition between the peacefulness of communion with God and the apparently "unspiritual" aspects of practical life. I mean, enjoying Him and working with Him have got to be balanced parts of one full, rich and surrendered life (*Lt*, 152-53).

In a later letter to this same student, she came back to this point of unity, of union with God in daily life, of finding the spiritual in the practical. After urging the person to take a regular time each day to pray, perhaps ten minutes in the morning at first, she added: "Hold on to this sense of peace and beauty, and in and with that, consider the duties, etc., of the day: surround them with that atmosphere as much as you can--and don't expect any very startling results at first" (*Lt*, 155)!

Another characteristic of her practical mysticism was a gentleness with oneself that leads us to a gentleness with others, a willingness to go at their pace. Underhill advised Lucy Menzies not to rush a spiritual directee to give herself freely at the beginning: "Let her go along gently, following her own *attrait*. She will probably do best on a sugar diet for a little while and in due course find out for herself that it isn't adequate" (8/10/25, *Lt*, 164).

Balance also characterized her advice for spending an hour with God since she suggested that it include a period of meditation on a New Testament reading, prayer about one's day, and spiritual reading.[7] Today women and men of faith set aside a time for daily prayer which may include a period of centering prayer, a period of meditation on the day's

Scripture readings, and/or a period of talking with God or Christ about one's day in one's heart or in one's journal.

Her way of seeing the infinite in the finite was based on a strong abandonment to providence whereby she sought God in everything and in everyone: "I am sure God has something to teach us in every situation in which we are put, and through every person we meet: and once we grasp that, we cease to be restless, and settle down to learn where we are" (11/21/1926, *Lt*, 173). This simple trust in God saw ordinary daily life as the medium through which God teaches us, and prayer as a way of remaining with God in confidence, self-surrender, and self-offering for those we love and who need us (1/28/1928, *Lt*, 179). Seeing God present in the visible was for her "the complete eucharisticizing of life" (1/19/37, *Lt*, 254).

At the same time, she was balanced enough to realize that sometimes one had to make a clean break with an emotionally involving friendship in order to live with serenity, open to the possibility that in the future it may be given back in a purified and peaceful form. Knowing the challenge of emotional detachment in her own life, she advised that in such a situation one continue to confide in someone for support and objectivity (8/1/1927, *Lt*, 174-75; 10/22/1927, *Lt*, 177).

Having decided to wait until after her wedding to become a Roman Catholic and then not to do so, Underhill was very aware of similarities and differences between Anglicanism and Roman Catholicism. In a letter to Margaret Robinson written shortly before Underhill's wedding, she wrote that the keys of the Catholic position, and so of the Anglican position as well, are the Incarnation and its continuation in the sacraments. In a letter writtenshortly after her wedding, she wrote to the same that the real presence of Christ is the central fact of the Mass; the full signification of the presence and the meaning of the Eucharist are based on communion, sacrifice, and adoration. In a later letter, she indicated her disagreement with Anglican clergy who argued against adoration of the Blessed Sacrament. In a followup letter, she recommended the Roman Catholic devotion of the rosary as a contemplative way of entering into meditation. Clearly she was drawn to the mystical and sacramental aspects of Roman Catholicism.[8]

Concerned about the inner life of the Anglican clergy, Underhill wrote a letter on this topic to the archbishop of Canterbury, Cosmo Gordon Lang, around 1929 or 1930, asking that it be read at the Lambeth Conference of bishops who met in 1930. Not knowing if it had been read at that conference, Robert Runcie, the former Archbishop of Canterbury, alluded to it at the Lambeth Conference of 1988.[9]

When consulted by someone who was feeling drawn to the Roman Catholic Church, Underhill granted that it was understandable for anyone who loves prayer because the Roman Church understands and emphasizes worship. But she countered: "The whole question, of course, is not 'What attracts and would help Me?' but 'Where can I serve God best?'--and usually the answer to that is, 'Where He has put me'" (3/20/33, *Lt*, 210). Both are valid for a fuller view. The correspondent had obviously touched a nerve. Underhill went on to affirm the Church of England's need for people who can pray and help others to do so, and to undermine leaving the Church of England for the attractive devotional atmosphere of the Church of Rome as abandoning the trenches and returning to the barracks, like Newman's spiritual selfishness. But this sounded more like an *apologia pro vita sua* than helpful advice. It was her task to help this person discern where God's call was, not to argue in favor of staying in the Church of England.

Her decision not to enter the Catholic Church, based on her conviction that she could serve God best where she had been put, probably influenced the advice she gave to one woman who felt drawn to enter a religious order. Underhill warned her not to hurry a decision nor to be influenced by the love and holiness she met unless a "steady and insistent pressure" urged her to this life (9/4/33, *Lt*, 216). By "pressure" she may have meant "impulse." This willingness to wait and be led by the Spirit marked her pragmatic approach to discernment.

Retreats

In her retreat addresses, Underhill exercised in other ways her spirituality for daily living. One way was her careful and judicious way of including Scripture references and suggested Scripture passages in line with the subject of the addresses she gave, as possible points for meditation before or after each of her talks. She actually listed seven sets of such texts for the retreat called *The Mount of Purification*.

A second way she showed her spirituality was in her suggestions for hymns to be sung before or after each talk, instead of leaving the choice up to the musician or haphazardly putting together a prayer service at the last minute. Thus she integrated her biblical and liturgical spirituality with her knowledge of mysticism.

Thirdly, in her retreat published under the title of *Abba*, she quoted from various mystics, mystical theologians, and authors of spiritual classics. For example, she drew upon the Old and New Testaments, Julian of Norwich, Ruysbroeck, Teresa of Avila, John of the Cross,

Martin Buber, Kierkegaard, as well as the Armenian and Roman liturgies.

Another way in which she integrated her background in mysticism with her reflections on the praxis of living the spiritual life was her use of quotations at the beginning of retreat addresses. For example, in the retreat she named *The School of Charity*, she prefaced each talk with a citation from such mystics and mystical theologians as Julian of Norwich, Teresa, John of the Cross, John Bunyan, Karl Barth, William Law, and Elizabeth Leseur. Yet another way in which she incorporated quite naturally and organically the writings and sayings of the mystics and the mystical theologians was to quote passages from them as points for meditation, as she did for the retreat called *The Mount of Purification* which includes points for meditation by Jacopone da Todi, Richard of St. Victor, Walter Hilton, J.N. Grou, Friedrich von Hügel, and John of the Cross. Her loving discernment of reality through prayer included her prayerful reflection on these works and her original synthesis between these works and Christian life in the world.

Other Spiritual Writings

In her other works on the spiritual life, Evelyn Underhill demonstrated her familiarity with mysticism and her personal experience of the spiritual life. She was convinced that spiritual formation should be a regular part of education for living the life of the Spirit in the world.[10]

In "Sources of Power in Human Life," 1921, Underhill claimed that the struggle for a personal spiritual life is the first step in all authentic social reform. Such a practical mysticism includes vision, that is, a wider horizon that the secret of existence is God, and an inner discipline which remakes personality and redirects consciousness by means of contemplation, self-mortification, and service. These elements mark the life of Christ who combined loving attention to God with practical service of others. The social dimension of spiritual consciousness supports discipleship and the corporate life and discourages individualism. We can capitalize on what psychologists call our collective suggestibility in order to tap into communal sources of power in human life that foster enthusiasm, unity of purpose, protection, and a nucleus which others can join (*Guide*, 69-85).

In *The Life of the Spirit and the Life of Today*, 1922, Underhill clarified that her purpose in writing this book was practical, bringing the classic experiences of the spiritual life into line with the conclusions of modern psychology, and suggesting some directions in which recent psychological research may shed light on the standard problems of the religious consciousness. She realized the importance of putting spirituality in dialogue with culture. In her day, that meant seeing the influence of psychology on religious experience. Today it means seeing the interconnectedness of all in God (*Spirit*, xvi).

Evelyn Underhill opposed the ordination of women at the 1932 Central Council for Women's Church Work because ordination could loosen the bond between Anglicanism and Catholicism, as she reflected on "The Ideals of the Ministry of Women," 1932.[11] Today she might have been swayed by other arguments in favor of women's ordination, above all, for the sake of the mission of the church which is the proclamation of Christ.

She described Christian ministry as a response to a call to service. This response needs to be full of suppleness and surrender. Our hidden prayer must be related to our active life as a root is to a tree. Women saints are caught up in selfless adherence to God and Christ. This makes them informal and free within the institutional frame. For her their best work is quiet and hidden cooperation with God (*Mixed*, 113-22).

Underhill's paper on "The Ideals of the Ministry of Women" is problematic for contemporary Christian feminists. Her resistance to women's ordination on the grounds that it would make a complete break with Catholic tradition reflected her Anglo-Catholic bias but also a seeming preference for institutional unity over and against the individual call and rights of women in the church. Christ's call to service overrode for her any consideration of women's status in the church, "and whether the shepherds accept us as trained shepherdesses, or more often regard us as auxiliary dogs--all that fades into silence" (*Mixed* 114-115). No, it no longer fades into silence. Today competent and well educated women are seeking ordination and being ordained as trained shepherdesses. Many are unwilling to cater to clericalism and to patriarchal attitudes.

Underhill said "No kind of assertiveness whatsoever can serve the purpose of the supernatural life. That merely blocks the Divine right of way; prevents the Spirit from getting through" (*Mixed*, 115). Today one can consider assertiveness the flip side of hope. We beg for the grace and do what we can.

She also felt "We surely cannot wish to give up the sacred privilege of the lowest place" (*Mixed*, 115). From the viewpoint of Ignatius' approach to the third degree of humility, she has a point which is valid for female and male clergy alike. But apart from desiring contempt, suffering, and poverty in identification with Christ, we women do wish to give up the lowest place and no longer consider it a sacred privilege but rather an unjust situation to be remedied. Underhill went on to observe that the women who have authentically served others have been simple and unpretentious: "The question of status, scope and so forth has never, I should think, entered their minds at all" (*Mixed*, 116). Today women are more conscious of the political overtones of life and of spirituality.

She found in women saints "something which we might call a maternal and domestic quality in their method, which seems on the whole to look more towards the prophetic than the priestly way of serving God and tending souls" (*Mixed*, 118). Is she saying that it is not priestly to be pastoral? This is an ambiguous statement. Affirming that women saints' work is quiet and hidden, she added a controversial opinion:

> Sometimes when it develops and becomes public and they get a status--and especially when they begin to tell people in general what they ought to do and how things ought to be done, and the mother of souls becomes a reformer--they seem to charm us less, and tell us less of God (*Mixed*, 118).

What is she saying and what does she mean? Catherine of Siena did not tell us less of God when she urged the pope to return to Rome from Avignon. Teresa of Avila did not tell us less of God when she began the Carmelite Reform with John of the Cross.

> Underhill went on to cite traits which are frequently characterized as feminine: Our home-making talents and our instinct for nurture, teaching, loving--the power of concentrating on the individual, on the weak or damaged, the intuitive touch on character and the understanding of it--these are the points at which women have something of real value to give to pastoral work (*Mixed*, 118).

It is not only or always women who bring these gifts to church ministry. Reflecting on how women saints fed some sheep, Underhill seemed to vacillate on her position about women's ordination when she added:

> A clear recognition of the standard they set is going to help women Church workers through their ups and downs, far better than any external change in our position can do. This change may turn out to be useful and desirable; but if the other side is lacking, it won't do much for the real life of the Church. All kinds of claimfulness are so foreign to the Christian genius, that every movement of this kind involved a certain spiritual risk; whereas every movement towards humility and hiddenness actually increases our real value to God and the Church. This does not mean softness or inefficiency; it merely means leaving ourselves out (*Mixed*, 119-20).

Perhaps her real insight comes out here: what she opposed was any kind of claimfulness that contradicts self-surrender. On that point I agree with her. For her suppleness means we are willing to undertake any job assigned to us. She added: "If a new era in women's life in the Church really is opening, do not let us come to it inwardly unprepared, because we are in such a hurry to begin" (*Mixed*, 120-21). This, too, might have been part of her resistance: the possible lack of depth and development of women's interior life, as she perceived it.

She urged a concentration on a growing sensitivity to God and gradual ignoring of our own preferences. In other words, cooperation with God depends on a disciplined life of prayer. Her fear of what she called assertiveness and the seeking of status was grounded in her plea for humility, for a healthy distrust of one's zeal for doing good for others, for "very loving and grateful sinners, entirely free from any notions about the importance of their own status and their own work" (*Mixed*, 121).

This paper would have been written very differently today. In spite of disagreeing with her major premise, I find there is much food for prayer in her points that can challenge women and men in ministry to live gospel values radically as well as realistically. Her living of her own multi-faceted ministry and her ideals for service in the church can invigorate a contemporary spirituality of ministry viewed as a ministry of empowering others to live gospel values in the church.[12]

In a February 4, 1933 letter to Mrs. Roberts, Underhill defended again her objection to women's ordination by reason of the break with Catholic tradition which it would involve. She argued that a development of an order of deaconesses can give women enough support and status for preaching, teaching, and church ministry apart from priesthood.[13] Given the development of women's self-understanding and the church's self-understanding, as well as the ordination of women priests and bishops in the Anglican Church, I trust that Underhill would have conceded her point today.

In the preface to the edition of her four broadcast talks, 1937, Underhill called the spiritual life the heart of all real religion, not an intense form of other-worldliness that is incompatible with common life. The essence of the spiritual life is to be, not to want, to have, or to do. She does not see it as an honors course in personal religion. It is the source of the purpose and quality of practical life, not an alternative to it like a fenced-off devotional patch that is hard to cultivate. The spiritual life is a free and unconditional response to the Spirit, not only individual self-improvement (*Spiritual Life*, 7-32).

Her insistence on seeking God in the details of daily life was revealed in the following assertion: "Most of our conflicts and difficulties come from trying to deal with the spiritual and practical aspects of our life separately instead of realizing them as parts of one whole" (*Spiritual Life*, 33). Our spiritual life is not a contrast to the worries and anxieties that may plague our practical life: "The soul's house is not built on such a convenient plan: there are few sound-proof partitions in it" (*Spiritual Life*, 33).

When we recognize our absolute dependence on God, inner and outer become one in our undivided response to creative love. The conviction of God's reality in our lives may come gradually or suddenly causing conversion. Renunciation of what is narrow and ambitious, and gratitude for the attraction of God deepen into a conscious communion at the center of our lives. These two aspects, mortification and prayer, mean that we must deal with ourselves and attend to God. The spiritual life demands total abandoment to God's purpose at the price of discipline and suffering; it is not a form of wish-fulfillment. The constant offering of our wills to God gives spiritual worth to our practical duties, professional work, social life, and leisure. What matters is the constant correlation between inner and outer (*Spiritual Life*, 34-123).

Conclusion

We can regard her legacy as her study of mysticism, her spiritual guidance, and her spirituality for daily living. Hers was a spirituality of the heart, a spirituality based on adoration, cooperation with God, and communion. She was interested in forming attitudes of heart not in refining opinions of the mind. Imbued with a listening heart, she was gifted to listen to others deeply and thoughtfully. Informed with an intellectual content, she was perhaps a preacher more than a teacher. Above all she was a pathfinder for our way to God.

Evelyn Underhill's study of mysticism is an aspect of her spirituality for daily living, a way of showing us yet again in the lives and writings of the mystics how to discover and reveal the transcendent in what she loved to call the homely, we might say homey, details of daily life. Her life and thought began and ended in experience.

In his introduction to *Collected Papers* of Evelyn Underhill, Lumsden Barkway, Bishop of St. Andrews in the mid-forties, wrote that Underhill's book on *Practical Mysticism* opened a door for him into his own personal relationship with God. He declared that she was a mystic as well as one who wrote about mysticism. She was rationalistic as well as receptive to the supernatural. He traced the development of her thought as follows: When she wrote *Mysticism* (1911), the two pseudonymous novels, and *The Mystic Way* (1913), she had gone beyond an early agnosticism, was Neoplatonic in her outlook, and took a modernistic view of the gospels. She was a Christian in a vague sort of way when she wrote *Practical Mysticism* (1914) and the two Ruysbroeck books. One can detect a change in *Jacopone da Todi* (1919) and *The Essentials of Mysticism* (1920). By 1922, her outlook had become incarnational, institutional, and sacramental, apparent in *The Life of the Spirit and the Life of Today* (1922), *The Mystics of the Church* (1925), and *Worship* (1936) (*Papers*, 13-19).

One can argue, on the other hand, that Underhill had moved beyond a Neoplatonic idealism when she wrote *The Mystic Way*. Instead of saying that she was Christian in a vague sort of way when she wrote *Practical Mysticism,* perhaps one could more accurately say that she was living a kind of religionless Christianity, that is, living the Christian life without any form of communal worship. One instance of her development from the a-historical approach she took towards the mystics in *Mysticism*, 1911, to a historical approach can be seen in her biography of John Ruysbroeck, 1914, in which she insisted that studying the mystic's prayer and teachings includes studying the nature and sources of his vision in the context of his life and environment (*Ruysbroeck*, 4). Another instance is in the introduction to her book on Jacopone da Todi, 1919:

> Lovers of the mystics too often forget that their lives have a local and temporal as well as an eternal setting, and can never be understood without reference to the history of the world in which they lived, the peculiar racial, intellectual and religious influences to which they were exposed.[14]

This biography and her essay on "The Future of Mysticism," 1918, reflect the shift that began after her disillusionment in 1917.[15] It is significant that Underhill was not alone in making the shifts she did in her thought, belief, and spirituality:

> She . . . expressed in her own pilgrimage the religious movement of the whole period as it proceeded from immanentalism to transcendentalism, from Liberal Protestantism to Orthodoxy, from private mysticism to public worship, from the individual to the institutional expression of allegiance, and from Theocentric to Christocentric faith.[16]

She experienced an intellectual conversion from Neoplatonism, Romanticism, and Bergon's vitalism to critical realism, as she indicated in the twelfth edition of *Mysticism*. Viewing Underhill as a mystagogue who passed on the meaning of the Christian mysteries to other Christians, Todd E. Johnson dates these shifts as developmental phases in her thinking, and perceives a third period during which she focused on the life and power of the Holy Spirit in the church and in the world:

immanence and vitalism (1891-1919), critical realism (1920-1929), and pneumatocentrism (1930-1941).[17]

Underhill lived the double life of Martha and Mary in the world, not in cloistered calm, but as wife of a busy lawyer, housekeeper, hostess, lecturer, spiritual director, and retreat preacher while at the same time leading a secret life of prayer, hidden with Christ in God.[18] A friend of hers commented: "It is the way she points to God and the God she points at, that matter. . . There is a wonderful fragrance of restraint about the Gospel stories. I have the same sort of feeling about Evelyn."[19]

In the preface to one set of her retreat addresses, Underhill included reflections that mark her as prophetic. She observed that there were two movements in her day, both of which were crucial for the future of religion. One was a surface immanentism which preferred altruism to adoration and humanitarian sentiment to love. While abounding in good works, this pious naturalism lacked the creative energy drawn from the divine. The other was a radical transcendentalism articulated in the works of Otto, Barth, and Brunner which so emphasized the otherness of the holy as to create an unbridgeable gap between the human and the divine, action and contemplation. For her the Christian doctrine of the Spirit could fill this gap by affirming the unity between the practical and spiritual dimensions of our lives while acknowledging our creaturely status before God. She preferred to dwell on purification and prayer rather than fellowship and service as a way of resorting to what she called first principles, a way of seeing life in relation to God, a way of stimulating the transcendental sense which she felt was the chief spiritual lack of the modern world (*Golden*, vii-x).

What are the current movements of our day that are crucial for the future of religion? We are familiar with if not engaged in the dialogue between laity and clergy, between spirituality and culture, between spirituality and theology, between science and religion, between East and West, among Christian denominations, and among world religions. Do we tend to prefer good works to adoration which focuses us on the work of God in the world? Do we so emphasize the otherness of God that communion with the divine seems unattainable? Are we so caught up in our churches with Christian fellowship and forms of service to others that we no longer talk about or make a place in our lives for the process of purification and prayer? Is the transcendental sense the chief spiritual lack of the postmodern world? If not, what is?

Underhill was keenly aware that a vague notion of God as spirit can reflect an adherence to the doctrine of the immanence of God which tends toward quietism and pantheism, away from adoration and divine

otherness. Naturalism can veer away from the self-revealing character of
the wholly other, settling for service to the other for the betterment of
humankind not for the greater glory of God. She stood for a firm
conviction of the interpenetration of God's Spirit and our spirit as the
basis of the practical theology of the future, not as a form of pantheism
but as a balanced Christian theology of the Holy Spirit that affirms God's
distinctness and immanence. The Incarnation is viewed as the greatest
insertion of Spirit into history.[20]

Underhill's insights make a significant contribution to pastoral
theology in a way similar to that of Thomas Merton and Henri Nouwen.[21]
The task of pastoral theology can be understood in the light of Karl
Rahner's description of the task of what he prefers to call practical
theology as bringing about the Church's self-actualization as it is and as
it ought to be in the fulfillment of its salvific mission in the world.[22]
Michael Ramsey, the late Archbishop of Canterbury, recognized the shift
that took place in Evelyn Underhill from the 1920s after which she wrote
not as the exponent of mysticism but as a doctor of the Christian Church.
Viewing her as far more than an echo of von Hügel, Ramsey noted the
significant contribution which Underhill made to both spirituality and
theology:

> She was able to use the insights she had gained from him and from her own
> studies for the expression of a theology and spirituality of a distinctively
> Anglican kind. Few in modern times have done more to show the
> theological foundations of the life of prayer and to witness to the
> interpenetration of prayer and theology. She has a place of her own, and it
> is an important one.[23]

He claimed that she did more than anyone else to keep the spiritual life
alive in the Anglican church in the period between the wars.[24]

Her instincts and intuitions were based on a solid foundation in the
scriptures and religious classics of the Judeo-Christian tradition. Since
we are living in an era which insists on knowing the implications of the
Christian faith for living in the world, I propose that her pastoral
relevance is that she discovered and revealed the eternal in the details
and duties of daily life. She was most interested in helping us deepen and
develop a real relationship with the living God that influences the way
we live the life of the Spirit in the church and in the world. She was
concerned with the church's self-actualization as it is and as it ought to
be. Her practical mysticism used the mystics as a source for inviting us
to see the spiritual dimension of the practical and the practical
implications of the spiritual life. For her the mystics live the praxis of
faith and theology. As we see in her letters and in her retreat addresses,
her pastoral approach to individuals and to groups adapted the Christian

tradition to particular needs and concerns, such as the need of priests for an ongoing personal life of prayer and the concern of her fellow Anglicans for an incentive to live gospel values in their Edwardian culture. She did not consciously take a pastoral approach during the first twenty years of her research and writing. But one can trace her pastoral insights and concerns from the beginning of her published work.[25]

What can be the impact of Evelyn Underhill today? Mary Xavier Kirby has written:

> An age of self-sufficiency needs her reminder of the interdependence of souls. An age of mediocrity needs her challenge of excellence; an age of irresponsibility, her insistence upon fidelity of duty; an age of frustration and depresssion, her values of steadfastness, perseverance, and courage; an age of anxiety, her assurance of God's personal love for all.[26]

Suggestions for Prayerful Reflection
Annice Callahan, R.S.C.J.

In 1988, the General Convention of the Episcopal Church in the United States added Evelyn Underhill to its liturgical calendar describing her as "theologian and mystic." Since she used biblical and liturgical texts as the basis and inspiration of her addresses and essays, it might be appropriate for us to end by praying the texts that have been suggested for the celebration of her feast on June 15:

O God, Origin, Sustainer, and End of all your creatures: Grant that your Church, taught by your servant Evelyn Underhill, guarded evermore by your power, and guided by your Spirit into the light of truth, may continually offer to you all glory and thanksgiving and attain with your saints the blessed hope of everlasting life, which you have promised by our Savior Jesus Christ; who with you and the Holy Spirit, lives and reigns, one God, now and for ever. Amen.

Psalm   96:7-13   or 37:3-6, 32-33
Lessons   Wisdom 7:24-8:1 John 4:19-24
Preface of the Dedication of a Church

1. In your opinion, what was Evelyn Underhill's contribution to mysticism? to spiritual guidance? to a spirituality for daily living?

2. What mystics' experiences and images of themselves, God, Christ, the Church, and the world stand out for you and shed light on your own?

3. In your opinion, what was Evelyn Underhill's contribution to a contemporary Judaeo-Christian spirituality of the life of the Spirit?

4. In particular, what can she contribute to women's spirituality?

5. What concrete action-step do you choose to take as a result of having read this book and reflected on Underhill's life and writings?

Readings

For a collection of Underhill's essays, lectures, and retreat addresses, see *Life as Prayer and Other Writings of Evelyn Underhill*, ed. Lucy Menzies (Harrisburg, Pa.: Morehouse, 1991), originally called *Collected Papers*. For contemporary editions of her 1937 set of BBC broadcast talks, see Evelyn Underhill, *The Spiritual Life* (London: Mowbray, 1955; Harrisburg, Pa.: Morehouse, 1996).

Notes

1. E. Underhill, *Shrines and Cities of France and Italy*, ed. Lucy Menzies (London: Longmans, Green & Co., 1949), 102.

2. On the process of conversion, see Annice Callahan, "Conversion in Daily Life," *Studies in Formative Spirituality* 12, no. 3 (November 1991): 333-344.
    On dimensions of conversion, see Bernard J.F. Lonergan, *Method in Theology* (New York: Herder and Herder, 1973), 238-44; and *The Philosophy of God and Theology* (London: Darton, Longman & Todd, 1973), 12-14, 17, 50-59.
    On psychic conversion, see Robert J. Doran, "Psychic Conversion," *Thomist* 41 (April 1977): 200-36; "Jungian Psychology and Christian Spirituality," *Review for Religious* 38 (1979): 4/497-510, 5/742-52, 6/857-66; *Subject and Psyche: Ricoeur, Jung, and the Search for Foundations*, 2nd ed. (Milwaukee: Marquette University Press, 1994), esp. 240-46; *Psychic Conversion and Theological Foundations: Toward a Reorientation of the Human Sciences*, AAR Studies in Religion 25 (Chico, Ca.: Scholars Press, 1981), esp. 178-93; and *Theology and the Dialectics of History* (Toronto: University of Toronto Press, 1990), 9, for the distinction between affective and psychic conversion.
    Underhill's use of the term "critical realism" is in line with Baron von Hügel's philosophy that reality has a dual nature, namely, the temporal and the eternal: the finite is a sacrament of the infinite. See *Fragments*, 28. For a contemporary understanding of critical realism, see Appendix: A Note on Critical Realism.

3. See B. Lonergan, *Method in Theology*, 130-31; "Theology in Its New Context," *Theology of Renewal* (New York: Herder and Herder, 1968), Vol. 1, 34-46; *Philosophy of God and Theology*, 12-14, 17, 50-59.

4. See E. Underhill, review of *A Literary History of Religious Thought in France* by Henri Bremond, *The Spectator*, 4 October 1930, 469-70, DGC.

5. See E. Underhill, *Lt*, 84, 179-81, 199-200, 235, 313.

6. At the same time, she was very willing to lend them her own copies. For example, to Margaret Robinson she sent a reading list of classics which included Augustine, Ruysbroeck, and Julian of Norwich. The same year she offered to lend Margaret her copy of Julian and recommended that Margaret read Augustine's *Sermons*. She lent Margaret a book of quotations by Plotinus. She also suggested a French edition of the life and works of St. Teresa, as well as an edition of Tauler. Two years later she lent Margaret her copy of Hilton and then that of Francis de Sales (*Lt*, 68-70, 101, 108).

7. See E. Underhill, 1/19/23, *Lt*, 311; 4/12/39, *Lt*, 270; 4/27/39, *Lt*, 273; 4/3/39, *Lt*, 274.

8. See E. Underhill, 5/12/1907, *Lt*, 63; 8/2/1907; 10/9/1907, *Lt*, 69; 12/30/1907, *Lt*, 71. Cf. Richard Leggett, "Evelyn Underhill: The Sacrifice of a Humble and Contrite Heart," *How Firm a Foundation: Leaders of the Liturgical Movement*, ed R.I. Tuzik (Chicago: Liturgy Training Publications, 1990), 70-80.

9. See Grace Adolphsen Brame, "Continuing Incarnation: Evelyn Underhill's Double Thread of Spirituality," *Christian Century* (October 31, 1990): 997-1000, in which the author admitted that she was the one who had found this handwritten letter in the Underhill archives in London.

10. See Alice Selby Boyack, "Evelyn Underhill's Interpretation of the Spiritual Life" (Ph.D. diss., University of Chicago, 1964).

11. E. Underhill, "The Ideals of the Ministry of Women," *Theology* 26, no. 151 (January 1933): 37-42, reprinted in *Mixed*, 113-122, and cited in D. Greene, *Artist*, 100, n. 23. Cf. Susan Dowell and Jane Williams, *Bread, Wine and Women: The Ordination Debate in the Church of England* (London: Virago Press, 1994).

12. See, for example, Paul Bernier, *Ministry in the Church* (Mystic, Ct.: Twenty-Third Publications, 1992); Urban Holmes, *Spirituality for Ministry* (San Francisco: Harper & Row, 1982); John Macquarrie, *Theology, Church & Ministry* (London: SCM Press, 1986); Patricia O'Connell Killen and John De Beer, *The Art of Theological Reflection* (New York: Crossroad, 1995); Dorothy Ramodibe, "Women and Men Building Together the Church in Africa," in Virginia Fabella and Mercy Amba Oduyoye, *With Passion and Compassion: Third World Women Doing Theology* (Maryknoll, N.Y.: Orbis, 1988), 14-21; Edward Schillebeeckx, *Ministry* (New York: Crossroad, 1981), and *The Church with a Human Face* (N.Y.: Crossroad, 1985); James D. and evelyn E. Whitehead, *Method in Ministry* (Kansas City: Sheed & Ward, 1995) and *The Promise of Partnership* (HarperSan Francisco, 1993); and Robert J. Wicks, ed., *Handbook of Spirituality for Ministers* (New York: Paulist, 1995).

13. See E. Underhill to Mrs. Roberts, 4 February 1933, Fawcett Library MS Collection, City of London Polytechnic, DGC.

14. E. Underhill, *Jacopone*, 18. Cf. D. Greene, "Toward an Evaluation of the Thought of Evelyn Underhill," *History of European Ideas* 8 (1987): 549-562.

15. On her going to pieces during the war, see E. Underhill to F. von Hügel, 21 Dec. 1921, TS, Underhill-von Hügel Collection, St. Andrews University, Archives, St. Andrews, Scotland, in *Artist*, 56.

16. Horton Davies, *Worship and Theology in England*, vol. 5: *The Ecumenical Century*, 1900-1965 (Princeton, N.J.: Princeton University Press, 1965), 144-45.

17. See *Mysticism*, 43; Appendix: A Note on Critical Realism; and Todd Johnson, "In Spirit and Truth," (Ph.D. diss., University of Notre Dame, 1996), 242-253, 256-258, 291-297.

18. See L. Barkway, introduction to *An Anthology of the Love of God*, 19-20.

19. In Lucy Menzies, Biography of Evelyn Underhill, XI.2, DGC. On her reticence about her interior life, see also E.I. Watkin, review of *Evelyn Underhill* by Margaret Cropper, *The Month* (July 1959): 45-50.

20. See *Golden*, 14, 20, 26-29, 36. See also Underhill, "A Way of Renewal: Study Scheme on the Holy Spirit in the Church," discovered by Grace Adolphsen Brame and included in an Appendix in Todd E. Johnson, "In Spirit and Truth," (Ph.D. diss.: University of Notre Dame, 1996), 298-302.
     On Underhill's understanding of the centrality of the Spirit in mysticism and liturgy, see, for example, Todd E. Johnson, *Mysticism and Liturgy in the Thought of Evelyn Underhill*. Julian Paper no. 8 (Waukesha, Wisc.: Order of Julian of Norwich, 1993). On Underhill's theology of the Eucharist as oblation in the Spirit, see Todd E. Johnson, "Pneumatological Oblation: Evelyn Underhill's Theology of the Eucharist," *Worship* 68 (1994): 313-332. On Underhill's theology of the Holy Spirit, see Todd E. Johnson, "Evelyn Underhill's Pneumatology: Origins and Implications," Unpublished paper presented in the Systematic Theology Section, AAR Convention, New Orleans, La., 23 November 1996; and "In Spirit and Truth" (Ph.D. diss.: University of Notre Dame, 1996).

21. On Thomas Merton's contribution to pastoral theology, see Anne E. Carr, *A Search for Wisdom and Spirit: Thomas Merton's Theology of the Self* (Notre Dame: University of Notre Dame Press, 1988), 3-7; and Lawrence S. Cunningham, "Thomas Merton: The Pursuit of Marginality," *Christian Century* 95 (December 6, 1978): 1183. In fact, Merton noted in his journal the influence which her book *Mysticism* had on him. See Raymond Bailey, *Thomas Merton on Mysticism* (Garden City, N.Y.: Doubleday Image, 1975), 44. Cf. Annice Callahan, *Spiritual Guides for Today* (New York: Crossroad, 1992), 97-116, 161-165.
     On Henri Nouwen's contribution to pastoral theology, see John S. Mogabgab, "The Spiritual Pedagogy of Henri Nouwen," *Yale Divinity School*

Reflection (January 1981): 4-6; and Seward Hiltner, "Henri Nouwen: Pastoral Theologian of the Year," *Pastoral Psychology* 27 (Fall 1978):5. Cf. Callahan, *Spiritual Guides for Today*, 117-135, 166-169.

22. On Karl Rahner's understanding of pastoral theology, see "Practical Theology within the Totality of Theological Disciplines," *TI* 9, 101-14; "Practical Theology and Social Work in the Church," *TI* 10, 349-70; "The New Claims Which Pastoral Theology Makes upon Theology as a Whole," *TI* 11, 115-36; and "Die Grundlegung der Pastoraltheologie als praktische Theologie," *Handbuch der Pastoraltheologie* I (Freiburg: Herder, 1964), 117 ff. Cf. Callahan, *Spiritual Guides for Today*, 61-78, 150-155.

23. Michael Ramsey, "Evelyn Underhill," *Religious Studies* 12 (1976):278; and "The Mysticism of Evelyn Underhill," in A.M. Ramsey and A.M. Allchin, *Evelyn Underhill Anglican Mystic* (Fairacres, Oxford: SLG Press, 1996), 13.

24. Michael Ramsey. "Foreword," in Armstrong, x.

25. On my hesitation to call her a mystical theologian, see, for example, David Knowles, *What is Mysticism?* (London: Charing Book Club, 1968), 11, where he wrote that like William James and von Hügel, Underhill made no attempt at a theological analysis of the mystical experience, remaining on the phenomenal level of recording and assessing the mystics' accounts.

26. Sister Mary Xavier Kirby, "The Writings of Evelyn Underhill: A Critical Analysis," (Ph.D. diss., University of Pennsylvania, 1965), 424.

Afterword

A Spiritual Resource for Today

I too have heard thy ceaseless song,
  I have discerned thy radiant feet
That flash in rhythmic dance among
  The squalors of the city street:
    And in its gutters every day
    Have seen thy ragged angels play.

For deep the secret world within,
  I feel thy stirring soft and strange,
And know all growing things my kin.[1]

Evelyn Underhill has been presented as a spiritual guide for the third millennium. This excerpt from her poem called "Invocation" published in 1916 reveals her sense of finding God in the poor and feeling a kinship with all creatures. Her seminal thoughts about our interdependence with other people, the earth, the universe, and God give her pastoral and ecumenical relevance, and put her in dialogue with representatives of contemporary movements in spirituality and theology, such as ecology, feminism, ecofeminism, the commitment to social justice and peace, liberation theology, the new cosmology which is putting physics in dialogue with spirituality, and other aspects of the postmodern paradigm which is showing the interconnectedness of all things in the universe. She anticipated these movements rather than introducing them.[2]

Her pastoral relevance for the third millennium is obvious to some and obscure to others. In this era where what counts is the now, she is a living memory of our Judeo-Christian heritage. In a consumer technological world, she summons us to save our hidden treasure in order to buy the pearl of great price, to wait for the Word instead of growing numb to words. In her genuine appreciation of art and architecture, she invites us to re-discover creative resources within ourselves that complement our scientific skills. In her sense of the beauty and sacredness of the earth, she opens us to all that creation-centered spirituality and ecofeminism are reminding us to value.

Her difficulty in espousing a cause kept her from becoming a feminist in her day, a choice she must have made freely, given the situation of women's emancipation in England at the turn of the century. Her metaphors for the spiritual life based on her experience as a woman living in Edwardian England are now outdated. Her volunteer work in the slums seems like a token gesture that overlooked the need for systemic change and social justice both for women and for the poor. Her difficult childhood and vapid marriage remained largely unconscious data for her. Her loneliness gave her an empathy with others who felt neglected or not understood. She continued to love, respect, and serve her parents and husband even though they could not return her love with any real empathy. In the same way, she counseled others to be faithful to their families and friends without expecting anything back. True to her times, she did not write about intimacy, much less about sexuality.

For Underhill, mysticism is a way of life, an organic process, not just intense experiences. We are responsible to respond to our relationship with God.

Evelyn Underhill helped others to see the practical implications of the mystics' spiritual ideals. She needed to discover them for herself first. She was disillusioned after World War I, became a pacifist, started visiting the poor in the North Kensington slums two afternoons a week, rejoined the Anglican communion from which she had drifted for many years, and started writing books on the spiritual life. She fostered her personal relationship with God in her daily life, and found her fellow Anglicans turning to her for spiritual direction and retreat work. One can detect characteristics of her spirituality for daily living which are aspects of contemporary Christian spirituality:

*meeting God in daily life: seeing the spiritual in the practical;
*choosing the disciplines of prayer, worship, service, and work
  with the poor;
*empowering ourselves and others as everyday mystics;

*honoring our body and our psyche: advice in dryness;

*embodying an image of our true self: the house of the soul;

*living our interconnectedness with the earth and the universe.

All of these approaches bring the mystics and ourselves as mystics into union with reality, that is, with ourselves, God, others, and the universe. They are aspects of a spirituality of daily life for laypeople.[3]

Her spiritual guidance was balanced. Her sense of embodiment enabled her to advise starting with our bodies and caring for them as a form of care for the soul. Thomas Moore, a psychotherapist, connects soul with depth, interiority, relatedness, personal substance, a sensitivity to the symbolic and metaphoric life, authentic community, and attachment to the world. He describes various ways of caring for the soul, such as the arts, homemaking, simple gestures, storytelling, nondoing, ongoing attention to what is neglected or rejected, respect for uniqueness, the use of creative imagination, sustaining experiences of absence and separation, making a home for emotions, images, and memories, allowing oneself to be affected by beauty. He is convinced that healing means feeding the soul, that is, observing its needs continually, letting it appear in the gaps and holes of experience. For him, living close to the heart strengthens soul power, which can emerge from depression, failure, and loss.[4] Although Underhill used some different points of emphasis and the vocabulary of her culture, she would have agreed with Moore's insistence that we need to care for our souls by cultivating depth and sacredness in everyday life. She would also have endorsed Moore's distinction between two approaches to the sacred and the secular:

> There are two ways of thinking about church and religion. One is that we go to church to be in the presence of the holy, to learn and to have our lives influenced by that presence. The other is that church teaches us directly and symbolically to see the sacred dimension of everyday life. . . For some, religion is a Sunday affair, and they risk dividing life into a holy sabbath and the secular week. For others, religion is a weeklong observance that is inspired and sustained on the Sabbath. . . The spirituality that feeds the soul and ultimately heals our psychological wounds may be found in those sacred objects that dress themselves in the accoutrements of the ordinary.[5]

His approach, in turn, supports Underhill's spirituality for daily living.

Underhill's conviction about the intrinsic unity between spirituality and politics connects her with contemporary theologians exploring the implications of creating a healed world. Rosemary Radford Ruether, a North American ecofeminist theologian, envisions a good society that fosters a life-sustaining community of human beings based on incremental shifts toward such transformations as renewable energy sources, seasonal patterns of food, organic methods of farming, a return to the land, the rebuilding of soils through composting systems, the empowerment of women, and genuine demilitarization. For this *metanoia,* we need to build strong base communities of celebration and resistance, that are nourished by being in touch with the living earth, the exercise of creative and intuitive powers, corporate liturgies, the engagement of the arts in the transformation of consciousness, pilot projects for living an ecologically healthful life such as the recycling of household wastes, and the formation of political bases of organizing and action.[6] Underhill's spiritual direction ministry, exercise of her creative imagination in her lectures and writings, and commitment to pacifism toward the end of her life were for her incremental shifts toward creating such a life-sustaining community. If she were alive, she would welcome the ecofeminist implications of a new global consciousness.

Underhill's practical spirituality of caring is challenged and enhanced by Dorothee Sölle, a German liberation theologian teaching in New York and a leader of the German peace movement, who has developed a liberation spirituality of sharing. According to Sölle, we need to learn from the poor how to become poorer and to choose poverty voluntarily, to advocate for victims of injustice with compassion, to mediate self-acceptance to women as Jesus did, to work for peace and justice taking the side of the poor against economic plunder, legal degradation, and political oppression, to discover the strength of the weak by singing of peace in the midst of war, and to thirst for liberation.[7] Underhill's spiritual leadership implies an ethical leadership which needs to be explored.

Underhill needed to enter into the experience of poor and oppressed people in the world. One prophetic voice in the church today is that of Hispanic women. In reflecting on poor and oppressed Hispanic women's stories of their understandings of the divine, Ada Maria Isasi-Diaz, a Cuban feminist theologian, and Yolanda Tarango, a Chicana feminist, have concluded the following:

> These understandings seem to question any and all theologizing of God as totally other--a never changing God. They negate any dualistic understanding of the human person: for Hispanic Women to feel, to understand, to believe is all one same thing. Hispanic Women have a very deep sense of being the church; for them the clergy is not in any way more religious than they are, or better members of the church than they are.[8]

Even though Underhill lived a privileged life, she may have identified with these understandings due to her intuitive experience of the touch of God as strength in her loneliness and her ministerial experience in the

Anglican Church of offering spiritual leadership to clergy as well as to laity.

Underhill's experience of volunteer work with the poor that led her to build friendship with the poor is reinforced and enriched by Mary Jo Leddy's experience of work with refugees that has enabled her to regard them as neighbors and friends. Unlike Underhill, Leddy felt drawn to live with the poor as well as serve them. In her book *At the Border of Hope: Where Refugees Are Neighbors*, Leddy invites us into the lives, memories, and dreams of the refugees with whom she has worked and lived at Romero House, a house for refugees in Toronto, Ontario. One may recall Evelyn Underhill's friendship with Mrs. Laura Rose as one reads Leddy's description of her friendship with Semira, an Eritrean woman. She became increasingly involved with Semira's family's struggle for landed immigration which revealed kinks in the system at the border of hope. Just as Underhill made accessible her scholarly study of mysticism in her pastoral ministry of spiritual direction, retreat addresses, and friendship with the poor, Leddy brings to bear her scholarly study of philosophy in her pastoral reflection on what she has learned from and with the refugees.[9]

Evelyn Underhill was a spiritual resource for Anglicans in Edwardian England. She is a spiritual resource for Christians today. Her spirituality gives us a way to live the life of the Spirit in faith, hope, and love. It enables us to embody the spiritual life in our attitudes, behaviors, choices, and encounters. It helps us to prolong the Incarnation in our daily circumstances, to find God in our humanity and on our planet earth. It invites us to be open to the Spirit's penetration in our hearts and at the heart of the universe. Her openness to ecumenism and to other world religions makes her an apt dialogue partner in our common search for the mystery of God in our lives. Her commitment to pacifism underscores the need for individual and international peacemaking. Her way of being with the poor opens a door for us to build relationships in compassion and communion, not to offer condescending charity. Her encouragement of nondevotional interests can refresh our energies and freshen our fervor. In all these ways she is a spiritual guide for the third millenium. In the future, she can be a spiritual resource for the world.

Let us end with her description of her spirituality for daily living in her essay on "Sources of Power in Human Life," in which she discussed two complementary aspects of authentic spiritual life, namely, its outer vision and its inner discipline:

Now a practical mysticism--by which I mean the spiritual development possible to the average man--offers just these two things; which are indeed two aspects of one transformation, since "we only behold that which we are." It shows us innumerable men and women who had the vision; who were aware of an unchanging love and beauty which really transformed their lives, so that they gazed more and more deeply into its heart. It offers to teach the method of self-conquest and of contemplation by which they remade their consciousness, and redeemed their lives from concentration on the transitory and unreal. It shows us their final state, in which they became fresh centres of creative life; receiving it--as an artist receives aesthetic joy--in order to give again (*Guide*, 74-75).

Notes

1. E. Underhill, "Invocation," *Theophanies: A Book of Verses* (New York: E.P. Dutton & Co., 1916), 117. Cf. Kathleen Henderson Staudt, "The Note of Failure in the Symphony of Grace: Reading Evelyn Underhill's Theophanies," The Evelyn Underhill Association Newsletter 4 (November 1993): 1-3.

2. On the interconnectedness of faith, theology, and praxis, see Dorothee Sölle, *Thinking about God: An Introduction to Theology* (Philadelphia: Trinity Press International, 1990), esp. 1-6.

3.For other books on spirituality written by laypeople for laypeople, see, for example, Elizabeth A. Dreyer, *Earth Crammed with Heaven: A Spirituality of Everyday Life* (New York: Paulist, 1994), which reviews such topics as asceticism, ministry, sexuality, and work in the light of historical and contemporary spirituality; Dolores R. Leckey, *The Ordinary Way: A Family Spirituality* (New York: Crossroad, 1982), which applies the Rule of St. Benedict to family life; Parker Palmer, *The Active Life* (San Francisco: Harper & Row, 1990), which develops a spirituality of work, creativity, and caring for laypeople; Frank X. Tuoti, *Why Not Be a Mystic?* (New York: Crossroad, 1995), which is a book on contemplative prayer; and Wendy Wright, *Sacred Dwelling: A Spirituality of Family Life* (New York: Crossroad, 1989), which explores the metaphor of "dwelling."

4. See Thomas Moore, *Care of the Soul: A Guide for Cultivating Depth and Sacredness in Everyday Life* (New York: HarperCollins, 1992). On "soul, see esp. 5 and 229. On ways to care for the soul, see esp. 12, 13, 16-20, 34, 39, 65, 172, 237, 242, 288, 304. On feeding the soul, see esp. 120, 122, 210, 235, 278, 280, 287. On soul power, see esp. 119-120, 126, 135.

5. Moore, *Care of the Soul*, 214, 219. In the Foreword to the thirteenth edition of *Mysticism*, Ira Progoff claims that Underhill's main contribution was in the realm of psychology, emphasizing a wholistic view of the effects of the spiritual on the material realm, and encouraging the forward development of the person. See Ira Progoff, "Foreword," in E. Underhill, *Mysticism*, vii-x.

6. See Rosemary Radford Ruether, *Gaia and God: An Ecofeminist Theology of Earth Healing* (San Francisco: HarperSan Francisco, 1992), esp. 254-274, 305-306; and Sallie McFague, *The Body of God: An Ecological Theology* (Minneapolis: Fortress Press, 1993), esp. 65-97. See also Steven Bouma Prediger, *The Greening of Theology; The Ecological Models of Rosemary Radford Ruether, Joseph Sittler, and Jurgen Moltmann* (Atlanta, Ga.: Scholars Press, 1995), esp. 103-134 and 217-263 on pneumatological implications of

236

Appendix

A Note on Critical Realism

In the twelfth edition of *Mysticism*, Underhill added that she would have focused on critical realism rather than vitalism had she rewritten that chapter (*Mysticism*, 43). What did she mean by critical realism? For her it was a refreshing corrective to her Neoplatonic idealism. By the time she wrote the twelfth edition of *Mysticism* in 1930, a group of Belgian and northern French Catholic philosophers and theologians had begun to establish a dialogue between Thomas Aquinas and Immanuel Kant, between the scholastics and modern philosophy, from the early 1900s until about 1925. It is probable that Underhill was referring to this group when she wrote her note in 1930 regarding how she would revise her chapter on mysticism and vitalism: "Were I now writing it for the first time, my examples would be chosen from other philosophers, and especially from those who are bringing back into modern thought the critical realism of the scholastics" (*Mysticism*, 43). My surmise is based on the fact that this was the only group undertaking this project at the time and her references to Joseph Maréchal's study of the psychology of the mystics in her work and in her general bibliography since Maréchal belonged to the Louvain school who were part of this group.[1]

Now with the late twentieth-century refinements in cognitional theory, one can speak, granted that it is anachronistic, of critical realism as a corrective to naive realism and idealism. The naive realist asserts the validity of human knowing , equates it with an intellectual seeing of objects out there, and attributes the objectivity of human knowing to the success of that seeing. The critical idealist agrees that human knowing would be an intellectual seeing, but she claims that valid knowing never occurs because the required intellectual seeing never occurs. The critical realist affirms the validity of human knowing, claims that valid knowing does occur, and argues that its objectivity is not a single property of one operation but a triad of properties found in distinct operations of experiencing, understanding, and judgment.[2]

Even though this transcendental Thomist understanding of critical realism was unknown to Underhill, one can applaud the turn she took and give it additional meaning. One can also propose that had she lived, Underhill might have been considered a critical realist in this cognitional sense.[3]

The critical realism of transcendental Thomism can shed light on definitions and distinctions connected with the study of mysticism. It can help to work out a much-needed definition of religious experience, mystical experience, and religious knowledge. It can help to establish that although experience is inseparable from interpretation, it is distinct from it. It recognizes that one can have an experience without explicit awareness of it. It asks whether there is a pre-interpretive phase of religious experience. It can distinguish religious experience as the inner core of the gift of God's love, which is common to all religions, and religious traditions which are culturally and historically conditioned. And it posits that there is a practical, intellectual cognition that is not theoretical.[4]

Notes

1. See E. Underhill's references to Joseph Maréchal, *Studies in the Psychology of the Mystics* (London, 1927), in *Mysticism*, in which she referred to his "balanced view," 242, calling this work "valuable" in her bibliography, 497, and repeating it in her Bibliographical Note to the Thirteenth Edition, 507. Cf. Etienne Gilson, *Réalisme thomiste et critique de la la connaissance* (Paris: Vrin, 1939) for a neo-Thomist rejection of the thesis Maréchal defended that there is something in common between scholasticism and the moderns; and Michael Vertin, "The Transcendental Vindication of the First Step in Realist Metaphysics, according to Joseph Maréchal," (Ph.D. diss., University of Toronto, 1973), esp. 30-54.

2. See Bernard Lonergan, *Method in Theology*, 76, 238-39, 262-65; "Cognitional Structure," in *Collection: Collected Works of Bernard Lonergan*, ed. Frederick E. Crowe and Robert M. Doran, 2nd ed. (Toronto: University of Toronto Press, 1988), 205-221. For this reference in *Collection*, I am indebted

to Michael Vertin, Conversation on April 6, 1993, at the Institute for Ecumenical and Cultural Research, Collegeville, Minnesota. Cf. Walter Conn, " Moral Conversion: Development toward Critical Self-Possession," *Thought* 58 (1983): 170-87, esp. 176-81 and n. 14; Michael Vertin, "Lonergan's 'Three Basic Questions and a Philosophy of Philosophies'," *Lonergan Workshop*, Vol. 8, ed. Fred Lawrence (Altanta, Ga.: Scholars Press, 1990), 213-48, esp. 217-19; and "Gender, Science, and Cognitional Conversion," Cynthia Crysdale, ed., a *Lonergan and Feminism* (Toronto: University of Toronto Press, 1994), 49-71.

3. This approach is in marked contrast with that of the critical realism that emerged in Great Britain and the United States in reaction to the new realism as an epistemology affirming that things are and that we can know what they are. These critical realists differed as to whether the sense-datum pointing to the object perceived is a mental existent or an essence. See, for example, Durant Drake et al, *Essays in Critical Realism: A Cooperative Study of the Problem of Knowledge* (London, 1920), and Roy W. Sellars, *Critical Realism* (Chicago, 1916). Cf., A.G. Rampsperger, "Critical Realism," *The Encyclopedia of Philosophy*, 1967 ed.

4. See B. Lonergan, "Religion," *Method in Theology* (New York: Herder and Herder, 1973), 101-24, esp. 115-24; "Religious Experience," and "Religious Knowledge," *A Third Collection: Papers by Bernard J.F. Lonergan, S.J.*, ed. Frederick E. Crowe (New York: Paulist, 1985), 113-45. Cf. Michael Vertin, "Philosophy of God, Theology, and the Problems of Evil," *Lonergan Workshop*, Vol. 3, ed. Fred Lawrence (Chico, Ca.: Scholars Press, 1982), 149-78, esp. 156-61. For a refinement of these points, I am indebted to Michael Vertin, Ecumenical Institute Seminar, Collegeville, Minnesota, April 13, 1993. See also Frank Fletcher, "Religious Experience in the Foundations of Theology," Ph.D. diss., University of Melbourne, 1982, copy at the Lonergan Centre, Toronto, Ontario.

Index